Conversations with Pauline Kael

Literary Conversations Series

Peggy Whitman Prenshaw
General Editor

GW00601782

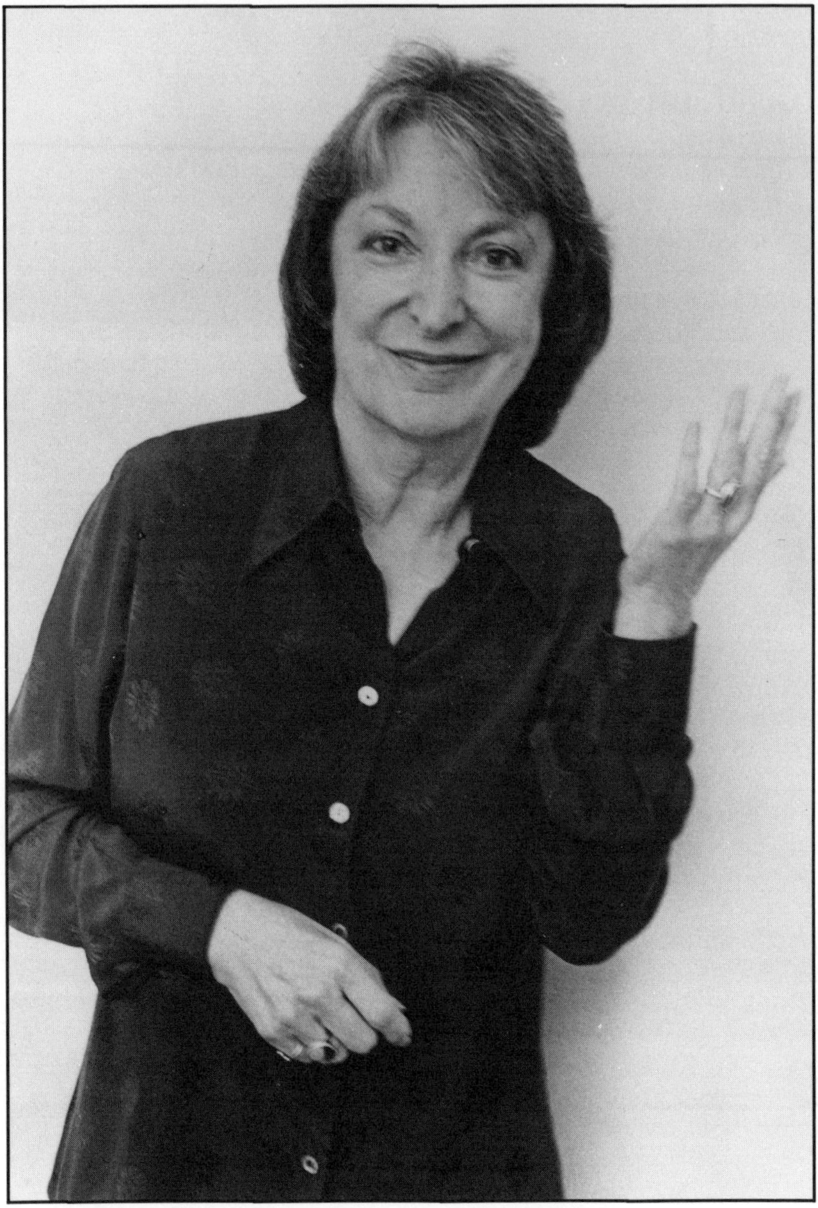

© Deborah Feingold

Conversations with Pauline Kael

Edited by
Will Brantley

University Press of Mississippi
Jackson

99 98 97 96   4 3 2 1

The paper in this book meets the guidelines for permanence and durability of the
Committee on Production Guidelines for Book Longevity of the Council on Library
Resources.

Library of Congress Cataloging-in-Publication Data

Kael, Pauline.
    Conversations with Pauline Kael / edited by Will Brantley.
        p.   cm. — (Literary conversations series)
    Includes bibliographical references and index.
    ISBN 0-87805-898-2 (cloth : alk. paper). — ISBN 0-87805-899-0
(paper : alk. paper)
    1. Motion pictures.   2. Kael, Pauline—Interviews.   3. Film
critics—United States—Interviews.   I. Brantley, Will.   II. Title.
III. Series.
PN1994.K24   1996
791.43'015'092—dc20   96-7200
                                                                    CIP

British Library Cataloging-in-Publication data available

Books by Pauline Kael

I Lost It at the Movies. Boston: Little, Brown, 1965.
Kiss Kiss Bang Bang. Boston: Little, Brown, 1968.
Going Steady. Boston: Little, Brown, 1970.
The Citizen Kane Book. Boston: Little, Brown, 1971.
Deeper into Movies. Boston: Little, Brown, 1973.
Reeling. Boston: Little, Brown, 1976.
When the Lights Go Down. New York: Holt, 1980.
5001 Nights at the Movies. New York: Holt, 1982; expanded 1991.
Taking It All In. New York: Holt, 1984.
State of the Art. New York: Dutton, 1985.
Hooked. New York: Dutton, 1989.
Movie Love. New York: Dutton, 1991.
For Keeps. New York: Dutton, 1994.

Contents

Introduction

The Kael cult, the Kael phenomenon: call it what you will, but Pauline Kael is a critic whose work has deeply mattered. Since her retirement from regular reviewing in 1991, and with the publication in 1994 of *For Keeps: Thirty Years at the Movies,* Kael's large body of writing has been the subject of several appreciations and critical examinations. In a provocative piece in *The Yale Review,* Jed Perl makes this assessment: "For those of us who opened the *New Yorker* every week or every other week for months and years at a time, looking to see what Kael had reviewed, how she had approached it, what exactly she had to say—we knew, even as the weeks were passing, that we were living in a golden age of criticism."[1] In *Artforum,* Greil Marcus offers a similar response, one that parallels my own. Marcus's immediate focus is Kael's first collection, *I Lost it at the Movies:*

> I look back to Kael's book—or, really, carry it with me, as I have since 1966, when I first read it—because like few books of criticism before or since it pays its promise in full: "You must use everything you are and everything you know." On page after page Kael's writing moves as if to match that pledge, to test its limits. The result, for a reader, isn't admiration or envy. It can be a kind of wonder: what would it feel like to write like that—to feel that alive?

Marcus adds that many people other than himself "are still trying to find out."[2]

Of course not all readers have shared the reactions of Perl and Marcus. Kael has generated her share of controversy. Yet even Renata Adler's bitter attack in a 1980 issue of *The New York Review of Books* is evidence of Kael's cultural significance. Few other twentieth-century critics have elicited anything like the response accorded to Kael; writers ranging from Norman Mailer to Alfred Kazin to John Podhoretz have felt compelled to respond to her intensely felt reviews. Speaking on behalf of other critics at a recent awards ceremony, Sheila Benson, formerly of *The Los Angeles Times,* said that "[Kael], more than anyone, made us aware of *the voice* in a review. Believe me, for writers who found their footing in the Seventies and Eighties, the hardest thing was *not* to sound like Pauline."[3]

Kael would, however, disparage the role of icon. She has in fact been one of the most consistently accessible of major writers. Over the years I have run into people who told me that they once wrote to Pauline Kael about something or other and that, to their surprise, she wrote back. As she points out in many of these interviews, Kael has relished all but the occasional hate mail that she has received throughout her career. She has also relished the fact that for more than twenty years she brought younger readers to *The New Yorker* and that, more often than not, she wrote against the tastes of a sophisticated and "literate" readership. Even prior to her retirement, a consensus view had emerged: Kael's relationship with *The New Yorker* is one of the most successful liaisons of twentieth-century journalism. As Mark Feeney observes in his feature interview for *The Boston Globe Magazine,* "Mismatched though the patrician *New Yorker* and pugnacious Kael may have seemed, the marriage turned out to have been made in magazine heaven. It was Fred Astaire and Ginger Rogers all over again: The magazine gave her class, she gave it sex appeal."[4]

Given that she has stressed the democratic nature of movies (she called them our "national theatre" in her prefacing remarks to *Deeper into Movies*), it is no surprise that Kael has been democratic in her response to requests for interviews. She has talked with student publications, with little magazines, with professional journals, with the big weeklies and monthly slicks, with daily and alternative newspapers, and with magazines for special audiences. This collection brings together over half of Kael's published interviews, many of which were conducted by other well established journalists and critics. The selections are not limited to conventional question-answer pieces; included also are feature articles based on interviews, a transcript of a 1981 debate between Kael and Jean-Luc Godard (it's great fun to see these two spar with one another), and a college newspaper's account of a less cantankerous conversation between Kael and Jonathan Demme that took place in 1988.

In her celebrated essay "Trash, Art, and the Movies," Kael argues that the "romance of movies" is found at least in part "in the adolescent dream of meeting others who feel as you do about what you've seen. You do meet them, of course, and you know each other at once because you talk less about good movies than about what you love in bad movies."[5] This impulse—this romance—accounts for much of the content of the interviews in this volume. In "It's Only a Movie," one of her few uncollected essays, Kael defends the lack of cultural anxiety or, rather, the ease with which we watch and talk about movies: "We go to movies because we want to," she insists; "That's the big thing and the starting point for any discussion. . . . the great advantage of film over the other arts, is that it has *not* been forced on us. It has been ours like jazz and popular music—something we wanted, not something fed to us."[6] As a movie lover (who can miss the eroticism in the titles of her books?), Kael also loves the talk that is a major part of moviegoing; and as anyone who has seen her in a question-answer session will affirm, Kael can cover a dense terrain in just one short hour.

Kael gave a number of interviews in the late sixties and early seventies during the years when she was becoming a national figure. She gave relatively few in the mid to late seventies, though she did lecture frequently at universities during these years. Since her Hollywood venture in 1979, a steady stream of interviews has appeared, with an average of about one each year. Though even some of the best interviewers bring up topics that Kael has covered repeatedly, she still responds openly and with care to even the most obvious questions (a perennial favorite is "how many times do you see a movie?"; Kael's response is always the same: "once"). In keeping with the conventions of the University Press of Mississippi's Literary Conversations Series, I have not deleted repetitions among the interviews. Anyone reading the collection from start to finish will see that each "conversation," whatever its repetition of another piece, is valuable within itself.

It is suggestive of Kael's approach to the film medium that one of the first pieces included here concerns not movies but books. In "Portrait of a Woman Reading," Kael makes the claim—one that might surprise her less attuned readers—that books are more important to her than movies: "I could live without movies much more easily than I could live without books, which would almost seem like a form of death." Kael goes on to make the kind of observation that, in the manner of H. L. Mencken or Dorothy Parker, has drawn attention to her unfailing ability to deflate the powerful and the pretentious. "You can see what living without books does when you talk to movie producers who depend on synopses," she tells Ann Geracimos; "Despite the power and money, they're tiresome people. I asked someone recently why a certain rich old director went on working, and the explanation was because no one would talk to him if he weren't in a position of power. That's the fate of bookless people; they bore each other with anecdotes." Kael is often required to spell out what should be obvious, that she is passionate about all the arts. In fact, one of her favorite questions is: "what do you do other than review movies?"

An early question-answer session with Leo Lerman in *Mademoiselle*

(Lerman was not credited when the piece appeared) is suggestive of
Kael's importance as a social commentator—as a critic of culture as well
as film. "Pauline Kael Talks About Violence, Sex, Eroticism and Women
& Men in the Movies"—the title of Kael's conversation with Lerman
contains the subjects that have drawn many readers to her criticism.
Interviewers in particular have known that Kael can be counted on to
respond to these topics in ways that fly in the face of received opinion
and that prompt viewers to re-examine how their reactions to a film may
have been shaped by its initial hype. In her *New Yorker* interview with
Hal Espen, for instance, Kael discusses the sexual politics of the popular
Thelma & Louise, which she calls "a revenge movie for women that
distorts the issues it poses much as the Charles Bronson *Death Wish*
movies used to." It's a peculiarly "class-unconscious movie," she as-
serts, and its "doomsday finish" strikes her as muddleheaded at best:
"The women punish men by killing themselves—they're heading for an
all-girl heaven."

Released in 1991 during a period of cultural conservatism, *Thelma &
Louise* may have seemed more radical than it is. Kael looks to an earlier
decade—the 1970s—as the great era for American film. Movies "played
an adversarial role" and, in a sense, became "the enemy" during that
decade, as she tells Ray Sawhill and Polly Frost. Kael wishes that movies
had remained the enemy. The interviews in this volume, and particularly
those that address social issues, provide a clear window into Kael's
politics and, specifically, her views on films with politically charged
content. A liberal humanist, Kael has not refrained from attacks on films
with either conservative or liberal agendas. Her remarks on *Thelma &
Louise* are another expression of the argument she presented in the
closing essay of *I Lost It at the Movies:* it takes more than liberal good
will to make a good movie.

Anyone who has followed her career will find that one of the interesting
features of this collection is the many ways in which Kael's interviewers
have conceptualized her work, the assumptions—sometimes ill-founded
but also often revealing—that they carry into an interview. Collectively
the interviews suggest some of the ways in which readers have responded
to Kael's writing and to her presence on the cultural scene. At times the
interviewers offer useful perspectives on Kael's sensibility or critical
approach. For example, both Polly Frost and Hal Espen bring up Kael's
love of jazz and its effect on her writing. Frost refers to Kael's distinctive
use of words and to her rhythms; and Espen tells Kael that he has
"always associated the unsentimental, fast, cool appreciation of virtuosity in [her] writing with jazz." Kael says the influence was never fully

conscious, but she does admit to Espen that her temperament is such that she "wanted to approximate something of the speed and feeling of jazz." It's a casual remark, but one that illuminates an important feature of Kael's style, and one that invites a re-reading of her reviews. Occasionally the interviews supplement the reviews. In this regard, a number of pieces respond to and expand on "Why Are Movies so Bad? Or, the Numbers," Kael's first broadside after her return to *The New Yorker* in 1980. In some instances an interview prefigures or anticipates an idea that Kael develops in a subsequent piece. In the early seventies Kael was commenting on what she found to be an alarming trend: a generalized fear of movies, of their power to arouse and disturb viewers. By the end of the seventies this tendency became the focus of a lengthy essay-review in which she described—and decried—a moviegoing public that, in the main, had come to prefer only "safe" forms of entertainment.[7]

Kael's interviewers have generally shared an overriding goal: to have her define her perceptions about what it is she does. What comes through in many different contexts is Kael's commitment to her craft, to the *art* of criticism. "Do you know how hard it is to be a good critic?" she asks screenwriter George Malko in one of the best of the early interviews. Though she has refused to score points for humility, Kael will freely discuss what she perceives to be her limitations. On the other hand, she is quite clear about the value of her collections, and about what it is that has motivated her to write: pleasure, for one thing, and the love of surprise, and the desire, which must be satisfied again and again, to understand why she responds as she does.

Something almost each of the interviewers share is a concern with the extent of Kael's power as someone who has monitored the industry for well over thirty years. Though Kael argues that only the voice of the critic stands between the advertiser and the moviegoing public, she admits to having had more influence than real power. A critic can help a small picture, she says in several interviews, but the critic can do little to affect the box office of a film the studios have chosen to sell.

Even Kael's earliest interviewers took note of her influence on other critics; and her more recent interviewers have tended to remark upon the hostility directed at those writers who have acknowledged a debt to Kael—dubbed in some quarters as the "Paulettes." Someone with a genuinely revolutionary sensibility will effect change; traditionally, a critic's clout has been measured, at least partially, by the very extent to which he or she has influenced others in the same field. Kael does not ignore the sway of her critical voice. "I admit I've had an influence on some of the younger critics," she tells one interviewer, adding that

xiv   Introduction

"some of it has been to the good because they've taken movies more
seriously and paid more attention to their writing." On the other hand,
Kael does not like to see other reviewers imitate her style (what critic
would?); and she acknowledges that some critics have been too much
influenced by her tastes: "I'll read a review and realize that the attitudes
are mine and they don't go with anything else in the review."[8] As for the
charge that she sits at the head of a critical mafia, Kael dismisses it as
nonsense worthy of Joseph McCarthy.

Highlights of this volume include Kael's in-depth interviews with Ray
Sawhill and Polly Frost, Marc Smirnoff, and Hal Espen; a detailed
discussion of her writing habits with George Malko; a probing exploration
of film aesthetics with Kristine McKenna; a consideration of the relationship between politics and film art with Pat Aufderheide; several accounts
of her relationship with William Shawn and *The New Yorker;* and a
number of reflections on her experience in Hollywood as an executive
consultant for Paramount Pictures. Of course an immediate pleasure of
the interviews is that they contain discussions of films like *Apocalypse
Now* or, more recently, *The Piano* and *The Crying Game,* that Kael did
not have the chance to review or that were released after her retirement.

Sheila Benson once heard someone say that "Pauline Kael has the
shortest chute from her brain to her mouth of anyone I've ever heard
speak." This comment, repeated in a recent tribute by Craig Seligman,
accounts for the readability of Kael's interviews. As Seligman observes,
Kael "may spend days on her reviews but they come out sounding like
first drafts or even tape recordings—in fact, the occasional interviews she
grants read as shrewdly and persuasively as her magazine pieces."[9]

Kael's criticism may be conversational in tone (a quality she has
consciously cultivated), but she still maintains that talk can merely
complement what the critic does in print. When Hal Espen asks her why
she doesn't give monthly interviews now that her health prevents her
from regular reviewing, Kael, somewhat baffled, gives this reply: "Because it's not the same. This is just off the top of the head—it's not like
giving yourself to a subject." She's right of course, but a crucial fact
remains: Pauline Kael reeling off the top of her head is still a major
critical force.

It was a great pleasure to work once again with Seetha A-Srinivasan,
Hunter Cole, and Ginger Tucker at the University Press of Mississippi.

Thanks are due to each of the publications and authors who gave their
permission to reprint. I am grateful to Betty McFall for locating those
pieces that required a seasoned sleuth. I am also grateful to Angelo Pitillo
for reading and discussing the interviews with me.

My student worker, Jared Wilson, and my research assistant, Julie Rice, provided help with the mechanical details; and four friends and colleagues—Adele Robertson, Franklin Cham, Michael Dunne, and David Lavery—lent their encouragement by following the project with great interest as it was taking shape. I wish also to acknowledge the Graduate School of Middle Tennessee State University for its generous support.

Finally, I must thank Pauline Kael for allowing me to edit this collection and for the suggestions she made along the way. This volume is a small measure of my thanks to her for sensitizing me to movies in ways that have enhanced all my perceptions.

This book is dedicated to Signe.

WB
September 1995

Notes

1. Jed Perl, "A Quarter Century with Kael," *Yale Review* 81.2 (1993): 105.

2. Greil Marcus, "Pauline Kael: *I Lost It at the Movies,*" *Artforum* 32.1 (1993): 141. See also Tom Carson, "Citizen Kael," *Sight and Sound* June 1991: 22–23; John Powers, "Pauline Kael and the Rise and Fall of the Movies," *L.A. Weekly* 5–11 April 1991: 16–23; Will Brantley, "In Defense of Subjectivity: The Film Criticism of Pauline Kael," *New Orleans Review* 19.1 (1992): 38–54; Steve Vineberg, "Critical Fervor," *Threepenny Review* Summer 1992: 25–27; Roy Blount, Jr., "Lustily Vigilant," *Atlantic Monthly* December 1994: 131–43; and Louis Menand, "Finding It at the Movies," *New York Review of Books* 23 March 1995: 10–17.

3. Speech presented at the 1994 awards presentation of the Los Angeles Film Critics Association, 17 January 1995.

4. Mark Feeney, "The Pearls of Pauline," *The Boston Globe Magazine* 11 June 1989: 52. Further references to interviews included in this volume will indicate the interviewer or the periodical in which the interview appeared.

5. Pauline Kael, *Going Steady* (Boston: Little, Brown, 1970) 89.

6. Pauline Kael, "It's Only a Movie," in *Film Study in Higher Education,* ed. David C. Stewart (Washington, D.C.: American Council on Education, 1966) 132–33; rpt. in *Performing Arts Journal* 17.2/3 (1995): 8–19.

7. See "Fear of Movies" in *When the Lights Go Down* (New York: Holt) 427–40.

8. William R. Katovsky, "My Dinner with Pauline," *Arrival* Spring 1987: 21. For reasons of space, I have not included Katovsky's interview, along with some other pieces primarily from the 1980s, the decade during which the largest number

of interviews appeared. Nor have I included Kael's remarks to Studs Terkel in three of his widely available anthologies. See *Hard Times: An Oral History of the Great Depression* (New York: Pantheon, 1970) 35, 346–47; *Working: People Talk About What They Do All Day and How They Feel About What They Do* (New York: Pantheon, 1974) 155–56; and *"The Good War": An Oral History of World War Two* (New York: Pantheon, 1984) 123–25.

9. Craig Seligman, "Tribute: Pauline Kael," *San Francisco Bay Guardian* 1 July 1990, *Image:* 24.

Chronology

1919   Pauline Kael is born on June 19, 1919, in Petaluma, California, the youngest of Judith (née Friedman) and Isaac Kael's five children.

1927   Moves to San Francisco when her father loses his farm in the stock market crash

1936–40   Attends the University of California at Berkeley as a philosophy major; abandons plans to attend law school and to teach philosophy.

1940–47   Lives in San Francisco and for several years in New York with poet and dance critic Robert Horan; is part of a group of young artists and poets, including Robert Duncan, who help to define the San Francisco cultural scene at mid century; experiments with filmmaking and with different modes of writing—plays, scripts, and essays; has an affair with poet and avant-garde filmmaker James Broughton.

1948–53   Gina James is born (fathered by Broughton). To meet expenses, Kael works as a seamstress, cook, ghostwriter, and at other jobs. Publishes her first piece on film in the San Francisco quarterly *City Lights*. A review of Charles Chaplin's *Limelight,* the piece is indicative of the strong, independent stance that will become a hallmark of Kael's career.

1955   Appears occasionally with Weldon Kees on his radio show; begins doing her own popular but unpaid show for KPFA, the Pacifica listener-sponsored station.

1955–60   Becomes involved with and eventually marries writer Edward Landberg; together they run the Berkeley Cinema Guild and Studio, the nation's first twin art movie house. "Movies, the Desperate Art" (1956) is included in Daniel Talbot's influential *Film: An Anthology* in 1959.

1961–62   Freelance pieces begin to appear with regularity in periodicals, such as *Sight and Sound, Film Quarterly, Kulchur,* and *Partisan Review.*

1963   Publishes the first of several reviews of books on movies in *The New York Times Book Review.* "Circles and Squares, Joys and Sarris" is published in *Film Quarterly.* An attack on Andrew Sarris's *auteur* theory, the piece initiates a debate that is still carried on in film schools and journals.

1964   Awarded a Guggenheim Fellowship

1965   *I Lost It at the Movies,* Kael's first collection of essays and reviews (many of which were originally broadcast on KPFA) is published. The book becomes a best-seller and a landmark work of nonfiction in the 1960s. Kael moves to New York City.

1965–66   Writes for *Life, Holiday, Mademoiselle, Vogue, The Atlantic Monthly,* and *McCall's.* A caustic review of *The Sound of Music* is often cited as the cause of her departure from *McCall's.*

1966–67   Writes for *The New Republic.* Two essay-reviews, "Movies on Television" and "*Bonnie and Clyde,*" are published in *The New Yorker.*

1968   Begins writing regularly for *The New Yorker.* Kael is assigned the Fall and Winter seasons while Penelope Gilliatt covers the Spring and Summer. *Kiss Kiss Bang Bang,* a second eclectic collection of reviews and essays, is published. Kael provides this note regarding the book's title: "The words 'Kiss Kiss Bang Bang,' which I saw on an Italian movie poster, are perhaps the briefest statement imaginable of the basic appeal of movies. This appeal is what attracts us, and ultimately what makes us despair when we begin to understand how seldom movies are more than this."

1969   "Trash, Art, and the Movies" is published in the February issue of *Harper's.*

1970   *Going Steady,* the first of eight collections of *New Yorker* reviews, is published. Kael serves as chair of the National Society of Film Critics and receives the George Polk Memorial Award for Criticism and the National Institute of Arts and Letters Award.

1971   "Raising Kane" appears in two successive issues of *The New Yorker* in late February, and, along with the shooting script and the cutting continuity from the film, is subsequently published in *The Citizen Kane Book*. The piece documents the contributions of screenwriter Herman J. Mankiewicz and cinematographer Gregg Toland, and provokes heated responses from Andrew Sarris in *The Village Voice* and Peter Bogdanovich in *Esquire*. Kael moves to the Berkshires in Massachusetts.

1972   Kael's most controversial review—of Bernardo Bertolucci's *Last Tango in Paris*—is published in *The New Yorker* on October 28. The film is hailed as a "breakthrough" and its opening night is compared to the 1913 premiere of Stravinsky's *Le Sacre du Printemps*. Kael receives honorary degrees from Georgetown University and Columbia College, Chicago (others will follow from Smith, Allegheny, Kalamazoo, Reed, Haverford, and the School of Visual Arts, New York City).

1973   *Deeper into Movies,* the first book on film to receive the National Book Award for Arts and Letters, is published. The judges provide this citation: "To Pauline Kael, whose sense of journalistic enterprise embraces not only her immediate subject, the movies, but also the world of popular culture and its reflection in society. Her prose style is lucid, funny, full of colloquial eloquence, and conveys a rare affirmation and caring. In citing *Deeper into Movies,* we honor a writer who has brought new vitality to the practice of criticism."

1974   Receives the Front Page Award for Best Magazine Column from the Newswomen's Club of New York. "On the Future of Movies," a lengthy consideration of how the film artist functions—or fails to function—within a corporatized art, is published on August 5 in *The New Yorker* as part of its "Onward and Upward with the Arts" series.

1975   Reviews Robert Altman's *Nashville* on March 3 in a cut that is roughly eight minutes longer than the film's final running time. The early review—a rave—is denounced by Vincent Canby in *The New York Times*. A *New Yorker* profile of Cary Grant, "The Man From Dream City," is published on July 15.

1976   *Reeling* is published. Because of the films it covers, including

Last Tango in Paris, Mean Streets, The Godfather II, and
Nashville, Kael will often cite it as one of her favorite collections.

1979   Takes a leave of absence from reviewing to work in Hollywood
        with Warren Beatty; decides against Beatty's proposal, but
        remains for five months at Paramount as an executive consul-
        tant; declines the studio's offer of a longer contract.

1980   *When the Lights Go Down* is published. Kael returns to *The
        New Yorker* on a bi-weekly basis as the magazine's only film
        critic. "Why Are Movies So Bad? or, The Numbers," which
        details her recent observations in Hollywood, appears in the
        June 23 issue. Renata Adler, a former reviewer for *The New
        York Times,* publishes a much publicized attack on Kael in the
        August 14 issue of *The New York Review of Books.* Rebuttals
        are provided by, among others, James Wolcott, Greil Marcus,
        and Michael Sragow.

1982   *5001 Nights at the Movies,* a compendium of short reviews
        written primarily for the "Goings On About Town" section of
        The New Yorker, is published. The book contains a preface by
        New Yorker editor William Shawn, who writes: "A master of
        synopsis, Pauline Kael has contrived to tell us between the
        covers of one book what eight decades of film are about and
        who is in them and behind them, and to reflect, swiftly but
        astutely, on what they signify. No one else has done that; no
        one else could have done that."

1983   Receives the Front Page Award for Distinguished Journalism
        from the Newswomen's Club of New York. Provides an intro-
        duction for *Three Screen Comedies by Samson Raphaelson*
        (University of Wisconsin Press).

1984   *Taking It All In* is published.

1985   *State of the Art* is published. On December 30 Kael publishes
        a negative review of Claude Lanzmann's *Shoah* over William
        Shawn's objections. Despite her contention that a film's subject
        should not preempt it from criticism, the review stirs some
        angry responses, including a rebuttal three years later from
        Alfred Kazin.

1989   *Hooked* is published.

1991   Receives *American Film's* Special Career Achievement Award.
        Retires from regular reviewing in early March; a number of
        tributes follow. Expanded edition of *5001 Nights at the Movies*
        and *Movie Love: Complete Reviews, 1988–1991* are published.

1993   *The Kael Index,* a resource for libraries, is published.

1994   Receives the Los Angeles Film Critics Association's Special
        Achievement Award. *For Keeps: Thirty Years at the Movies,* a
        1300 page anthology of selections from previous collections, is
        published. In her Introduction, Kael writes: "The week-by-
        week flow is gone, but you can still get the sense of how movies
        interacted with public life, and you can get the critic's first
        flushes of discovery. I'm frequently asked why I don't write
        my memoirs. I think I have."

1995   Receives the Independent Feature Project's Gotham Award for
        her "extraordinary career in film criticism." "It's Only a
        Movie" (1966) is reprinted in the May-September issue of
        Performing Arts Journal.

Conversations with Pauline Kael

Perils of Pauline
Newsweek / 1966

From *Newsweek* 30 May 1966: 80–81. © 1966, Newsweek, Inc.
All rights reserved. Reprinted by permission.

Movie critic Pauline Kael plays no favorites: she snaps angrily at the
puffed-up Hollywood epics just as readily as she pans the arty art film.
The 46-year-old Miss Kael is a bitter opponent of all cinema cults, yet
there is a Kael cult. Until recently, however, her fame has been underground, her reviews appearing mostly in such magazines as *Film Quarterly* (circulation: 5,500) and *Partisan Review* (circulation: 15,000). When
she said at last year's New York Film Festival, "It's nearly impossible
for a serious film critic to make a living wage in the U.S.," she was
speaking very definitely from experience. "In ten years I made under
$2,000 from film criticism," she explains. "It's always been for fun and
love, never for profit. I've never made a living as a critic until now."

Last year Miss Kael went mass. Her collected reviews, *I Lost It at the
Movies,* sold 150,000 copies in paperback, and as the resident film critic
for *McCall's* (circulation: 8.5 million), she made around $20,000 a year.
Then last week, she lost something else. *McCall's* paid her contract
through January and fired her. The trouble, it seemed, was that Miss
Kael changed her audience but not her position. She blasted *The Sound
of Music* as "the sugarcoated lie that people seem to want to eat." About
Our Man Flint, she wrote, "If your local critics or TV reporters are kind
to this film, you might bear in mind that 78 of them were invited on a
publicity junket to Jamaica, as part of the film's budget." (*Flint* producer
Saul David then sent a letter to the reviewers attacking Miss Kael for
attacking them.)

In the June issue, she speaks for the last time in *McCall's,* and knocks,
among other movies, *Born Free,* as "a tear-jerking account of a trembling,
stiff-upper-lipped, emotionally frustrated woman's obsession" with a
"lion that is just a big sweet puttytat."

Her review of *Sound of Music* drew a bundle of letters, almost all of
them negative. But Robert Stein, the editor of *McCall's,* insists that is
not why she was fired. "I knew that she was extremely critical when I
hired her," he said last week. "But her reviews became more and more
uniformly unfavorable—not only to all films, but questioning the motives

3

of the people who made the films. The reviews became less and less appropriate for a mass-audience magazine. I still think she's one of the best movie critics around. My hiring her was, I thought, a noble experiment. The experiment did not work out."

Considering her bellicose reputation, Miss Kael took her dismissal with uncharacteristic charity. "From the beginning I thought I was the wrong person for their readers," she said, "but they were willing to take the risk. I had realized that I would sock the ladies right between the ears, but what the hell is the point of writing, if you're writing banality."

Banality is one of several grounds on which she faults her rival reviewers. She has little regard for them, from her sop sisters on big-city dailies to the far-out *cinéastes.* "It's hard to find a first-rate critic on an American newspaper," she told *Newsweek*'s Ruth Ross. "How do you become a newspaper critic? Most critics are switched over from some other desk—often sports or the city desk. I think *The New York Herald Tribune's* Judy Crist is tough, which is more than you can say for most men critics. . . . I have certain disadvantages. I'm hard to take, because my point of view is strong."

"I'm available," she concluded. "I guess I'm up for grabs."

Portrait of a Woman Reading

Ann Geracimos / 1969

From *The Washington Post Book World* 23 February 1969: 17.
© 1969, Washington Post Book World Service/Washington Post
Writers Group. Reprinted with permission.

Ann Geracimos: What is the first book you remember?

Pauline Kael: I can't even think in terms of there being a first. I can't
remember the first movie I saw, either. I've always had omnivorous
reading habits. I was the youngest in a large family. We lived on a farm
30 miles north of San Francisco and then when I was eight, we moved
into the city. I read *The Decameron* and *The Sheik* when my older
brothers had them around, and the Kathleen Norris or Willa Cather or
Sherwood Anderson my older sisters were reading the same time I was
reading fairy tales and Oz books and those girls' series. I saw movies the
same way because I went with my parents or any of my brothers or
sisters who would take me along.

By the time I was about twelve I'd given up on raiding one of my
sister's acquisitions because she had such rotten, dull taste. *Collier's* and
Liberty magazine and pulp Westerns. She's a very bright woman—an
educator—yet to this day I can't understand how she can read what she
does. She whips right through best sellers the same way she read *Liberty*.
I just got a trickle of stuff from my brothers, but I got great loot from my
other sister, who's an English teacher.

In San Francisco there was always a public library close by, and we all
made our trips, sometimes daily, and when I finished my haul I'd see
what my sister—the literate one, not the one who used books like
fodder—had brought home.

Geracimos: What books, if any, have influenced you?

Kael: Consciously, I have no idea. But I'm sure I've soaked up
something from the people I like. Maybe you can tell what influenced you
from what people can see in your work. I haven't read R.P. Blackmur's
The Expense of Greatness for 25 years, but someone told me recently
that a review of mine reminded him of Blackmur. I feel closer to
American writers than to the English and I think this shows in my prose,
which often embarrasses me because it's so plain. I'd rather read a
heavy, clumsy writer like Dreiser than someone like Styron. Maybe that
shows, too, probably badly.

Geracimos: How have your reading habits changed over the years?

Kael: When I was in high school, I read Dashiell Hammett and James M. Cain, and popular nonfiction, too, like Gene Fowler. I don't read that kind of thing anymore. And now I despise anecdotal books and semiunwritten reminiscences. I can't read the kind of books people tell me are so easy to read, like *King Cohn*. I try and I can't get through them.

Movies do that better, that whole world of the superficial look at things. I don't think as highly of Hammett or Chandler as many of my friends do. Maybe it's because that whole minor function of literature is taken over for me by movies. The glamour and romance of Fitzgerald do not interest me now as they once did. Maybe that's getting older, maybe it's because movies—particularly the new French directors—do that kind of thing so well. I read for all the kinds of thought and observation you don't get much of in movies. I read a lot just to try to know what's going on in the world.

And then, of course, I read the new work of friends. Not just because they're friends, but because I want to. When I was a child I didn't know anyone who had ever written a book; now I hardly know anyone who hasn't. I think we're often drawn to the work of friends for the same reasons that we're drawn to friendship with them—that we have a temperamental affinity with their way of seeing things.

I like to read the new work of people whose other work I know and like. When a new magazine article or a book review by Alfred Kazin comes out, I want to read it right away. Once I'm interested in somebody's mind, I want to see where it takes him. When I got interested in an author, I always read everything of his I could get hold of and everything about him I could find, before I went on to something else.

Geracimos: Which writers did you read this way?

Kael: Melville and James and Proust and Céline and Henry Adams and George Eliot and Virginia Woolf, Stendhal, Hardy, Dostoevski, Strindberg, and a lot of others. The writers, whose work I was content to read a volume at a time intermittently over the years, were those whose minds I wasn't drawn to, and the awful thing is that I never have caught up with all the volumes of theirs that I didn't read then. So I have gaps in Faulkner, for one, and especially Conrad, who has always given me trouble.

There are people I've read in volume after volume—like Joyce Cary or Dorothy Richardson—not because I thought they were great, but simply because I was interested in what they were trying to do as writers and the kind of contemporary material they seemed to be, well, processing.

When I was a teenager, my older sister—the one who teaches English—

was appalled at the way I tore through a man's life work in a day or two. I mean it didn't take long to read someone like Synge. She chided me when she saw me go right through that edition of Shaw's *Nine Plays* one after another in a day and said that I would never remember anything. But she was wrong: I do remember and I certainly remember enough to know which ones I don't want to re-read. If I hadn't read so much during those years when the days seemed to be so long, I wonder if I'd ever have had the time again, because I've always worked at awful jobs. I didn't start to make a living as a writer until after my first book came out in 1965.

Geracimos: Are there any special subjects you prefer to read about?

Kael: My field was philosophy of history in college, but I always read fiction and poetry, too, and my friends were English majors. We argued over Pound and Joyce and read and talked about books like *The Confessions of Zeno,* or Nabokov's *The Real Life of Sebastian Knight* when they came out in New Directions editions. Reading the same thing as friends and reacting to that reading was a more intensive experience than other kinds of reading since and so may have been more formative.

Geracimos: When do you read?

Kael: All the time. I mean that just about literally. When I was a child I used to read under the covers with a flashlight after my mother had turned off the lights. I still feel furtive sometimes when I stay up to finish something and know I should be getting sleep instead.

Geracimos: Did books lead you to want to write about films?

Kael: No, I don't think there was a direct connection there. Movies were what you did with other people: books you read alone. I had worked in experimental moviemaking in San Francisco with James Broughton and others, and we all talked about movies a lot, too. That's how I got started on criticism.

Geracimos: Aren't there more and more movies in which books, the physical presence of books, play a large part?

Kael: Yes, but I don't know that it's very important. Piles of books, characters named after people in books—this sort of thing converts books into a form of gesture. It can be charming and amusing but it can also be just exhibitionism, like a girl on a vacation trip carrying smart luggage, or a homosexual carrying a serious magazine to set off the right signals. Books used emblematically—or for resonance—well, it's not really such an interesting idea.

What's more interesting is the influence of movies on books. In 1968 the major literary event was Mailer's *The Armies of the Night,* in which Mailer saw himself as the hero of a movie, and a documentary was indeed being made about him as he took part in the events. And *Myra Breckin-ridge,* which, I think, belongs among the minor classics, with *Miss Lonelyhearts* and *Gentlemen Prefer Blondes,* is a Hollywood novel—the best, I think, since *Day of the Locust.*

Geracimos: You have written that the best movies are usually not derived from first-rate books. Is there an example of any first-rate novel you have seen translated successfully to the screen?

Kael: Some of the Japanese directors have come startlingly close to the novels. But with English and American novels, no. Although a sensitive director can sometimes give you scenes that illuminate the book if he can't convey the whole structure or the writer's style and complexity. There's a scene in Jean Renoir's version of *Madame Bovary*—the scene at the opera—that shows the rapturous banality of Emma's response, and it seems almost to get to the essence of the material.

Scenes like that are so rare. The general attempt is to get the broad outlines of the plot. Movies generally simplify and distort even relatively easy works like Liam O'Flaherty's *The Informer.* Even a novel like *The Ox-Bow Incident* has much more ambiguity and more depth than the movie version. The original story of *Blow-Up* by Julio Cortázar is much more complex and fascinating than the movie. I wish someone would make a movie of it. It's a good thing movies provide so many elements that books don't, or they would just be shallow versions of books.

Geracimos: Which is more important to you, books or movies?

Kael: Books. I could live without movies much more easily than I could live without books, which would almost seem like a form of death. You can see what living without books does when you talk to movie producers who depend on synopses. Despite the power and money, they're tiresome people. I asked someone recently why a certain rich old director went on working, and the explanation was because no one would talk to him if he weren't in a position of power. That's the fate of bookless people; they bore each other with anecdotes.

Raising Kael
Hollis Alpert / 1971

From *The Saturday Review* 24 April 1971: 48–49, 60–61. Reprinted by permission of *The Saturday Review* © 1971, S.R. Publications, Ltd.

If anyone should ever do a study of film criticism in America, the month of February 1971 undoubtedly will take on historic significance, for that was the month that John Simon and Andrew Sarris traded swings at each other in the Drama Section of the Sunday *New York Times,* readers responded pro or con, or anti-both, and Pauline Kael's long essay *Raising Kane* took up most of two successive issues of *The New Yorker.* In a curious way, the events were related. The quarrel between Simon and Sarris basically had to do with the validity of the *auteur* theory of film criticism. Miss Kael's study of the origins of that landmark of American cinema, *Citizen Kane,* had considerable bearing on the argument. The ramifications of the theory are too Byzantine to be discussed here, nor is Sarris to be held responsible for all the interpretations and misinterpretations of his notable field work. Enough, one hopes, merely to say that the *auteur* theory has helped make the film director into a figure of cultish hero worship.

Since Orson Welles rates high in the *auteur* rankings, Miss Kael's essay exploded among auteurial circles and film buffs generally like a dynamite blast in the halls of the U.S. Senate. Welles, her essay made clear, was not the sole creative force behind *Citizen Kane.* And it strongly implied that the stout prodigy had, over the years, acquired a lot of the credit and glory that by rights should have gone to a Hollywood screenwriter, long dead, by the name of Herman J. Mankiewicz. Her research led her to the conclusion that Mankiewicz (the older brother of director Jospeh L.) was the initiator of the ground-breaking film, and at the very least an important participant in its creation.

None of this could have been expected to go down nicely with Welles adherents, and a counterattack is said to be brewing. Sarris, for one, feels that her interpretation of certain facts is questionable. He also reports that Peter Bogdanovich, a film-maker and cineast who is preparing a book on Welles, with the collaboration of the master himself, is violently opposed to Miss Kael's conclusions.

But for those who have managed to stay aloof from the critical wars,

9

Miss Kael's 50,000-word essay is an uncommonly fascinating piece of
film scholarship, a compendium of nostalgic gossip, and a suspenseful
intellectual narrative that for at least one reader among the hundreds who
have written her is "an elegant thriller." What she has also done is to
raise the sadly neglected ghost of Herman Mankiewicz, turn him into one
of the most interesting people ever met, and restore him to his deservedly
high place in film history. How all this happened to come about is a story
in itself, one of its oddest quirks being that Miss Kael never intended to
write it.

Who exactly is Pauline Kael and what makes her write so long and
well? Dispersed throughout her three books of film criticism are little
tidbits of autobiography, and perhaps we can connect them with some
help from the lady herself. One thing she makes no bones about is her
age. She is fifty-one, and sees no reason to hide the fact. "I don't know
any way," she says, "to discuss the movies you saw when you were
young if you conceal your age. And I don't know why women have to be
so hung up about age, anyway." So, she was born in 1919 in the town of
Two Rock, California, some thirty miles north of San Francisco. Her
father, a rancher, moved his brood of five children (she was the youngest)
to San Francisco, where she attended local schools, then moved on to
the University of California at Berkeley. She majored in philosophy, read
voraciously, and gobbled up movies, although, in those days, she had no
idea of her eventual vocation.

She was, however, interested in writing, and tried plays, film scripts,
and literary essays. "I had no money," she says. "In the East people
know how to get started in a career, whereas in the West you simply try
to write." She wrote and had a crazy-quilt variety of jobs. She set up an
art book department in a San Francisco department store, sold books,
worked at Houghton Mifflin's San Francisco branch office, assisted with
the making of experimental films, and, for two years, worked at home as
a seamstress, putting in hems and shortening men's pants. The reason
that she had to work at home and, as she puts it, "had so many crazy
jobs" was the serious illness of her daughter, Gina, who could not be left
unattended. An operation restored Gina's health, and the two now share
an apartment on Central Park West in New York with a dog and a cat.

Pauline Kael's first published writing in San Francisco's *City Lights*
was, as it happened, an essay on movies. She also began doing broadcasts
on movies for KPFA, the Pacifica Foundation station in Berkeley, and
soon developed a following. One listener, a man who owned a movie-
house in Berkeley, wrote her; he was having a rough time with the
theater, and she began the programing and managing of it. Once under

her wing, not only did the theater become a phenomenally successful operation, but it became two theaters. So many were turned away that a second room was opened. The Cinema Guild and Studio became the models on which others have since based their twin art houses. In addition to selecting the programs on what might be called eclectic principles, she wrote the program notes to fit exactly the space for each film on the monthly calendar she printed. Herewith a sample of early Kael:

BRINGING UP BABY: Katharine Hepburn's first comedy, made in 1938, rescued her from the tremulous anguish in crinoline which had made her one of Hollywood's surest guarantees of financial disaster. Lunatic comedy of the 30's generally started with an heiress; this one starts with an heiress (Hepburn) who has a dog and a leopard, Baby; Cary Grant is a paleontologist who has just acquired the bone he needs to complete his dinosaur skeleton . . . Grant (Cary) winds up with Hepburn and no paleontologist ever got hold of a more beautiful set of bones. . . .

In 1961, she went back to her radio reviewing, and some of these broadcasts were reprinted in *Film Quarterly,* a West Coast publication that brought her to the attention of East Coast critics, mainly because she often took issue with their judgments. ''People have used this against me in a funny way,'' she says now, ''as though I were doing it out of spitefulness. But, out West, when we got the movies, they'd already been reviewed in the Eastern press and everyone was seeing them in terms of a sort of impacted New York opinion, which was largely Bosley Crowther's, and movies he hadn't liked nobody went to see. And, so in order to try for a fresh approach to certain movies, I tried to clear away the Eastern view, my aim being for people to look at movies somewhat differently from the delivered dicta. People insistently misunderstand this, as though you go out of your way to pan your colleagues.'' She came to New York in 1965, and her first job was for *Life.* That year was the first in which she managed to make a living as a film critic, a big help being the success of her first collection, *I Lost It at the Movies. Life* also commissioned her to do a long study of the making of *The Group,* a film based on Mary McCarthy's novel. She turned in a brilliant 25,000 words, and *Life* turned it down. Being Pauline Kael, she now realized, was becoming perilous. Work with *Atlantic, Vogue,* and *McCall's* followed. When she and *McCall's* parted company because of editorial disagreement, she moved on again, this time to *The New Republic,* replacing

Stanley Kauffmann, who had gone to *The New York Times* as its drama critic.

She was hardly happy at *The New Republic*. The editor, she says, would cut her copy without consulting her, and sometimes wouldn't use it at all. "I quit the magazine in some despair," she said, "and had no idea what to do. I had come to the conclusion that it was just about impossible making a living as a movie critic. I was lying in bed with the flu, I was busted, when a telephone call came from William Shawn of *The New Yorker*." The call from Shawn came, much like an episode in *The Perils of Pauline*, in the nick of time. The movie spot on *The New Yorker*, he told her, was open because Brendan Gill was taking on the theater column; would she consider sharing it, on a six-month basis each, with Penelope Gilliatt? "I didn't at all mind," she said, "and it's worked out ever since."

About two-and-a-half years ago, Marc Jaffe, the editor of Bantam Books, asked her to do a brief introduction for a paperback edition of the script of *Citizen Kane*. The firm had acquired publication rights from RKO and Orson Welles. Miss Kael declined on the grounds that she had, the year before, written a long piece on Orson Welles. She recommended someone else. Months went by, and the writer she had recommended failed to come up with anything. "So I said I would do it. There were other directors I would have rather studied, Renoir for instance, but when I got involved in it I became *really* interested. The Hearst material I was already familiar with, but because my job was to introduce the script I started investigating the writing, and that took me into the whole role of the writer in film-making. From being absorbed in the project, it became a kind of madness, made all the more strange because I was giving months and months of time to something I couldn't make any money on. In fact, I soon dissipated the fee for the job [$750] just on telephone calls."

The passages in *Raising Kane* that have caused the most furor in movie circles have to do with the diminution of the Welles role in the writing of the script. Not only did he not write it, she makes clear, he didn't even think of the idea. She quotes the secretary who was present throughout and typed each draft: "Welles didn't write (or dictate) one line of the shooting script of *Citizen Kane*." Welles, wrongly or rightly, has won only one Academy Award, and that was for his "co-authorship" of the famous film. Miss Kael adds, "Under the present rules of the Guild [for script credit] Welles's name would probably not have appeared." But she goes further. Even that vaunted *style* of the film, which has so impressed succeeding directors and critics everywhere, she traces not to Welles, but to his cameraman, the late Gregg Toland. While I talked with her, she suddenly showed me some stills and asked me which film I thought they had come from. They looked as though they might have come from *Citizen Kane,* but they were stills of an earlier film, *Mad Love,* photographed by Gregg Toland.

Here, then, was strong evidence for what many have long suspected: that neither authorship nor credit has been fairly apportioned, more often than not, in the film world. And it is not merely a matter of personal vanity. Audiences are being cheated when talents are robbed of their just recognition, for the opportunity to continue working in film often depends on that recognition. Directors, aided and abetted by film historians and critics, and by their own publicity, have emphasized themselves as the primary creative force in film-making. Sometimes this is, of course, true. On the other hand, if one adopted the *auteur* director point of view, one might all too easily assume that all the rest involved—writers, technicians, actors, producers—are merely automata through which the director is expressing himself. Several contemporary directors, misreading Sarris, cheerfully espouse his theories, although they hardly apply to them at all. (His theory aims, mainly, at a unified way of looking at films of the Thirties and Forties.)

Nevertheless, Miss Kael is more than anxious to give Welles a great deal of credit for *Citizen Kane.* "The key was Welles," she said. "He was the catalyst. He made it possible for so many frustrated Hollywood talents to give of their best. Marvelous as Mankiewicz's script was, the picture might have been an ordinary picture with some other director . . . and, certainly, with some other actor as Kane. But it is wrong to think that Welles brought it all out of himself. He brought it out of others also."

Her research took her, off and on, close to two years. "I talked to everyone I thought could help me," she said. "But I was very selective about whom I interviewed. Mainly, I guarded against people I felt might be too emotionally involved." She did not talk, for instance, to Herman's younger brother, Joseph L. Mankiewicz. An important clue came from Sam Zolotow, who had been on the *Times* when Herman Mankiewicz had worked there in the mid-Twenties. "I got a lot of help from the secretary, Mrs. Rita Alexander, who had taken the dictation from Mankiewicz and done the typing from start to finish. It was one of those funny things; it turned out she now lived only four blocks from me."

One person she did not contact was Welles himself. "He has talked about *Kane,*" she said, "over the years, here and in England, and I felt there was nothing to talk with him about. I know what he has to say."

Once into the writing, she knew she was going far beyond her original assignment from Marc Jaffe, who informed her that her contract allowed her to retain magazine rights. "About seventy-five pages into it, I wanted

to see if *The New Yorker* would be interested in publishing it, and I went
to see William Shawn and asked him if he would like to read some of
what I was doing. I handed him the seventy-five pages, he asked me to sit
down, and he started reading. After twenty pages he looked up, said,
'I'm buying it,' and then went on while I sat there." Jaffe, with an
important script and an important essay on it in hand, then arranged for
Atlantic-Little, Brown to bring out a hardcover edition, to be published
in September, at which time the fuss over *Raising Kane* should become
louder and more furious.

A good deal of the currently intense interest in film criticism is due to
this same dedicated lady, who feels that movies are worth as much time
and attention "as any art form that involves the emotions and minds of
people, and affects their lives." With no stipulations on the length of
what she writes for *The New Yorker,* she has been able to go into the kind
of careful analysis she feels is her forte as a writer on film. "But people,"
she said, "constantly refer to film criticism as though it were new. There
was tremendous interest in Agee's criticism, and people read Otis Ferguson back in the Thirties."

Since she makes it a point of seeing six or seven films a week, her own
writing is often done in the late hours. She does it in longhand, scribbling
away sometimes until dawn breaks over Central Park. She has never
learned to type. The best Christmas gift she ever got was when her
daughter announced to her that she had secretly learned to type and
would henceforth do her typing. While some unhappy film-makers call
her venomous, and reviewers will occasionally refer to her work as
"bitchy" (a description conveniently applicable to the writings of a
woman), she feels it would be callous and stupid to neglect the evidence
of her eyes and ears. "People talk about how great movies are," she
said, "and they never go to them. It's a minority audience now, and that
minority seldom sees more than six movies a year."

She can be as formidable in person as in her writing. The film-maker
who tangles with her had best have strong defense positions. Those who
happened to be present when she and Norman Mailer discussed his films
were treated to a rare example of intellectual infighting. Women's Lib is
not a subject that interests her, nor are other women's organizations. "I
love what I'm doing."

If there is a question most often asked her by those she meets, it is the
meaning of her title, *I Lost It at the Movies.* "What," I once asked her,
"did you lose at the movies?" I treasure the answer she gave me. "Oh,"
she said with a sigh, "there are so many kinds of innocence to be lost at
the movies."

Pauline Kael Wants People to Go to the Movies: A Profile

George Malko / 1972

From *Audience* January–February 1972: 38–48. Reprinted with permission from George Malko.

If fate ever condemns you to suffer through a really bad movie, pray that some quirk of same puts you in a seat next to Pauline Kael. She cannot make what is happening up there on the screen go away, but she can jolt you into a kind of super-awareness of why what you're looking at doesn't succeed. That is the experience she recreates so tellingly week after week in her reviews for *The New Yorker*. It is a combination of the visceral and the cerebral, and it succeeds in making you *care*, in making you realize, for example, why you want to machine-gun the screen after seeing something unusually ghastly. "Soldiers have done that during wartime," Miss Kael recalls matter-of-factly. "They've shot up the screen. They did it during World War II, at a movie called *Four Jacks and a Jill*. And they did it at other pictures, too. They shot up the condescending, patronizing, patriotic pictures."

Miss Kael imparts her special presence no matter where she sees a movie, in a crowded commercial theater or in a by-invitation-only screening room. Take one particular screening: It is maybe half-an-hour into the movie, people around you are starting to mumble things like, "Oh, *Jesus*," in that disgusted tone of voice that says they are really tired of being used, again, and next to you Pauline Kael, a small lady who has to move from one seat to another when anyone at all big-shouldered sits in front of her, sinks even lower in her seat and, eyes still glued faithfully to the screen as for the fourth time now a hypodermic needle slides lubriciously into the veins of a compliant actor willing to portray the agonies of addiction, says with more weariness than annoyance, "Oh, my God . . ."

A heavy, at times emotional sigher, Miss Kael is not the critic who talks most relentlessly during movies. "A lot of them talk," says Charlie Powell, former National Publicity Manager for Columbia Pictures. "The classic is John Simon. He mumbles to himself in German through the whole film." Miss Kael is not quite like that. But when she has really had it with a picture she lets you know. Watching a particular drawn-out scene in which nothing at all is happening, she sits up and whispers, really only to herself. "They're dishrags up there." And then at a certain moment, weary of talking either to herself or the movie, she whips out a small pad and a pencil and begins taking notes furiously: short notes scribbled hastily, eyes never leaving the screen, hand working across the tiny piece of paper, finger flipping to the next page, hand writing on and on, eyes on that giant screen, head dropping for one moment only to see if, by chance, she has written right off the edge of the pad and onto the purse and raincoat lying on her lap.

This lack of reserve prompted Cinerama Releasing Corporation not too long ago to initiate a policy of individual screenings for each critic because her remarks were affecting her fellow critics. As one of New York's top independent film publicists, who prefers to remain anonymous, says, "They [her fellow critics] like Pauline a lot and they respect her a great deal, and when Pauline says, 'Oh, my God, what a load of crap!' and *they know* that that's going to be in an anthology in six months"—he has to laugh at this point "—I think it affects them."

Out on the street after the screening, Miss Kael asks, "Can you imagine somebody taking someone to a movie like that?" She doesn't wait for an answer but muses about what can possibly be gained from seeing the movie she has just seen. Yes, drugs are death, and addicts lifeless, she says, but the movie has been so relentlessly, so monotonously depressed and undeveloped. "*They* are killing the audience?" And Pauline Kael desperately wants people to go to the movies.

There is a kind of ferocious tenacity about the way she acts on this conviction, a fanaticism about what a film is capable of being, that makes movie executives cringe in the privacy of their corporate sanctuaries and publicists worry about who she's going to rend asunder next. They seem to think of her as a nagging terrier who, jaws locked and hold secure, hangs on until the lumbering Hollywood-made behemoth is brought, whimpering, to its knees. But rather than admit this they speak of her with an odd blend of pragmatism and circumspection because, as former *Newsweek* film critic Joe Morgenstern puts it, "They'll need her on their next movie, and they know it." They say things like, "When she likes one of your films you're very happy about it, when she doesn't you're very unhappy about it. At times she's infuriating, at times she's quite lovable, depending upon what she's saying about your picture."

Miss Kael is aware of the power of her position. "With a new movie," she says, "if you point out too many of the things that are the matter with it, people will use that as an excuse not to go. If you get *anything* out of a movie, I mean if there's anything there to be gotten, help people to get it. Never give them the excuse to stay home if there's anything there on the screen. There are so few movies that really offer you anything that's fresh, that's different, that's exciting. And there are so few movies where the life and death of that director makes a difference in the history of the art."

A few weeks later this conviction is put to the test. The father of her twenty-two-year-old daughter, Gina, is in New York—Miss Kael is divorced, three times according to some published sources, four according to others who refuse to be identified—and invites Miss Kael to some kind of a film-people dinner in Chinatown. At the last minute she calls and begs off because she feels it is much more important to go back and see Robert Altman's newest film, *McCabe & Mrs. Miller,* which she has already seen once, and has written about at great length and with thoughtful enthusiasm. She wants to see the movie again to be sure her sensibilities haven't failed her, that some unrecognized state of mind hasn't influenced her unduly. She is, she admits readily, worried about the movie's future and feels her review is important to its survival. She is seeing it again so she can say, as unequivocally as possible that, yes, she is absolutely sure it is damn close to being a masterpiece. Going into the screening room she says, "I've rarely wanted a movie to succeed as much as this one." So Gina's father is left to go to the dinner alone and Pauline Kael is in the screening room waiting to find out if she was right.

If seeing a bad movie with her is a small adventure of survival, seeing a good one is no less illuminating, even though she says not a single word and jots down only four words of notes during the entire showing. Her enthusiasm for what the director has put onto the screen produces in her a radiating silence and incredible attention. There is also a certain anxiety, since she feels she's still alone in her affections. When the picture ends she has confirmed all of her excitement, and now, standing up to leave, senses the indecisive optimism hanging in the air. People are saying things like "Interesting," and "I *really* think it's going to do well," with about as much conviction as a skier with a double spiral fracture who keeps telling everybody he's going to be back on the old boards in no time. She excuses herself to walk over and say a few words to Robert Altman, telling him once again how much she loves the film. They talk quietly for a moment or two and he seems to appreciate her words. He must know she's not lying because she didn't hesitate to tell the world how little she thought of his previous film, *Brewster McCloud.* As Miss Kael leaves the screening room the talk is definitely not about big box-office; nobody is willing to declare, for the record, that this one's going to be a hit. But by returning to see it a second time, Pauline Kael has honored both Bob Altman and his achievement.

Miss Kael's faith in movies does not mean she is beyond throwing in the towel when a particular picture turns her off completely. "I walk out all the time," she admits candidly. "I walked out on *Quo Vadis,* for example. But I'd never walk out on a movie and then review it without indicating that I'd walked out; I mean, I wouldn't pretend, because suppose the last ten minutes were brilliant and I didn't see it? Which, you know, is conceivable, although rare. Generally speaking, if it's so bad I walk out, I don't mention it. That generally means it's going to flop anyway. There's no reason to kick a guy when he's down."

Miss Kael goes to the movies constantly, even during those six months each year when Penelope Gilliatt replaces her as film critic for *The New Yorker.* During her own six months she is under constant pressure. "Say my deadline is Tuesday, which it is," she explains, her voice barely suggesting the urgency which pursues her from screening to screening. "If I go to the movies all week I may not see the movie I want to cover till Monday night. So then I stay up Monday night and get the review in on Tuesday. I *may* see it Sunday afternoon; I may see it Saturday. I see a lot of movies for every one or two I write up; or the two or three. Very often I make notes during a movie, but I don't remember to look at them when I write the review. You want to be sure you won't forget something, but then who has time to look at his own notes? You write fast if you're a critic."

She writes all of her reviews in longhand, sitting on a straight-backed chair on the seat of which is a doubled-over bed pillow. Her desk is a large drafting table with a gawky-looking elbow-lamp attached to one corner. Scattered over the table's broad surface are various small rocks, sea shells, and an antique double-welled inkstand with both wells filled to overflowing with paper clips; there are scraps of paper with scribbled notes, a diary, jars of pencils, and a large electric pencil sharpener. A copy of the *Random House Dictionary* sits on a four-sided book hutch next to the drafting table. When the phone rings, she answers it almost immediately, even when working. She laughs or commiserates readily with whoever is calling about whatever it is that is going to happen or was meant to happen, keeping the conversation headed steadily toward termination. She will, if disappointed by some bit of news, utter a very ladylike and precisely enunciated "Oh, shit," managing, unlike that famous Radcliffe girl who died at the tender age of twenty-five, to lend the expression genuine personal charm.

It often takes her most of the night to finish a review. Behind her, through the double doors leading into her bedroom, Bushy, the surviving male of a much-loved pair of wizened-face basenjis, burrows among the blankets on her bed and keeps her faithfully silent company. When she has finally finished, she leaves the review for Gina to type up in the morning. By the time Miss Kael awakens, the typescript is finished and she checks it over, adding phrases here or there if she decides she hasn't made a point with sufficient emphasis or grace. This meticulous attention to both detail and style is the reason so many people read her not only to find out what she thinks of a movie, but because she's a genuine writer. As one former senior studio executive didn't hesitate to say: "I think it's generally accepted that Pauline is one of the finest writers and critics working today." Former Columbia Pictures executive Charlie Powell says, "I think Pauline is one hell of a writer; I think she's as good a film *writer* as there is."

When she has finished her corrections, Gina retypes the review. Then, toward six in the evening, a messenger from *The New Yorker* appears to pick it up and take it directly to the home of William Shawn, the magazine's editor-in-chief. "Shawn has to go through it and take out any dirty words," Miss Kael says merrily, as if enchanted to acknowledge her respected editor's fame as a somewhat conservative man. Two hours after he has received her review he calls, usually to say no more than that he has received it and everything is fine. He may go so far as to say, "It's a good piece," which for Pauline Kael means, as she admits, "a good night's sleep." She explains, "Shawn is a great editor. He really is what a writer looks for; it's what you never think you'll find: an editor who gives you space, who doesn't let anybody pressure you, and who pays you. You know: space, freedom, and pay . . . *God*."

That softly uttered *God* is not to be taken lightly. Pauline Kael has been hassled one way or another ever since the day people in the movie industry realized this disarming-looking, small-featured and bespectacled woman who had spent twenty-five years fighting to write about movies the way she wanted to write about them, was here to stay. When Mike Nichols' *Carnal Knowledge* is being screened in New York for critics and that ephemeral crowd known as the taste-makers, she finds herself being kept out of all the screenings. Though this occurs during her six months off the magazine, she has agreed to do the week's review because it is fairly common knowledge around the film industry that Nichols and Miss Kael's fellow *New Yorker* film critic Penelope Gilliatt had been close friends at one time, and *The New Yorker* does not want to be suspected of printing either a very good or a very bad review of *Carnal Knowledge* for reasons that have nothing to do with the film's excellence. So Pauline

Kael calls the distributor every day for almost a week, asking when she can come and see the picture. There is always a reason why she can't, and she's wearily accustomed to all the ploys. "They no longer say 'We won't let you in,' " she says. "Now, they often don't ask me until the last minute. Or they somehow manage to 'overlook' me so that I won't make my deadline. They just maneuver so somehow they forget to ask me, and if I phone, and say 'I really need to see it,' they say 'Oh, we're sorry. We're not holding any more screenings. It was an oversight we didn't ask you.' All that kind of stuff." She shakes her head in disgust, then, looking as if she's about to burst out laughing: "My daughter's been invited by friends to see movies that the studio men told me they hadn't screened yet! The fact is, they know I can see it on opening day and still get the review into *The New Yorker,* but what they're afraid of is that newspaper critics in other parts of the country may be paying a little attention to me. If *possible,* they like me to be late, that's all."

Eventually, because she must see *Carnal Knowledge,* she calls John Springer, press representative for Mike Nichols. Springer is genuinely upset at what is happening and assures her she will be on the following evening's list. When she arrives, her name is not on the list and the functionary at the door refuses her entry. She patiently explains that John Springer has arranged for her name to be on the list, constantly interrupting her quiet argument to turn and greet people she knows as they file past her into the screening room. When Springer himself appears, she appeals to him. Springer takes the guard aside and they converse for several moments in hushed voices. "They cater to the press they know they can count on," Miss Kael observes with intentionally serene indifference. "They prefer people they can trust; they know there are certain people they can influence, you know, indirectly, nicely. Nothing overt." Springer comes back, apologizes for the misunderstanding, and motions her into the now packed screening room. She watches *Carnal Knowledge* sitting on a folding chair in one of the aisles.

A few days later, looking back on the whole silly business, she says, "They're such poor judges, they never know what I'll like or what I won't like." A former studio executive agrees, "You can't really find why she didn't like one picture when she did like one like it a short time ago." Then, perhaps because this sounds as if he thinks Miss Kael irrational, he feels compelled to add: "I guess everybody's human."

Particularly human are those film industry executives who continually find ways of hedging their reservations about the actual extent of her power. Says a vice president of one of the major studios, "I don't know that she makes or breaks movies." Says Charlie Powell, now assistant to

Hollywood producer Mike Frankovich: "Most movie people honestly feel that with the exception of two or three critics around the world, criticism doesn't hurt or help most films, that there's only a certain type of film that a review such as Kael's will affect. That goes for all average Hollywood films, with the exception of a four-star review in *The Daily News*—Wanda Hale's review is a goddamn sight more important than all the other reviews put together. We're not for a specialized audience; the mass audience never even heard of Pauline Kael. I also contend that a lot of people who read her aren't moviegoers anyway, they're just readers, clever readers who see two pictures a year. She doesn't affect us one way or the other. I don't say it arrogantly, I say it realistically."

A New York publicist disagrees: "You read Pauline everywhere, and you see Pauline everywhere, and she goes on television shows, and she goes on Barry Gray [a popular radio talk show in New York City] and the other critics regard her with a good deal of awe, and if the executives had any brains—and they don't—they would recognize that if you go around the country and talk to most of the young critics, you'll find they became interested in film because of Pauline Kael. You talk to Gary Arnold, in Washington, or Roger Ebert, in Chicago; I mean they are Pauline Kael's children, whether she knows it or not. She's had an enormous influence on the business when you have someone who's as iconoclastic as Arnold reviewing in a city like Washington where the other critics write like idiots. Her influence on that level has become enormous. And she also sort of made film criticism a legitimate concern for literate young men. Not only because she's a good writer, but also because she wrote about film as if she liked it. People sort of assume the lasting review will be Pauline's. That's the enduring review, that's the one that's going to be collected." The man pauses, and then, experienced enough to be a realist, adds, "I like Pauline a lot though I don't like to see her walk into my screenings. Under any circumstances."

Certainly the most famous Pauline Kael cause-célèbre involved her review of *The Sound of Music,* which appeared in *McCall's* in 1966, during the few months she was its reviewer. "The audience for a movie of this kind," she had written, "becomes the lowest common denominator of feeling: a sponge." When, soon thereafter, she was fired from the magazine, a lot of people were convinced it was because that particular review had produced enormous pressure from Twentieth Century-Fox. A film industry executive close to the episode at that time denies it: "I can say categorically that it's absolutely untrue, that no one involved with the studio raised a finger. I ran into her at that time at a meeting that was hosted by the Motion Picture Association for Jack Valenti, and she had

just been fired a week or so before, and she and I suddenly found
ourselves in the center of a ring of people expecting a big brawl. I think
she was very bitter and was under the impression—or chose to believe—
that we had gotten her fired. I told her then that this was not true, that we
hadn't done it. The picture had mixed reviews—I mean it wasn't all
pans—but I would say the serious critics tended to pan it, and by that
time we knew we had a hit of phenomenal proportions; another highbrow
blast would not affect business."

Miss Kael herself has never insisted she was fired just because of her
Sound of Music review. "It was because of a lot of movies," she says.
"There was a definite change of policy on the magazine and I was part of
the policy they dropped."

Bob Stein, who was editor of *McCall's* at that time and who, with the
change of policy, was moved upstairs to the position of senior vice
president, agrees only too happily that it was much more than *The Sound
of Music* that got her fired. "It was really more complicated than that,"
he says. "We had signed her as a reviewer on a six months' basis. It was
admittedly an experiment, because she wasn't by any stretch of the
imagination a natural choice for a mass magazine reviewer. But we were
trying to do better things in a lot of areas in the magazine and we thought
we would try her. What happened over a period of some months—and I
should say that I was a great admirer of hers before I hired her and I'm a
great admirer of hers still; I read her reviews religiously—but what
created a problem for us, was that she was doing short reviews of a lot of
movies, which is not her best running time."

Miss Kael remembers wanting to prove that the generalizations made
about the fifteen million women who bought and read *McCall's* were
wrong, that they had views of their own and were open to fresh opinions.
She failed.

"When you're editing a large magazine," Stein explains, "it's very
hard to isolate your responses on any single thing because you're dealing
with so damn many at the same time, and God knows I may have
transferred my problems about *other* things to Pauline, but I did get the
progressive feeling that there was a nasty edge to some of the things she
was doing, and what sticks in my mind is when it just got personal. For
example, she would criticize Lana Turner for getting old, and she would
criticize producers for what their previous occupations were—things like
that—which seemed to me not in line with the kind of reviewing of hers
that I admired. I don't know what particularly brought it on. My own
guess is that reviewing for a mass magazine, she seemed to have some
need to make it clear how independent she was. She would say: 'Doesn't

Paul Newman have anything better to do than make a picture like
Harper?' Okay, she's the reviewer and I'm not. She can say *Harper* is a
bad picture from here to doomsday and deal with the picture, but I did
find that she would continue to sort of gratuitously attack people *ad
hominem* for their motives, their backgrounds—God knows, poor Lana
Turner for her age—and I really objected to that. That's a luxury I didn't
allow anybody else who was writing for the magazine. It's not too
characteristic of her, and may very well have been a symptom of her
unease, that she was in a cramped position somehow writing for the
magazine. I tried, even at the time, to make it clear that I wasn't mad at
her, that it wasn't *The Sound of Music.*'' Stein stops abruptly. "First of
all,'' he says quickly, "the movie people don't have any hold on mass
magazines. They never did. They used to advertise, they haven't adver-
tised for years. So even if you tried to picture the situation at its most
venal, what force could their complaints have had? Probably, perversely,
we would have gotten tougher about backing her up if they had put some
pressure on us. No, it's just that I got uncomfortable with what she was
doing and I didn't think it was right, and I'm sorry, and even looking
back at it from this distance, it's one of those things I don't know about.
I may have overreacted.''

"As a matter of fact,'' Stein goes on, "that piece on *The Sound of
Music* was one of the ones I liked best. I was quite pleased with it
because that seemed to me to be a very proper thing to be doing in a
mass magazine, to deflate something that was that popular, that many of
the readers either had seen or might see. So I had really no objections to
that and I don't know how the story ever got started that it was about
The Sound of Music, except that I suppose it made a good story that a
big, sloppy mass magazine like *McCall's* wasn't going to let anybody
criticize a big treacly movie like *The Sound of Music.* It wasn't about that
at all.''

An executive who was involved with the episode from the studio's side
says, "It's possible she was fired because the editors concluded that she
was out of touch with the readership that they were catering to. And their
view of criticism was of something to be a guide—what to see, what not
to see—rather than what to think about.''

In any case, the major studios were delighted to see her go. "If I hadn't
gotten the job at *The New Yorker,*'' Miss Kael says bluntly, "I'm not sure
that I'd still be a movie critic. There was a period there when I wasn't
allowed into screenings, when four of the majors were keeping me out,
and they effectively drove me out of the monthlies.'' (Most people seem
to have forgotten that she used to contribute to quarterlies such as *Sight*

and Sound and *Film Quarterly,* and monthly magazines such as *Harper's,
The Atlantic, Holiday, Mademoiselle,* and *Vogue.*) "You can't write for a
monthly magazine," she explains, "unless you see the movie when they
first screen it. You can write for a weekly, but they kept me out of the big
important monthlies."

The animosity expressed toward her seems to have been grounded in
more than her outspoken criticism. As the New York publicist explains,
"Pauline doesn't play any of the games. She doesn't dress New York,
she isn't polite and social—none of those things. I remember when she
first came to New York, which would've been six or seven years ago. She
showed up at something wearing a dress with a hole in it, under her arm,
and it was really The Scandal. I remember her showing up that way, and
everybody being just totally horrified, just really horrified that she would
do this. You look at the other female critics and by and large they're a
fairly chic, social group of ladies who play the success game very hard,
and on one level or another are susceptible to all sorts of inducements.
Sometimes just attention does it: sending a car."

"I don't fraternize in general," Pauline Kael says, less as a statement
of principle than of fact. "I don't do interviews, and I try to avoid most
actors and actresses. They don't understand what criticism is about: they
think it's all just personal bitchery."

"Pauline," says the publicist, "plays *none* of those games at all.
There's just no way anybody can get to Pauline, they've got nothing to
offer her; because she isn't interested in the movie business, she's
interested in the movies."

"The most common way that movie critics are bought," she says late
one evening, "and I mean *bought* in the specific sense, is that the
producers hire them to write a movie script. The movie script is never
made. It's put on the shelf. But they give them eight thousand dollars, or
ten thousand dollars, or fifteen thousand dollars for it, and, that man is
able to buy a house in the country, or a farm, or *something.* He's got a
little bit of property, and he's perpetually beholden to those producers,
and those companies, because they've given him that little bit of dough.
Once you work for them, you are *theirs.* It's one of the reasons for not
writing movie scripts. Chances are the movie'll never get made, or will
be rewritten. I mean, the chances of their using your script are rather
slim. It's one thing if as a critic you get to know a director and you know
what he wants and you write a script for him. But if you deal with the
producer, or a company, to write a script for them, they're simply buying
you. Chances are it's twenty-five thousand dollars in the bank and that's

the end of the transaction. But you are *their* man. And I will not be their woman."

"She's had offers," says Bob Mills, Miss Kael's literary agent. "I don't know about writing, so much, but as an assistant director, a 'technical advisor.' There have been a number of inquiries of that general nature."

Those who go for it don't surprise or upset her. "Most of the critics who do that are not good critics," she says simply. "The good critics who are writers in any sense—Gavin Lambert, for example—some of their work gets made. I mean Agee's work, some of it at least got made and the rest got published. Penelope Gilliatt, her film *[Sunday Bloody Sunday]* is made. But the critics who get 'bought' by the studios are not surprised when the films are not made. There are many, many, many who have done this. And I think they deceive themselves."

It is, as even Faulkner and Fitzgerald have been ready to admit, the money. "I am staggered," she says, "by the fact that a mediocre writer, who gets *one* movie on the screen, can then command a price of a hundred, or a hundred and fifty thousand, to adapt a novel. He doesn't even have to *write,* he just has to do reconstruction. You know how hard other people work for money. I mean, no one else *sees* that kind of money. It's only in show business—or now in music—that people make amounts like that. It's totally irrational. But these second-rate, *fourth-* rate writers, who've never written anything or published anything under their own name—maybe a couple of television adaptations or television originals—six months of their work, constructing a screenplay out of a novel, are apparently worth a hundred thousand dollars to somebody. But that is *incredible* in terms of the salaries in this country, and how other writers live. I mean, most good writers never come *near* money like that!" Then she adds, with a tiny note of unexpected regret. "And it took me so long even to make a living as a writer at all."

Her resentment, what there is of it, is directed not so much at the years she struggled to achieve her present eminence, but at the energy it all consumed. "I've made about *twelve* starts," she says. "The awful thing is that they consume your best years. They took away the energy I need now."

In order to survive over the years she was a cook and a seamstress— "God, two years as a seamstress! Do you know what that does to you? You know, not only your eyes?"—and she wrote advertising copy, first for Houghton Mifflin and then for American Book. She sold baby photo-graphs and insurance over the phone from home for seventy-five cents an hour, and she gave music lessons, and tutored people in what she

remembers as "weird fields I don't know anything about, like anthropol-
ogy." She sold books—"what writer hasn't?"—and ghosted books,
preferring to forget their titles because, this said with a quick laugh,
"there's ethics in crime."

Pauline Kael was the youngest member of a large family and lived on a
farm thirty miles north of San Francisco. "I remember my father," she
wrote toward the end of a long review of *Hud,* a review directed in part
at those critics who found the character of Hud to be that of a dangerous
social predator because of his *indulgences:* "I remember my father taking
me along when he visited our local widow: I played in the new barn
which was being constructed by workmen who seemed to take their
orders from my father. At six or seven, I was very proud of my father for
being a protector of widows . . . My father, who was adulterous, and a
Republican who, like Hud, was opposed to any government interference,
was in no sense and in no one's eyes a social predator. He was generous
and kind, and democratic in the western way that Easterners still don't
understand . . ." Miss Kael has never written so boldly of her mother
because she feels to have been much closer to her mother than she was
to her father. But it was an inner closeness rather than the remove from
which she knew her father. He was more considerable as a subject for
her opinions; her mother was . . . her mother.

When she was eight, the family moved into San Francisco. She read
voraciously all through high school and college. At college, she majored
in philosophy of history, but most of her friends were English majors and
she remembers arguing with them endlessly about Ezra Pound and James
Joyce. She was first drawn to film criticism when she worked with such
underground film-makers as James Broughton. Her creatively formative
years were centered at Berkeley, where, in the late 1950's, she successfully managed twin art-movie houses: the "first twin art-movie houses in
the country," she says with pride. She was married, not very happily,
and living in a home where the prized possession was a gigantic 35mm
projector sitting in the middle of the living room. It was, as one person
remembers it, a monster of a machine, with a throw that "went right
through the living room, the dining room, into the kitchen."

Less palmy days are remembered in unusual terms. "I never saw *The
Greatest Story Ever Told,*" she says unexpectedly, as if to tell herself it
really happened once upon a time, "simply because it was rather expensive to go to see. At this point it seems rather beside the point. But I was
embarrassed one day when I had lunch with the director, George Stevens,
and he wanted to know what I thought of it."

She clearly remembers her success as an advertising copy writer because she gave it all up so suddenly. "The *day* they were putting up the partition and putting my name on the door I went in and quit in tears because I suddenly saw myself behind that partition for years. And I didn't *want* that, I wanted to write." The moment seems oppressively vivid, and she shakes it off. "The main thing is fighting off the successes that trap you. That's the really weird part of it."

Late one afternoon she finds herself trying to explain why she hasn't considered imitating her French counterparts, critics like Truffaut and Louis Malle, and become a director. "I wanted to do those things thirty years ago," she says patiently. "Now, it would be very stupid—" She catches herself in mid-sentence, and then, angry now at having to answer this unpleasantly familiar question. "Why aren't people satisfied with the fact that I try very hard to be a good critic? Why when someone works for a long time to become a good critic is it necessary to say, 'Why don't you become a screen writer? Why don't you become a director?' Do you know how hard it is to be a good critic? The whole thing that sustains me in writing is to tackle new ideas, new subject matter, new areas: but the whole thing of changing myself and becoming something else . . ."

She slows, and explains further. "As you grow older, you have to accept the fact that the steps you've taken have turned you into a certain kind of person. When I ran theaters, I had the kind of business sense to deal with the film companies. I no longer have the kind of disposition I'd need to deal with the unions, and all of the tough men, and the crews I'd have to deal with if I became a director. If I went into directing, or into something actively involved in making movies, I'd have to go back into business." She understands what it takes to be a director in this country. "He has to be, a good part of him, a businessman. Or work, as a team, with a producer, who keeps the business pressures off him. It's what's killed most American directors. They don't have anyone to take off the business pressures; they spend all their time setting up the deals, rather than making the movie. If Sam Peckinpah had someone to handle the business he could be a truly great director."

She laughs suddenly, reminded of something. "By the way, I have this thing which I point out to Gina: when directors come to see me, and very often they do—often I've never met them before—they always come into the apartment and sit down in a certain chair." She points to it, a simple straight-backed chair, one of four around a table. Sitting in that chair you get a breathtaking view of Central Park, including the entire breadth of the reservoir which, toward dusk on almost any day, takes on a mellow, almost somber, tone, with two or three seagulls floating placidly on its surface. Beyond the reservoir, resting among the trees like some concrete conical hat, is Frank Lloyd Wright's Guggenheim Museum. And around it all is the anomalous serenity of the park as seen from this distance. "The first time Peckinpah ever visited here he came in the room and sat down in that chair. And it's not because I was sitting opposite. Often directors sit down before I do." She laughs again, pleased by how she noticed this absolutely lovely thing, pleased to know how right a touch it is. "I think," she says, "it's so they can command the vista. Peckinpah sat in that chair, Kershner sat in that chair, Wyler sat in that chair, Mazursky sat in that chair, Altman sat in that chair. They have *never* sat in another chair in the house. Recently, a director—and it made me very nervous—came in, and sat in *that* chair—" she points to another chair, more of an easy chair with arms, which faces in a different direction, "—and I thought to myself, 'He's going to have a flop.' It really made me nervous."

She talks as directly as she writes and while being all sweetness and light about Sam Peckinpah—"I voted for him as the best director of the year that year"—suddenly veers like a car in which the driver has floored the gas pedal for no apparent reason, and says, in answer to an innocuous comment about Ken Russell's *The Music Lovers:* "You really feel you should drive a stake through the heart of the man who made it. I mean it is so vile. It is so horrible. I know all sorts of people who didn't believe my review, went to see it, and they phoned and said, 'You didn't make it bad enough. It's the most horrible thing I've ever seen!' "

Pauline Kael has never retreated from a printed review—she stands by what is published—but she is willing to admit a factual error on those rare occasions when she makes one. She is so seldom wrong because, as Joseph Morgenstern points out, "Her knowledge of movies is encyclopedic." But she has been wrong, and when the writer or director whom she has slighted has written to explain the mistake, she usually responds immediately and openly. Novelist James Salter, who is also a screenwriter and director, wrote her after she had criticized something in his screenplay for *Downhill Racer.* He explained that the passage she had singled out was not his and hadn't been in the original screenplay. Several mornings later, as Salter recalls, his phone rang at his home in Aspen, Colorado, and a cheerful voice said, "Hi, it's Pauline Kael." She wanted him to know she appreciated his letter, and was sorry she had misattributed the passage in question. "It's pretty tough," she explained, "but you have to go by the credits on the screen."

What does she think of her colleagues? "I think there are three or four pretty good ones," she says. "I think at the moment Gary Arnold is

good. I think Canby [Vincent Canby of the *New York Times*] has been
perceptive. I think Andy Sarris [Andrew Sarris of *The Village Voice*] has
some marvelous perceptions from time to time. I disagree with his theory
about film aesthetics, but he has interesting things to say."

Sarris, unfortunately, does not return the compliment. Vincent Canby
admires her, and Joseph Morgenstern, former film reviewer for *Newsweek*, says, "She opens up questions that nobody else opens up." *Life*'s
Richard Schickel recently wrote a very long piece for *Harper's* in which
he expressed his admiration for her enthusiastic devotion to films. But
when *The New Yorker* published her two-part article on *Citizen Kane*
which now serves as the introduction to the published original screenplay,
Andrew Sarris answered it with a long diatribe designed both to criticize
her for what she had set out to do, and to set things straight as regards
Citizen Kane and what *really* happened. At one point, embroiled in
demonstrating why she was being "maliciously misleading" in denying
Orson Welles the full director's credit—author of it all, creator of the
look and style, which can be taken as a simplistic definition of the *author*
theory—he wrote: "What I find peculiar . . . is the malignant anti-
auteurism in the writings of Kael . . . as if auteurism were an established
religion that had carried the day."

When that appeared in *The Village Voice*, a friend called Miss Kael
and read it to her over the phone. She listened, her mouth moving in a
familiar half-smile, broadening and narrowing as if words and half-formed
phrases were crowding her mind. When the caller had finished she sighed
and said, "I wonder what's wrong with him?" She added a small shrug,
a grace note of regret, and said, "I hope everything's all right at home."

It is a dig, yes, inspired in part by two embarrassingly self-revelatory
articles written by Sarris and his wife for *Vogue*. While Miss Kael herself
can be relentlessly confessional when arguing a point about a certain
film, she loathes that special contemporary glorification of personal data
bared solely for the purpose of advancing celebrity. (Still, what could be
more personal than the following from a Pauline Kael review: *"When*
Shoeshine *opened in 1947, I went to see it alone after one of those
terrible lovers' quarrels that leave one in a state of incomprehensible
despair. I came out of the theater, tears streaming, and overheard the
petulant voice of a college girl complaining to her boyfriend, 'Well, I
don't see what was so special about that movie.' I walked up the street,
crying blindly, no longer certain whether my tears were for the tragedy
on the screen, the hopelessness I felt for myself, or the alienation I felt
from those who could not experience the radiance of Shoeshine. For if
people cannot feel Shoeshine what can they feel?")*

One comes to realize, finally, that for Pauline Kael, writing film criticism is not only a chance to write about the way we live in this country at this particular moment. It is also, very often, a necessary act of protection. "You have to recognize what is important for the art of the movies," she says. "The movies that have the big publicity budgets and the advertising, they will take care of themselves. I mean, the critic is the answer to advertising, mostly because the advertising *protects*. The critic is the only protection for the *art* of the film for which there isn't a big budget and a lot of advertising. A movie like *The Conformist* is *exactly* the kind where you've got to help that director [Bernardo Bertolucci] keep working because he is a major talent. It was the same with Godard's early films, or *Bonnie and Clyde*, or *China Is Near*, or Bob Altman—when Fox didn't know what they had in M*A*S*H—or Fred Wiseman's documentaries. If there's a chance that you can help, you do. And so the deficiencies you minimize, I mean just instinctively. If you're sane you just *have* to."

Pauline Kael Talks About Violence, Sex, Eroticism and Women & Men in the Movies
Leo Lerman / 1972

From *Mademoiselle* July 1972: 132–33, 173–78. Courtesy *Mademoiselle*. Copyright (c) 1972 by the Condé Nast Publications, Inc.

Editor's Note: Pauline Kael is passionate about movies. They are one of her life's deep centers. She and her daughter, Gina, also love opera, flowers, Art Nouveau glass, beasts: in residence, Bushy, a tan & white dapper dog (that's he, left, drawn by the projectionist in a movie house Pauline ran in Calif.) and Kiss, a slinky black cat. "I published my first piece in 1953 . . . a review of Chaplin's *Limelight*—which I did *not* like." And she's been writing about movies ever since, most recently and extensively for *The New Yorker*. Gathered Kael: *Going Steady; I Lost It at the Movies; Kiss Kiss Bang Bang; The Citizen Kane Book*. Coming Kael: a huge gatherum which "reads like a history of the past three years in this changing industry."

Pauline Kael: Some people are staying away from movies because of the violence, and on the other hand, the drug generation reacts differently from the way some of us do. Violent behavior on the screen may stir them; they may experience it as a jolt and enjoy the excitement of it.
Mademoiselle: My friends go to a movie like *El Topo,* but they're not really excited by the violence. It's that if you don't enjoy it, you aren't chic.
PK: Some of the violence in *El Topo* is funny. But a lot of animals are killed in that movie, and that's *not* funny. Those animals are really being killed. It's a very creepy thing to hear a young audience laughing and reacting at the same level to the surreal comic incidents and to actual death. They may *want* to believe that it's all fake. The movie that shocked me the most deeply, the one I really could barely deal with in print was Polanski's *Macbeth.* The murder of Lady Macduff, the torn bodies scattered around, the pieces of children's bodies, like a chicken yard, the knives constantly going into flesh had me shaking afterward. I felt numb. When I came home my daughter thought I'd been mugged. Yet there

31

were schoolchildren in the theatre—they're going in busloads to see it—and they didn't seem to be bothered by it. They may take it as *theatre*, that is, as unreal, in the same way TV violence is unreal to them. Perhaps even death in war on the news may seem unreal to them when it's juxtaposed with commercials & TV Westerns. I think I reacted to the possibilities of suffering in a way the schoolchildren didn't.

MLLE: I have a young friend who is in his twenties and he said to me, "People getting shot, I don't call violence anymore. But the garrotings in *The Godfather,* and what goes on in *A Clockwork Orange,* in *Straw Dogs* and *Dirty Harry,* that I call violence."

PK: Well, it's all violence, of course, but in *The Godfather,* I felt you were meant to experience the violence as horror, and I did, and I think that's a valid use. But when you are supposed to be turned on by the violence, I mind that. I feel that Polanski is on dangerous ground, on a new borderline, because one experiences the brutality in his films as the *norm* and as meaningless.

MLLE: What is some sort of working definition of objectionable violence?

PK: Perhaps—and this is very rough, with lots of exceptions—when there is really nothing in the movie but the excitement of violence, so that you wait for it and long for the next eruption.

MLLE: When it manipulates you?

PK: Well, it's too easy to use that word for what one dislikes. The spaghetti Westerns work the audience over, but they're not designed to be taken at any deep emotional level. And there are horror movies that are often frightening fun for the young audience. They may take them as a kind of paranoid, head comics. And, as you suggest, they can feel that it's "hip" to laugh at bloody death in *El Topo,* to enjoy brutality and to take it as a sensual pleasure. It *is* a sensual pleasure that way.

MLLE: In *The Conformist* there was violence but it was part of it.

PK: Oh yes, and also the quality of the violence in *The Conformist!* You experienced intensely every violent action as pure horror. You didn't want the girl, Dominique Sanda, to get killed. *Z* was a brutal melodrama and yet every single violent act you experienced with pain. You did not want any of those people to suffer. Whereas the tendency of thoughtless movies—especially *action* movies in which violence has become routinized, conventionalized—is to make you *want* the brutality. You're waiting for it, practically ready to cheer in *Dirty Harry* or *The Cowboys.* And I think this brutality is disassociated from suffering—that is, from your own suffering, because those maimed or killed appear to be subhuman or ridiculous—as in *Straw Dogs*. So instead of being sensitized to pain, you're desensitized.

MLLE: Also in *Z* you could calculate good guys and bad guys.

PK: Well, we weren't supposed to admire those who imposed their will on others. We became more aware of suffering and what it meant, in that movie, even though it was an exciting melodrama. Whereas in *Dirty Harry*, the whole thing is to watch Clint Eastwood, the *good* guy, giving it to everybody. It's the easiest way to make a movie. It's the basic, primitive cops-and-robbers formula, which in itself has always had a dangerous element. Adolescent boys and fantasizing men enjoy identifying with the strong man, the man who lives by his fists or his fast gun.

MLLE: Women too?

PK: I don't think women enjoy these movies the way men do. There has always been the battle, you know, in families, that women don't like men's action movies, and the men often went to Westerns or racing pictures and other action-genre films alone. When I started reviewing movies, I pointed some of this out in analyzing the *auteur* position which glorified men's action movies; I pointed out that there were no women *auteur* critics. It's men who haven't grown up in their tastes, men who retain their adolescent fantasies, who still go to movies for chases and big fights, and all that boy-boy punching around in Western saloons. There is nothing for women to identify with in most of those action films. The actresses are up there worrying and delaying the big sequences with lines like "Please don't go to the underground meeting tonight." Or, "I don't know if I'll be waiting for you." Or, "Be careful!" At a film like *Grand Prix*, the women were sleeping all over the theatre, and the women on the screen were essentially sleeping too, because they were slowing down the action.

MLLE: Do we really have more violence today in films than we did?

PK: This last year, particularly, has been rough. And we've also been getting rightwing movies that glorified violence. People sometimes say that when you pan movies with Eastwood or Wayne, you're panning them for their private political views. But when I review their movies I'm not concerned about their offscreen views, only because their offscreen views are in their movies. *Dirty Harry* and *The Cowboys* are selected and shaped in terms of what these stars want to say, and of their own image of themselves. It isn't simply a matter of politics, but of how the political ideas shape the content of the films. Last year, I found the complacent liberalism of a movie such as *The Sporting Club* objectionable, too.

MLLE: *Straw Dogs?*

PK: *Straw Dogs* has taken what was submerged in many action pictures

and made it into a demonstration of a thesis. Directors like Kubrick and
Peckinpah and Polanski have been influenced by the thesis about man's
development—he is violent by nature—that has become popular in the
last few years. They love the idea of man, the predator; it gives them a
kind of intellectual justification for putting more kicks into movies. I think
Peckinpah is a considerable artist, but what comes out in his movies is a
confusion of mind, and a justification for *machismo*. A great many
Hollywood directors—by their whole way of life—get into thinking that
way. They do think of starlets as whores: it's an easy attitude for show-
business people to get into. This is probably going to change (possibly
we'll get something worse—a naked, aggressive sexual hatred), but they
do still fall into it, and the power of the movie director increases
this sense.

MLLE: About sex and violence? Do they equate?

PK: No. They don't at all. I would enjoy seeing sex on the screen that
was erotic. But most of the sex on the screen isn't sensual; it isn't
erotically suggestive; it isn't great fun. One of the reasons that young
Americans have loved Bertolucci's *The Conformist* so much is because it
is *really* sensual. Bertolucci would be a wonderful director of erotic
material. He has the feeling for it, and also he's young and has the
energy. He's sensual not only in the feelings of the men and women
toward each other, and the women toward each other in that movie, but
visually. It's in the color and the style. He touches almost all our senses:
this is why I think he's probably the most talented young film artist in the
world today.

MLLE: Compare it to *The Last Picture Show*.

PK: It's a good movie but there's no real sensuality in it, and what's
there is strictly from a male point of view and a very limited one. The
scenes between the boys and girls are poorly felt, unfelt, really; and the
girls are put down at a very simple level. They're mostly mindless, for
one thing, except for the scheming young vixen and the older women—
Ellen Burstyn and Cloris Leachman. The picture is about male adolescent
desperation and loneliness, with no special responsiveness to the female
adolescents or tenderness toward them.

MLLE: Is it an honest movie? Does it show people as they really are?

PK: Is that a fair question? I think it showed McMurtry's experience
probably pretty honestly. . . . The number of European movies with a
sensual understanding of women is rather limited too. There is one
Godard movie, *Two or Three Things I Know about Her,* which really
shows you how much he loves women. There is a physical awareness of
the heroine, of her body and flesh, that is very unusual.

MLLE: Truffaut?

PK: Truffaut, yes. And yet I feel less so. There's more exploration of women's minds and emotions in Ingmar Bergman's work. But, altogether, it's *very* uncommon in movies, partly because movies have grown up with simple, old-pulp formulas. There really was no place for sensuality in the men's action films. How does sensuality fit in a Western? But comedies often became romantic comedies. Even though there is no real physical contact in *It Happened One Night,* there is a sense of happy, romantic love that touched the imagination of the audience. And when Rogers and Astaire began a dance—well, their dances are perhaps the most exquisite courtship rites we've ever had on the American screen. Pure romance. Not sex, but an idealized sex that for the audiences of my generation seemed *better* than sex. They were *wonderful.* They were sex with wit. . . . One American director who has just shown a sensual approach to the medium, and quite surprisingly, considering the genre, is Coppola, with *The Godfather.* His approach is rich: he has a sense of texture. English movies are not especially visual or erotic, but how would they be? Think of their cities, or of English painting. The English—it's all speech.

MLLE: Did you find *Women in Love* erotic?

PK: In a peculiarly awful way—a kinky way, and kinkiness on the screen has no real resonance. But in *The Godfather*—the family relations, the way people move, and the scene with the girl in Sicily—there is eroticism there. Coppola is going to be a sensual director. Billy Friedkin, who did *The Boys in the Band* and *The French Connection,* won't be. Of the major ranking older directors, the *least* sensual is Stanley Kubrick. That's what was fundamentally missing in his *Lolita,* though it was successful in most other ways. Robert Altman is a sensual director, especially in *McCabe & Mrs. Miller.* Mike Nichols? I felt B'way effectiveness all the way through *Carnal Knowledge,* rather than sensuality. He knows the value of a sensual kick, but that's not the same thing as being a sensual director. You can feel the calculations in every scene. *Carnal Knowledge* has the views of sex that men like to give each other in locker rooms. That's what they pretend, but that's not how they really are with women. When you hear businessmen talking on planes—that's their image of themselves, and what the advertising culture tells them they should be—consumers of women. But that's not how they are.

MLLE: Going back to sex in the movies today. You see so many bedroom scenes, you see violent sex, and I was thinking back to the days of Doris Day, when the virgin triumphed. I was wondering if that reflects the way young people have changed. It's like, when we go to a movie, we say, "Well, if Ali MacGraw, a fine Radcliffe student is doing it, well. . . ."

PK: I'm not sure it's as simple as that. The Doris Day routine of flirting with the idea of bed but never getting there was as commercialized as the new plunking into bed. What upsets a lot of people in these new movies, and bores them finally, is that sex is dehumanized and made impersonal and mechanical, and it's no fun that way. Or rather, it's fun occasionally (both off- & onscreen), but it's not very memorable. Many men probably enjoy hard-core pornography. I don't think women do, as much. There are few—often no—women in the hard-core theatres. I've gone to the $5 theatres, where you see people in various positions performing, and I've been the only woman there, and I don't stay for very long. And yet the same men go again and again. But I think it's a relatively small audience. I've been told that some married couples like to go, not to the hard-core, but to the soft-core, because it gives them new ideas of what to do together. But I think the large audience wants sensuality and eroticism, not just hard-core, mechanized pornography.

MLLE: When we're living during a Vietnam war, why are there no movies about that violence?

PK: Movies rarely deal with social issues directly. The war comes out indirectly. It's come out in a whole series of movies that are based on American self-hatred. Everybody can feel what the war has done to us. But wars are seldom dealt with (except in propaganda terms) while they're going on. *All Quiet on the Western Front* was made many years after World War I. Vietnam we experience indirectly in just about every movie we go to. It's one of the reasons we've had so little romance or comedy—because we're all tied up in knots about that rotten war. It would take a great artist to deal with it directly, and an artist takes time to think it out. *War and Peace* wasn't written during the Napoleonic period, either. I just don't know how a movie artist could deal with the Vietnam war now. The journalistic side is on TV. As for the major issues and what it's doing to us all, there may be great movies that will deal with that—but first, we must get out of it.

MLLE: How does *Sunday Bloody Sunday* fit into all this?

PK: What bothers people in *Sunday Bloody Sunday* is the basic premise. No one really believes that the woman, the way her character is given to us, would be involved with that boy. She would *have* to be a woman who is loused up in certain ways, to be involved with him. You can believe in the relationship of the two men; even sensually, it's convincing. But the relationship of the boy and the woman is not. She's shown to us as absolutely normal, that's the whole premise of the picture, *that they are all normal.* And yet we can't quite believe in her normality.

MLLE: I was thinking of something like *Women in Love,* which had a lot of appeal to young people. A young man my age admitted to me the other day that he loved his best friend, and that's a startling thing for someone to say. One reason the young related to that movie is because they're trying to be open-minded enough to even entertain the idea of a homosexual relationship, but not necessarily a physical one.

PK: I'm old-fashioned enough to think that it's not on a sexual basis, unless there is some sex involved, or unless some horribly repressed sex is involved. Love without sex is something else. I love lots of people. For example, I love Jean Renoir. I really love him, and very personally. I adore him. I think he *knows* I love him, and yet it's a completely nonphysical relationship.

I hope we have more richness and sensuality in movies because that has always been one of the reasons to go to the movies. And gaiety. But gaiety has to wait for the war to end. It's very difficult to make a happy movie now, though I thought *Made for Each Other* a funny movie, and parts of *Bananas* are very, very funny, and the year before that, *The Owl and the Pussycat.* This year, there isn't much comedy. This seems the time for a comedy of sexual role confusion. *Some Like It Hot* tapped it slightly. We all *need* to be able to laugh today at sex confusion. We're very confused *now* when we see 14-year-old boys with eye makeup, and we don't even know if they are homosexual anymore. You can't tell anything!. . . . I see girls in this building going out, and very often [an enormous sigh] the girls are trailing behind the boys and you just know they're not going to have any fun. Girls now miss the courtship rites. We had wonderful places to go to eat and dance—dinner dancing is one of the great joys of life—it's heaven.

MLLE: But what's so sad is that we're afraid to admit that we like to do that.

PK: That's heartbreaking. I don't often see boys carrying flowers anymore, and even though some of that stuff was a lot of conventionalized silliness, some of it was absolutely wonderful.

MLLE: When I look at a Humphrey Bogart movie, or a John Garfield one, well, that's an Event!

PK: Probably part of it is because the sexual differentiation in those movies is very satisfying to the viewer. It's very satisfying to boys to have an image of how it is to be a man, and it's very satisfying to girls to see how a man would treat them. Girls still adore Cary Grant in old movies, even though he's sexually slightly ambiguous, and slightly pas-

sive, because he has elegance, and that's also why they adore Sidney
Poitier. Poitier is clearly a man, and he's like a black Cary Grant—he has
style and physical grace.

MLLE: Are there any younger men like that on the screen?

PK: That's a tough one. George Segal is very likeable but his appeal is
comic and lightweight. Paul Newman has that innate male courtliness and
gentleness in him. It will be interesting to see what Al Pacino does next.
I'm sure at least some of the next male stars will have that unmistakable
masculinity which permits the man also to be gentle, and makes women
and girls feel secure. I thought Robert Redford would be a big star, but
now I think he may have missed his chance. But I do think that this
generation wants what Bogart had, what someone like Garfield had. The
men gave the appearance of being secure in themselves as men, and
that's very important to women. It's going to become *more* important as
things become more insecure in our culture, as I think they may become.
Girls are going to want this image on the screen and they are going to
need it.

MLLE: What will the male audience want from the women on the
screen?

PK: There's much more confusion about that. I'm not at all sure I
know what men want, because men—particularly in the last five years—
and teenage boys have become very unsure of themselves *vis à vis* women
and girls, and I think they are insecure about what their roles should be.
Probably the Women's Liberation Movement has not affected women as
deeply as it has affected men. It has shaken men in their presuppositions,
and that's going to be a problem.

MLLE: So what you're saying is that we really need stars.

PK: Of course we do. Everybody wants stars. You hear in the media
about how all that moviegoers now care abut is *The Director*! But *The
Director* needs stars to work with, to embody his conception. Everybody
wants to see people on the screen who have special intensity, and special
gifts. You go to see something like *Alice's Restaurant* and it's sort of
interesting, but Arthur Penn obviously couldn't bring enough out of Arlo
Guthrie, so there was no full subject in the movie. . . .

The Bebe Daniels movies of the twenties were daredevil-girl stuff.
Bebe was a newsreel camera woman, a journalist, a racing car driver.
Her comedies would come out every few months—they were a continua-
tion of the serials, which often featured active, adventurous "tomboy"
heroines. It was the Lillian Gish kind of women who were frail flowers.
We small kids adored the daredevils, though the flowers weren't *always* a
pain. There were a lot of good periods for women in movies. And there

were times when women were the top stars too. Garbo didn't get into all that trouble by being a shrinking violet. She got into all that trouble by screwing around. And in the '30s, the girls we in the audience loved were delivering wisecracks. They were funny and lovely because they were funny. A whole group of them with wonderful frogs in their throats. They could be serious, too. There was a period in the early '30s when Claudette Colbert, Ann Harding, Irene Dunne and other actresses were running prisons, campaigning for governor or being doctors and lawyers, and it was not until after World War II, when men came back and women were displaced because of the competition for jobs, that the women on the screen changed and became bunnies and cute prostitutes. People don't necessarily learn this from watching old movies on TV because they see things in a jumble and they can't distinguish the different phases. In *Private Worlds,* Claudette Colbert played a psychiatrist who had difficulties with the director of the hospital, Charles Boyer, a European who didn't understand an American professional woman's freedom. That movie had a woman screenwriter. Many fine movies that dealt with women's problems had women screenwriters, and often you *can* feel the difference in the movie. After the War Freud started being misapplied. That's when Rosalind Russell, who had been tough & wisecracking, had to discover at the end of her movies that she had to give up her job and get her man. That's when Ginger Rogers, in the poisonous *Lady in the Dark,* discovered she was running the fashion magazine because there was something the matter with her. This Uncle Tomming killed the endings of a lot of movie comedies because nobody could believe it when Rosalind Russell had to become helpless. Movie women never did recover. Claudette Colbert had been strong, and Jean Arthur, and Katharine Hepburn, Carole Lombard and Joan Blondell and Barbara Stanwyck. Bette Davis demonstrated that women of intensity and drive were exciting to men. She was never any man's inferior. The audience experienced the energy of a woman who was unmistakably female, yet she had charge to her, and she was smart. She rarely played a dumb woman (and wasn't convincing when she did). The fact of her intelligence and her force really represented some kind of liberated American energy. But the '50s and '60s were very bad for women on the screen (and not so good for the self-image of women off-screen either). They played prostitutes most of the time—like Marilyn Monroe and, later, Shirley MacLaine—or nothing. It's a bad joke. That's why there are so few women stars left. But now we do have Streisand, who has a great comedy spark and is very independent, very strong. We have Jane Fonda who has the great acting drive that Bette Davis had. Some women are very uncomfortable around

Streisand, and Minnelli in *Cabaret,* because they've grown up with this thing of giving everything over to the man and the man running the show. These strong women's personalities upset them.

MLLE: Do you think we're ever going to see the return of the male being the victim of feminine wiles, as it went on years and years in movies?

PK: I hope not, because that was the worst. It was degrading to both sexes. If you were acting opposite someone like Kirk Douglas in the '50s, what was there for a girl to be? Did anybody believe all that butchness the men put on? I find it very unappealing and it's boring—those rugged blank faces. I've always rather liked Burt Lancaster, though, and I thought he was beautiful in *The Leopard,* as well as in American films, particularly early in *The Crimson Pirate.* He's a graceful man inside all that *macho.* Most men would probably become much sexier if they gave up that *macho* pose. It has been a trap for the male actors. It's turned Kirk Douglas into a laughing stock—all that fake muscularity. The big-muscle men can rarely use their bodies sensitively and the big muscles can be ugly. You know they come from weight lifting and that throws the role out of whack.

Of course, there have been obstacles to women doing what they wanted, but there have also been paths and loopholes that we have been able to find. Some women couldn't get jobs on magazines and newspapers, so they became agents. So some of the best agents in America are women. It was almost impossible for women to become directors, but they became script girls, and then from that, when talkies came in, they became screenwriters. I don't think anyone—man or woman—starts out in life intending to be a critic. Most directors started out wanting to be actors. You discover your aptitudes as you go along, and you also discover what the jobs really involve. I think my work is right for me. . . . Not too surprisingly, when a woman becomes a critic, the terms in which she is customarily described indicate the condescension and hostility that men seem to be unaware of. Whenever one of my books is reviewed, the same terms come up. I am described as bitchy or nervous or shrill or as impressionistic—that's a favorite term. "Impressionistic" suggests, of course, that the woman doesn't really have a good mind, but that she somehow takes off sense impressions though she can't organize them. If you think of my writing over a period of time, it's far more analytic than that of most of the critics, and that's probably my most serious limitation. But people think of that as a masculine trait, and I don't think I've *ever* been described as analytic. It's astonishing how much nonsense men movie critics can write while thinking of themselves as the possessors of fine masculine intelligences.

Pauline Kael on the New Hollywood

Pat Aufderheide / 1980

From *In These Times* 7–13 May 1980: 12, 23. Reprinted by permission.

Pauline Kael is the premier movie critic in the U.S. Since she began writing about films as a broadcast and print critic (and also film programmer) in 1953, and especially since she became a *New Yorker* critic in 1968, she has consistently challenged, fascinated and enraged readers with her incisive, provocative opinions on movies.

Film criticism is an art form that has perilously few serious, regular practitioners, and most of them are dismally narrow in focus. Kael avoids two standard pitfalls—a high-cultural pedantry that tries to raise the subject to the technique; or a cheery populism that ignores the hard questions. Further, she sees American film as unique, not only because it is accessible to and seductive of mass audiences, but because Hollywood grew up in and produces for a democratic society.

In an earlier anthology Kael wrote, "The words 'Kiss Kiss Bang Bang,' which I saw on an Italian movie poster, are perhaps the briefest statement imaginable of the basic appeal of movies. This appeal is what attracts us, and ultimately what makes us despair when we begin to understand how seldom movies are more than this." In another anthology, *Deeper into Movies,* she wrote, "I try to use my initial responses (which I think are probably my deepest and most honest ones) to expose not only what a movie means to me, but what it may mean to others: to get at the many ways in which movies, by affecting us on sensual and primitive levels, are a supremely pleasurable—and dangerous—art form." That double edge of movie art is never far from her reading of particular films.

Her most recent collection of reviews, *When the Lights Go Down* (Holt, Rinehart and Winston, $9.95 paper) provides the same wealth of information and a chronological overview of film—for the period 1975–1980—that her former anthologies have.

It is rich in small, punchy pleasures. Take her review of *The Deer Hunter,* which she called "An astonishing piece of work, an uneasy mixture of violent pulp and grandiosity, with an enraptured view of common life." Its male characters with their Boy Scout Americanism she found "American cousins of hobbits." She described the Vietnam helicopters as "Walpurgisnacht locusts coming down on your head." Noting the film's attitude toward women, she called the bridesmaids "plump—stuffed with giggles." And she noted her De Niro's "sea-to-shining-sea muscularity."

The collection also contains the other traditional attraction of her anthologies, a longer essay. This time it's a profile on Cary Grant's career, which functions as much as a historical essay on film styles and on changing images of the masculine as it does as a personal assessment. But it doesn't have the bite of an essay like "Trash, Art, and the Movies." For that we can look to the much-debated "Fear of Movies" essay also anthologized here, which accused *New Yorker* readers of hiding fears of social and racial tension behind a sanctimonious indictment of violent films.

Kael has long defended the passion and energy of American filmmaking against those who would censor or dismiss it. But now, of the two paths of commercial film—one, toward safe banality, the other toward a technician's approach to emotional manipulation—neither is likely to generate the kind of greatness in moviemaking that she was able to find in, say, *Bonnie and Clyde*.

Then, against a tide of protest against the film's violence, she argued, "Our best movies have always made entertainment out of the anti-heroism of American life." Yes, she wrote, the film was violent and audiences "*should* feel uncomfortable, but this isn't an argument *against* the movie." Her defense of filmmakers' right to make audiences uncomfortable goes on, but the films often don't bother to claim the right.

This was the year in which Kael, long the only critic who garnered the respect of the Hollywood filmmaking community on a weekly basis, finally left film criticism for filmmaking—if only temporarily. Taking a five-month leave of absence from the *New Yorker,* she became an "executive consultant" with Warren Beatty under a Paramount contract.

Now that period is at an end and Kael is at a point of decision.

Pat Aufderheide: *Will you return to writing film criticism?*
Pauline Kael: I'm torn because the movies are very bad now—especially in the last couple of years—and writing regularly about movies is very painful if the movies themselves are not stimulating, particularly if you've been writing for as many years as I have.

Reeling, the book just before this one, covered a wonderful period in movies [the mid-'70s]. And the first part of *When the Lights Go Down* covers a wonderful period, but they get less interesting as the book goes on.

I think a lot of what's happened is simply that the movie companies have been able to take the risk factor out of financing movies, by selling them in advance to TV, international TV, cable, Home Box Office, as well as selling them in advance to theaters. They will not take a risk on projects that are not desirable for TV. They want to get all their money guaranteed in advance.

They can do that using TV stars like John Ritter or Henry Winkler. They can use big name stars, and they can set up projects with readily paraphraseable themes that are easy to sell to TV. About the only studio-made picture that took a risk recently—and it was a very small one—was *Breaking Away*, because it had no stars and no obvious theme. And it happens to be one of the few good movies of the year.

I thought the best American movie of the year was *The Black Stallion*. Without Francis Ford Coppola arranging financing for that it would never have been made. Of course he knew Ballard—they were at UCLA together—but it took courage to give more and more money to get things right because it took much longer than they anticipated. A regular studio would probably have cancelled production.

I also liked *The Warriors,* and if the studio had realized the problems they were going to have with it, it would never have been made.

I thought *Richard Pryor, Live in Concert* had the great performance of the year. Richard Pryor gave a performance millions of miles ahead of the performances nominated for the Academy Awards. And Bette Midler gave the performance that stood out among actresses. *The Rose* was not a great picture, but she was doing things that had never been done before, something original.

But the studios are very happy with utter conventionality. Because then they don't have to worry about making another soundtrack for TV, or dirty words, or violence or sex. They are terrified of anything that will not readily satisfy the networks.

The only time it's fun to write about bad movies is when they're being universally praised and you know they'll make a lot of money and you want to tell people why you think they're being suckered, or if a picture has a huge campaign and people are taking it as a work of art and you think it's not very good.

Are conventional movies being made to suit the era, or does the economics of the industry define the conventionality?

I think it ties in together. The younger generation has grown up under the ratings system, and they have only seen G and GP films. So almost anything that has a little bit of shock value can knock them out. Previous generations could go to any movie. But since the ratings system was set up the kids see mostly dull pictures. So if they see something a little crazy they get very excited about it.

Animal House has a kind of crazy, silly energy. A gross-out is fun, it's amusing. I understand why kids go to *Dawn of the Dead*. If you've been taught respect for propriety and blandness and suddenly you see all these heads being splattered—and it's obviously artificial—you get the giggles.

Older people often take violence in movies awfully seriously, when the audience doesn't necessarily take it that seriously. Obviously the violence of *Mean Streets* is very different from the violence of *Dawn of the Dead*. *Mean Streets* and *Taxi Driver* are both wonderful movies that upset people on a different level. It upsets you the way art often does.

I don't see how you can have art that investigates certain areas of experience without upsetting people. I mean, *Macbeth* is very upsetting. *King Lear* is almost intolerable, if it's done well.

When you wrote in the NEW YORKER *that people are afraid to go to American movies now, there was a tremendous backlash.*

Yes. The readers of the *New Yorker* have been putting down American films for years, and going to very bland foreign films. I loved pointing out that it used to be exactly the reverse. They would go to foreign films for sex because it wasn't there in American films. Now they go to foreign films because there's nothing there but genteel, polite sex, whereas American films are free enough to deal with social and economic tension, and they don't like being upset by those tensions.

To raise the issue that Michael Wood did in the *New York Times Book Review,* of whether my approach to movies is "populist chic"—although he decided it wasn't—sort of misses the point. It's precisely the readers of the *New Yorker* I'm addressing with that argument. You wouldn't make that argument to blacks in a Broadway theater. It's exactly those educated people who are self-protective and who are going to foreign films instead of seeing the day-to-day reality of some American films, who don't want to be upset.

They feel they've been through a lot during the war years. There's been all this violence, and they're afraid of the tensions in the city. They want to keep the race issue down. When they go to the theater, they want everything to be nice and sweet.

But art that does not deal with the tensions in a society is not art. It's just a repressive, cheerful kind of German kitsch. The Germans are the most sentimental people in the world in their movies. If you look at their movies of the '30s and '40s you want to choke—they turned out pastry shop musicals. The greatness of American films has always been the freedom to get at what was going on in the society.

But educated people have more and more pulled back. In part I think this is a reaction to the fact that the self-hatred did become intolerable in American movies for a while. The culmination is *Apocalypse Now,* which is an orgy of self-hatred. It doesn't look at the facts of the war, of what we were doing there. Instead we are carriers of metaphysical evil, we are demons. And that was the attitude in a lot of American films during the war years, even Westerns that deal with an early period of American life. The Americans are racists who shoot up the Indians for the careless joy of it—in *Little Big Man,* for instance. It was a sophisticated criticism. The Indians, for instance, would have Vietnamese faces. The key girl we saw killed in slow motion in *Little Big Man* was definitely an Oriental.

The directors were making points. And it got to a point where people felt oppressed when they got up from the theater. They felt guilt-ridden, but they didn't know what to do about it because the movies never examined facts. They just thrust guilt in their laps.

But now it seems movies and TV want to swing totally back to an earlier period and not absorb the skepticism, say, that you felt in the *Godfather* movies. *The Godfather* is the fullest examination of the American experience in American movies.

In cop movies and a lot in men's adventure and action films, directors thrust violent confrontations at you, and almost any American you saw at any period was a son of a bitch. They were very self-righteous, showing Americans what America really was, that sort of thing. It was a tendency in the culture, not for any particular group of filmmakers. Chicness was to attack the squares.

You look at a movie like *Coming Home.* It isn't enough that the husband is a hawk, but because he is he must not satisfy his wife in bed—that kind of naiveté. And all the wives of hawks are women who don't want to work in military hospitals. Actually we know that a lot of these women worked very hard to take care of those men.

So it's that kind of simplification. If you're a right-winger in any sense you're a total nothing. If you're on the left you're right in everything.

Is it left or is it liberal, or moralistic?
   Mostly liberal, but in some cases it's left. Because there's nothing directly political you may not see that they're really left wing, that movies in those years did represent the lib-lab point of view.

I would say the first big movie to swing the other way is *The Deer Hunter*. That and the Clint Eastwood movies do represent a right-wing consciousness. It's not explicitly political—they're just right wingers.

But most of the movies were the other way, definitively. Certainly there were a lot of moralistic films. But it's more than that. If you saw *Midnight Cowboy*—the society was shown as corrupt, desperate, callous. America would have been shown as different in an earlier period. That kind of thing happened during the Vietnam period.

Every city film had that—it covered the screen. And older people resented it. Movies seemed to them to be too free in language. They didn't like the way America was represented; they didn't like the new actors. They always say there are no stars anymore, because they couldn't accept Al Pacino and Dustin Hoffman as stars. They wanted those perfect, good-looking guys with an English accent and WASP profiles. They had Robert Redford, but he was the only one, and he was doing lib-lab movies where he was the perfect gentleman.

Very ugly things go into those movies in order to protect that beautiful WASP image. Think of *All the President's Men,* of the ethnic prejudice of that movie. Robert Redford was always the one saying to the witnesses they were trying to get to talk, "You don't have to talk to us if you don't want to," and the Jewish one was always pushing and tricking them. And the way that journalism was represented was preposterous—the assumption that those two did it singlehandedly, when obviously their great success depended on having an informer.

Did your work in Hollywood change your impression of how movies are made?

I got a more specific understanding. In a lot of movies I had seen that fell apart, I had thought there never was a decent script. In many cases, I discovered, there was a remarkable script. It was that the director wandered off from them.

I began to see more and more that the real need is for better producers, and I began to see why Warren Beatty and Paramount were interested in having me come out to Los Angeles.

There seem to be almost no producers who watch every detail of a picture. I know I couldn't do it. It's past the point in my life when I could take on that kind of responsibility. It takes a patience and a toughness I don't think I have. But the industry needs the kind of producer Warren Beatty was on *Bonnie and Clyde* and *Shampoo.* And I regret to say that when he's directing he does not have that kind of producer.

Most of the people who take the title of producer on movies are the executive producer, which means they help set up a real creative tension with the director, to keep them from missing the point, to keep from losing track of the structure.

In picture after picture I think, "Why wasn't there somebody there?" For instance, *Coal Miner's Daughter* has a wonderful opening and then none of the themes are sustained or carried through. Or *Bound for Glory*—there was a good script and the director wandered off from it for about 45 minutes, and the end of the picture went down the drain. Or *Being There,* which for the most part follows the script. Suddenly at the end Peter Sellers is wandering in the water. Well, in *Coming Home,* also directed by Hal Ashby, Bruce Dern wandered off into the water. It's a preposterous director's conceit. The only reason anyone can think of is that Hal Ashby lives at Malibu. *New York, New York* had a wonderful script, and then it got rewritten and improvised on and the whole point got lost.

Directors often don't have the structural or literary sensibility that went into the creation of those characters in the first place. You can't put the writer in charge, because he's so literal minded that he insists that the director stick with his script, even when the director has made the point without using all his dialogue.

It is the producer's function, not to coerce the director, but simply to be there and create a tension so that if things are going wrong someone is there who can point it out. And to do that requires a lot of patience and diplomacy.

The reason there aren't more good producers is because the deal has become so important. They're getting their money anyway; they're getting it presold, so nobody worries about artistic unity. The executives of the studios don't care very much. Most of them are quite honest about the fact that they aren't terribly interested in movies.

They used to care. They often had appalling taste—vulgar, corny, bland, cheerful, phoney. But they took great pride in pictures. Nowadays, you wouldn't get the job by talking about movies, but by providing reassurance to your superiors and never indicating to them you might know more about movies or care about them more than they do.

We can't tell yet what the younger producers might do. Coppola is still releasing through the commercial structure. Lucas has very commercial taste. Neither has as much freedom as they might on their own.

Coppola didn't do a good job of producing Apocalypse Now.

You can't produce and direct at the same time. I think if he had had a producer with independent power, they would never have started production until the script was finished. And then I don't think the picture would ever have gone into production, because there is no way to transfer *Heart of Darkness* to a movie today.

It's the story of a white man who goes native, and the horror is his reversion to barbarism. But of course we no longer think of blackness and going native in the same terms. We think of those people as having their own culture. We don't think of being in the jungle with no clothes on in the same way English readers of that period thought of it.

None of the mechanics of the movie makes sense. You could not have the Martin Sheen character go upriver to him on a little boat while planes are carrying messages and supplies to him. The showcase sequence of the helicopters comes early—how can you go further than the craziness that the Robert Duvall character plays?

The film has no structure. There's no possible confrontation between Sheen and Brando, because Sheen is already a coldblooded killer who murders an injured girl, so what has he got to change into? When it turns out that the injured girl only moved to protect a puppy you want to say, "Oh Francis, the old puppy number."

I think the people who love it are taking it as a head trip. They're going to get stoned on the sensual imagery. The movie's feeling for bombs bursting is like what Mussolini's son-in-law talked about, about how he loved the bombs bursting over Ethiopia. I think people who loved this one loved the carnage too. It sure doesn't make you hate war.

Do you believe that newspaper and magazine film critics play an important role?

Yes, although it depends on the critic. In general I think people are hostile to critics, because they hear the stars and directors on TV jumping on them.

But it's so silly, because without criticism you're completely at the mercy of advertisers. The influence of the critic is so small compared with the power of the advertiser. There are critics who make a lot of difference to their communities. Gary Arnold of the *Washington Post,* for instance, has enough followers to take an obscure film and get people excited about it.

Not that journalism is in good shape in this country. News writing is awful. Everyone imitates the *New York Times,* and when it adopted all those sections—which was a kind of imitation of *People*—everyone else did. Now there's less space for other kinds of news and for criticism of the arts, and instead they want personality coverage.

The proliferation of gossip and unchecked rumors in journalism is startling. A lot of things are going wrong, and some of it is the result, I think, of Woodward and Bernstein. People are on the tail personally of people in office, but they don't investigate issues. They worry about whether a president stumbles or uses the wrong word, or they jeer at his family. That really began to grow with Lyndon Johnson, because of the Vietnam war. It became a form of protest to jeer at the president, and now it has a kind of validity.

I don't think the national magazine critics are doing the job they could, mostly because most of them don't stay in it for very long. They don't get involved in their art form enough to take the space to write. They have it if they want it. It's been years since anyone has complained that my *New Yorker* articles are too long.

The only chance for new work, innovative work, work that's disturbing in any way, to reach the public is if a few critics get behind it. Movie studios would be perfectly happy making the same kind of big star-ridden boring movies year after year. There would be no chance of new life in the industry.

The Critic's Critic
Sheila Benson / 1980

From *The Pacific Sun* 11–17 July 1980: 5–6. (c) 1980 by Sheila Benson. Reprinted by permission.

"Pauline Kael has the shortest chute from her brain to her mouth of anyone I've ever heard speak," a tanned, steel-haired writer said flatly, walking back to the parking lot. He had come to Berkeley's Pacific Film Archive for one of her infrequent Bay Area speaking engagements, this one sparked by publication of her most recent collection of reviews, *When the Lights Go Down*.

It's now official: Film critic Kael has returned to *The New Yorker* "on a flexible basis" as the sole critic at the magazine. (She formerly shared the job.) She has begun her tenure with an exhaustive appraisal of *The Shining* and an in-depth analysis of the business side of movies (lousy).

That night's Berkeley audience heard the news, however, just as it was hatching. It was an audience with a peculiarly hungry air, as though it had been absented from felicity for entirely too long. Kael to many is *the* voice of *The New Yorker* and that voice had been silent while she spent five months in Hollywood as an "executive consultant" at Paramount. In person, as in print, her words come in a disciplined torrent, reflecting the mind of a philosophy major, which Kael was at U.C. Berkeley in 1940.

When a questioner asks whether her time in Hollywood changed how she looks at movies, she replies with a friendly astringency. "It hasn't changed how I look at movies; what's on the screen is what you look at. I think I understand better now how they get to be as bad as they get to be. I understand . . . how certain people get to be in a position to run a studio: The qualification is getting the job. And the way you get the job is if you know how to provide reassurance to your superiors at every step of the way, if you make them feel safe and completely non-threatened. There are practically no heads of studios who have any interest in movies at all, and they are open about admitting this. Some of them are brilliant bureaucrats—they know how to manipulate the talents of other bureaucrats. They know how to market films, how to make deals for television and how to say, 'No, *I* might like to see that film but I can't sell it.' That sort of man would feel very threatened by someone who really had imagination and wanted to take risks.

"For instance, Peter Yates spent between five and seven years getting financing to do *Breaking Away.* If he had not made *The Deep,* a horrendously sleazy movie, he probably would never have had the opportunity to do it. *That* kind of man does not get a job as an executive. So the war between the directors and the executives goes on."

Surprisingly small, Kael faces the audience without a lectern, one hand holding tightly onto a handkerchief like a *lieder* singer. Up close you see that the hand that reaches for a water glass once or twice while she speaks trembles slightly, like the ripple in a race horse nerved up for the gate. She had laid down only a few ground rules this evening. She will not talk about specific critics—but critics in general, ah, that's quite another matter.

"I've been rather depressed to notice the strong class biases in the way the press has reacted to certain movies," she broadsides. "They have middle-class taste, they write in very proper middle-class terms and they tend to dismiss as exploitation or as somehow gross or offensive movies that express the attitudes of youth or under-class attitudes.

"If you look at the reviews of *Saturday Night Fever,* you can see the derision behind them. Certainly you can see it in pictures like *The Warriors;* it's a key example. I'm interested in how the press condescends to any movie that has a sexual context. Take *Cruising:* they treat it as if it were preposterous or simply exploitation, and they deny their own emotions. I think it would be fine if they said, 'This gets into areas I can't deal with—I was upset looking at the movie,' but they don't do that. Very often they take the surface attitudes of the movie and don't go beneath that.

"Look at *Mr. Goodbar,*" she continues to her intent audience. "The reviews almost never dealt with the sex drive that might lead people to go to bars at night. Instead, the terms of the film were accepted: that because she's lame and has a father with repressive ideas she's doing this terrible thing—going to bars. They never seem to assume that maybe women go to bars for casual sex. People don't want to acknowledge that sex without love can be terrific. You don't always want an emotional involvement. Sometimes you just want sex."

Reflected sexual attitudes bother Kael in another way. "I don't think movies have gotten *near* the sexual revolution yet," she cautions. "They're terrified of the kind of rage many men feel and the kind of impotence which is becoming endemic on college campuses among men who are terrified because so much is expected of them. It would be very interesting to have movies deal with some of this. We shouldn't settle for

a *Ms.* magazine editorial disguised as a character that we get in the Meryl
Streep role in *Kramer vs. Kramer,* for instance.

"The press should be more aware. There should also be more awareness on the audience's part," she scolds mildly, advocating that audiences assert themselves by writing to studios and to film makers to
express strong reactions to movies.

Shifting gears slightly she fields questions about political films. "It's
interesting to see how liberals think. Take *All the President's Men:* Here's
this wonderful WASP, and he's running around with this small, pushy
Jew. The WASP keeps saying to the witnesses, 'You don't have to tell us
anything.' The Jew tricks them and forces them to talk. That is Hollywood liberalism. Well, these are not very interesting attitudes, we should
be going a little further in dramatic writing."

A woman bravely rides the waves of laughter which follow to ask about
The New Yorker. The news that Kael would return creates a murmur in
the audience. "I needed a break," Kael adds. "I'd been working there
twelve years, of course only six months a year. After a while you begin
to feel maybe you're getting into a rut. You don't want to start saying the
same things, boring people, drying up in the job. There are not that many
movies that provide you with a lot of stimulation and when movies are
bad it is *hell* to write about them. . . . You long for something original and
new that comes only a few times a year.

"If I'd had an opportunity to review *Apocalypse Now* or . . . some that
opened in the other six months I wouldn't have left. But as it was, I
thought maybe I should get out of my own head and the isolation that
comes from sitting at your own desk working that hard.

"People don't realize what the life of a movie critic is on a magazine
like *The New Yorker.* They think you lead"—the words are stressed
tartly—"an active social life." She details the reality: 4000 to 5000 words
every week between her department and the capsule reviews up front, a
dash to the city from several hours away, "a mess of movies," and then
solitude at a desk again.

"When you have something good, it writes itself, nothing is more *fun*
than using your brain. But suppose you confront, say, *King of the
Gypsies*? What can you say? And how do you make a creditable piece of
writing from bad movies? If you have pride in your writing, and I do, it
becomes an incredible chore.

"It's my feeling," she goes on firmly, "that no one should trust any
critic who does not take the art form he is writing about seriously enough
to write a decent paragraph. I simply do not trust the observations of
people who write sloppily or in illiterate hyperbole. I can only believe in

people whose level of observation in prose does justice to the art of
motion pictures or any other art he is writing about. But in order to live
up to that requirement, you *kill* yourself sometimes if the subject is
a bummer.

"Now," she says thoughtfully, "I can finally have the job all year, but
it comes a little late in life. You wonder, given the conditions of New
York, how long you can sustain that. There's also the specter of elderly
writers who never come up with a fresh phrase. Perelman went on getting
great reviews every time he brought out a book, but did anyone *really*
develop an interest in Perelman from the pieces of his last 20 years? You
have to confront these biological processes and figure out whether you
should quit when you're doing well or wait and rot in the job.

"The terrible thing about *New Yorker* readers," she says in mock
exasperation, "is that they read me but they don't go to what I tell them
to. They really want to hear about the latest Fassbinder or the newest
piece of art by Robert Bresson. You can't lure them to *Carrie*. In all the
years I've been there, not one of the writers or editors ever said, 'Gee, I
went to that movie you wrote about last week, and was it exciting!' The
only people who do that are the messenger boys who live in the slums.
The most awful thing I've ever heard there was one of the editors who
said, 'When you pan something, you're really great, but when you
recommend something, forget it.' That is enough to kill you as a writer."

During the question period, people in the audience bring up the names
of favorite films like babies for a politician to kiss, anxious to check their
reaction against hers, wanting a private Pauline Kael review to take home
with them.

A woman asks if she's seen *My Brilliant Career*. "I will, I will," Kael
answers with a small sigh, "but something tells me. . . . You see, I'm
tired of women who go out to forge their destiny apart from men. There
are reasons, maybe, for the sexes sticking together. I can't conceive of
how a woman goes out to be an artist by isolating herself from men. The
women artists I know are generally very deeply involved with men. I will
go see the movie, but I have an instinctive feeling it's popular for the
wrong reasons.

"Everyone is applauding *Hide in Plain Sight*, the *Rachel, Rachel* of
this season," she says in answer to another query. "We're supposed to
respect it because it's about blue-collar workers and how they really are.
Well, it's a Hollywood directors's idea of how they really are: they have
no *talk*. Part of the difference between educated and uneducated people
is that educated ones are sometimes quiet. And here's James Caan
playing a worker like *The Man with the Hoe*—he can't express anything

but 'huh.' I don't expect everyone to like *Laura Mars* and be pleasurably excited as I was, but I expect them to be honest enough to say that *Hide in Plain Sight* is a drag."

Kael's mind and mentality have been on display for an hour-and-a-half, virtually without letup, a mental fireworks show. The feeling toward her in this place, which regards itself as her jumping-off spot, is unexpectedly voiced as a young woman stands and identifies herself: Natalie Cooper, a film maker with a first work in progress.

"I've been down there [to Hollywood]," she says, "and I've had no one to emulate or salute, but I keep your books near my bed. You, paradoxically, are my hero.

"And you're not going to burn out or rot in the job," she continues steadily. "Because in addition to your intelligence, your humor and your humanity, you are a very sexy writer."

And for the first time that evening, Kael is without a word.

The Economics of Film Criticism:
A Debate [between] Jean-Luc
Godard and Pauline Kael
Camera Obscura / 1982

From *Camera Obscura* 8/9/10 (1982): 162–85. Reprinted by
permission of Indiana University Press.

Partial transcript of a debate held at the Marin Civic Center,
Mill Valley, California, May 7, 1981.

Jean-Luc Godard: All right, you want me to begin?
Pauline Kael: Please.
J-LG: Do you know how long this is supposed to go on?
PK: As long as they are interested.
J-LG: I was told it was going to be about an hour or an hour and a half,
and I thought that's not very long; I thought it was going to be two or
three or four hours. . . . When I was thinking about this event I tried to
train myself by reading some of your articles on recent movies, so at
least we would have something in common with the audience. I read
something about *Melvin and Howard, Raging Bull* and *Heaven's Gate,*
and I wanted to talk to you about them and also about an article you
wrote six or seven months ago, called "Why The Movie Was So Bad."
Maybe we can begin with that.
PK: Fair enough. I think there was perhaps a negative implication when
you said you had prepared yourself by *trying* to read some of my articles
(laughter). To us that means you couldn't stomach it, but I hope that is
not the case.
J-LG: No, no, because I don't speak well English or American *(laughter)* and I am really trying to listen to you and to myself speaking in a
foreign language and today, after thirty years in the movies, I am more
involved in making pictures, so it is very hard for me to listen and to talk
in a foreign language.
PK: I've heard you talk well enough in English to have confidence. I
wish you would give me some sort of foothold here by telling me how
you reacted to what I've written in these past few months.
J-LG: Well, just five minutes ago you told me that I should not hold

you responsible for all American film criticism, but I think you are, in a way, just as I feel responsible for the movies I see even if I have not made them.

PK: Oh, no, I won't accept that. I can't believe that you personally feel that you are responsible for the work of somebody whose work you hate.

J-LG: Well, let's take this article, for example. You wrote about why movies are so bad, and you attack (and I disagreed with you) a good fellow you mentioned by name who was Vice President of some conglomerate. You made him responsible for everything that is bad in the movies. I said to myself, "How can one man be responsible for. . . .?" I mean a movie is made by a hundred people at least. It's like war. Nixon is responsible, but the American people are responsible for electing Nixon.

PK: Well, let me explain what I mean about the people at the top having that much influence. If the people at the top of the movie company are not primarily interested in movies, but come either from agencies or law firms or the business community itself, if they are from the Harvard Business School, as many of them are, and they are put in to rationalize the business, and if they look strictly in terms of how much money they can get out of a project before it goes into production, that is to say of how much they can be sure of from television, from overseas television, from cable, from cassettes, they know they can get the most money from pictures that have stars or have a big bestseller property. Those pictures are the easiest to market, and so it is the marketing decisions that determine which pictures they will make. And often if a picture comes along that they did not have much confidence in and really couldn't sell in advance, they don't do anything for it so that a picture like *Melvin and Howard* or, say, *All Night Long* or *Atlantic City* doesn't get anything like the promotion of those movies that they are sure of. As a matter of fact, they are embarrassed to be connected with those movies because they assume those movies are going to fail financially and so, inadvertently, they *make* those pictures fail.

J-LG: Yeah, but it's not a good reason. It's right, but it doesn't describe the reality of making a movie. They alone are not making the movies, the movies are made by the audience, the movies are made by the cinematographers, by the union people; they are all responsible . . . I mean why don't they sell American cars today?

PK: Jean-Luc, let's put it this way. . . .

J-LG: No, it's because who is obeying this order? I try never to obey it. That's why. . . .

PK: You don't work in a big studio system.

J-LG: I wish I could *(laughter)*.

PK: But the reason you can't is the reason I am explaining. It's the same reason that an American Godard could not work in the big studio system.

J-LG: But it is not the reason not to give me a picture to make.

PK: I am trying to explain something about the way movies are made in the Hollywood structure. I was not talking about regional or independent filmmakers. Actually, *you* work much more like the regional and independent filmmakers in this country. You've never made a film that had to be a mass success in order to get its money back (except I believe *Contempt*), and I think that was probably your last experience with something like the studio system.

J-LG: No, it was my first experience with an American producer, that's why *(laughter)*. . . .

PK: But, I mean, won't you even agree. . . .

J-LG: I am trying to explain that the title of our article should have been "Why Are *Movies* So Bad?" You as a critic, and myself as well, are responsible. But especially in America, *you* are more responsible, I think, if a picture is bad. This is because the critics are so powerful here and they are not using their power; or, rather, they are using their power in the same direction that the businessmen of the movies are.

PK: I think that's true to some degree because essentially they are working for the same companies that make the movies and also, of course, they tend to be impressed by big name directors rather than to look at the quality of the individual film. But it is not true for all American critics just as it is not true that all American directors who work for the studio system give in. Many of them fight it and hold on to what their vision of the picture is. But, getting back to trying to analyze why movies in general in the country are so bad and seem possibly to be getting worse with the whole advent of cable television and big sales to commercial television—in the last few years they have become worse because I think there is less chance for any unusual project to get financed now because of the conglomerate control of the studios.

J-LG: Yeah, but then you have to forget about making movies that way and to do it another way. If you can't do it in the States you do it elsewhere.

PK: You know it's not that simple. A lot of people have ideas that are large scale ideas.

J-LG: Where do they get those ideas from? *(laughter)*

PK: Well, you are associated now with Coppola who is an example of a man who really works best on a large scale, not necessarily as large a scale as that of *Apocalypse Now*, but he does have an epic kind of vision.

He is not a small picture man, not really. I don't think *The Conversation*
is his best work and I certainly don't think *Rain People* is his best work.
I mean, he is dependent on the studios' system of financing and releasing.
I wish that he had been able to keep his independence, but he hasn't
been. Well, because you work in a different way you assume that
everybody can. I mean that's the trouble with talking about artists. They
feel their way is the only way.

J-LG: No, not at all, but it's the only way that you can still exist. This
is the only way. I never made a picture, I never dreamt of making a
picture, I have always made what is possible.

PK: But there are people who fight the system and win. Some good
movies come out of Hollywood.

J-LG: That's true.

PK: Most people when they start on a project hope to be able to make
that good movie. For one thing they don't want to have to go through
what the regional and independent filmmakers do, which is making a film
and then spending two years flogging it around the country to get their
money back. It's a terribly self-destructive way often, because with the
studio they had a distribution guarantee, at least the hope of distribution,
but if they work alone it is too defeating for them to spend all their time
virtually distributing the film themselves.

J-LG: For example, let's take a picture everyone, I think, including me
(but I'd like to defend it) considers a bad picture, *Heaven's Gate*. I don't
know what you have said about the picture, but I read some articles by
Vincent Canby and other people, and I think they said a lot of good
things about the *Deer Hunter* which I think was not that good; just as
Heaven's Gate is not that bad *(laughter)*. Even if it's a failure, in my
opinion, failure is much more interesting than success because it is like a
sick body. You can look at it and examine it and then say what's going
wrong or not. I think *Heaven's Gate* is a very good example. It has a lot
of magnificent things that the director cannot follow through on—for very
obvious reasons which we can analyze. But the reviewers never say that,
and never try to help even someone who is very arrogant, as Cimino is,
to make a better picture next time.

PK: Well, let me first say that I was not as enthusiastic about the *Deer
Hunter* as most of my colleagues, nor was I as condemnatory of *Heaven's
Gate*. I did point out that I thought the picture was a failure, but that it
was made by an artist. He is a man with talent. On the other hand when
you say a failure is more interesting than a success, when it is a $40
million failure it also depends on who finds this failure interesting.

J-LG: I do because with the $40 million, I could do forty pictures *(laughter/applause)*.

PK: That's part of the reason for the hostility against Cimino.

J-LG: A $1 million picture is a very expensive picture for me. I would be secure for the rest of my life *(laughter)*.

PK: You've just shifted ground.

J-LG: No, but I am thinking that in that picture what was interesting was they got lost. Maybe I would like to talk to you about it because it concerns me as a moviemaker and I am interested in America, which I consider as my home for its mood and my link with Francis—he has a studio and he tries to make a home out of his studio, and I have a home and I would like to make a studio out of it. This is the only link I have with Francis. But I think all good American directors—Scorsese, De Palma, all the famous ones, they are as lost as I am; we are not turning out the pictures we could turn out. I could deliver a much better picture, Martin could, Francis could, but we are not. Michael Cimino, too, could deliver a much better picture but he is not able to. When I saw *Heaven's Gate* two days ago I thought that he was trying to make a picture in America when a big picture—like Griffith—is no longer possible. It's like seeing an artist who is crippled but doesn't know it. It is very interesting; because Michael is inventing it as he goes along, he is only capable of turning out a few shorts within a three-hour movie, but those few shorts are much more interesting than a lot of shorts in other pictures because it makes you understand what making a movie is. He is trying to make an American movie and that is very interesting.

PK: I can't quite follow what you are saying, because you are saying that these people are not able to do the films that they are able to do.

J-LG: That's true.

PK: In that case it's a paradox and I guess we just accept it.

J-LG: No, directors today go too far, whether it is made in Europe or by an Italian or a Spaniard, the better he is, the more he exaggerates. Francis exaggerates, I mean, he was going to make a nice little comedy just for the studio; he was secure, there was no problem, it would recover the money from *Apocalypse* in the long run, and then, suddenly, a $4 million picture turns into a $25 million one. This is an indication that something is going on and we have to look at it because it is our future—at least mine as a moviemaker. De Palma, too, who is gifted, goes too far when he puts his talent into such a lousy script.

PK: I think De Palma works relatively inexpensively so I don't know what you mean exactly. Most of De Palma's films, except *The Fury,* which was still moderately priced by Hollywood standards, have been done very cheaply.

J-LG: Well, he exaggerates in that he doesn't care about the script, and for him it would be a very good thing to take more care with the script.

PK: Well, he wrote his own script for the film and I thought it was rather good.

J-LG: I think it is a mistake because he goes too far, especially in the last one, *Dressed to Kill.* I like De Palma because he really works with the image; he starts with the image, and that's good, but he shouldn't have such disdain for the story.

PK: So did Hitchcock.

J-LG: No, no, this is not true, at least in two or four or five of his best pictures.

PK: Well I would say most of his films of the last twenty years of his life have very mediocre scripts. Even in some of the earlier films, he wanted to get in certain episodes and the scriptwriter maneuvered the script to that point (the script having been left to the poor screenwriter). If you look at movies like *Saboteur,* or *Foreign Correspondent,* you can see the script is just maneuvering around these episodes. But this I think is distracting us. I still don't quite understand your point when you say American directors *exaggerate* or go too far. I don't know whether you mean economically, technologically, or what, since there is a world of difference between De Palma and Coppola.

J-LG: In every way—they are making pictures which are either too big for them or too small for them, and they don't have a normal relation to their creation. It's like someone who has very important things to say, but who speaks so fast that we can't hear him.

PK: But what is a normal relationship? I mean, how can any artist determine that? Most of them vary from one project to another—Coppola has worked big and he has worked small. Now by temperament he seems to be working on a larger scale. But how can you ask a man to deny and fight his own temperament? Maybe it's on the largest scale that his greatest work will be done.

J-LG: To me, when you spend $40 million on a picture like *Heaven's Gate* or *Apocalypse Now,* it's not on a large scale, it's on a small scale. Because on *Apocalypse Now,* I mean $40 million—an American embassy in Saigon spends a lot of money every morning *(laughter).* Very early on I became my own producer. And I discovered that, in making movies, movies are not made to make money, they are made to spend money *(laughter).*

PK: Well I think there is some truth to that, even from the studio point of view.

J-LG: And Francis is a great spender *(laughter)*.

PK: But there is a kind of magnificence about that. Some of these people have made a tremendous amount of money for the studios. In the case of say, Spielberg, and Lucas and many of the others, they have brought in hundreds of millions of dollars to the studios. So if they get a lot of ideas and want to try them out, and the picture gets expensive, they do have moral justification. They also know that when they make a lot of money on a picture, that money is not going to be put back into moviemaking. The conglomerates are going to take that money and buy another industry, or a company somewhere, a papermill or a shoe business. So I don't worry too much about Transamerica's loss on *Heaven's Gate* because Transamerica has made enormous profits on some other movies. If it were a case of the money, . . . if it were $40 million that you and other filmmakers could have that was being wasted, it would be something else. But it's very hard to control a certain kind of director now. A man like Cimino is a visionary kind of director. In the case of *Heaven's Gate,* everybody in the studio was terribly scared during production. But there *was* no way to control him because you can't fire a director who has the movie in his head. It's not like the old days, when you could fire him and replace him with another contract director who would just pick up the script at a given point and start shooting. There was no way that picture could have been stopped. So they *had* to let Cimino keep going. I mean they tried to pull in the reins on him.

J-LG: They could have, but they didn't want to. They were very eager to spend that amount of money. They even probably earned a lot of money on interest, because they control the bank that loaned the money *(laughter/applause)*.

PK: No, I think not in this case. And I think that executives are scared shitless when a picture runs over budget like that because chances are a few heads are going to roll afterward. Everybody knows how frightened the executives are when a picture starts steamrolling ahead like that. I remember over a year before the opening, everybody in Hollywood was talking with bated breath about what was going to happen on *Heaven's Gate* because the company had simply lost control of the director, and they had to go with him in hope that he would pull something out. But I think you're being a little unfair to the critics as well, in the case of what happened with *Heaven's Gate*. I did think Canby's review was rather brutal. On the other hand, the fact is the picture does not have one good scene, or one good character, and it goes on for several hours *(laughter)*. I think it's very interesting visually, but there is *nothing* that can carry it with an audience. If the company had thought that the critics were wrong, they would have put in millions in advertising and they might have recouped on the picture. A lot of terrible movies get by if the companies believe in them. But they didn't believe in it, and that is why they listened to the press. I mean, you take a picture like *Blue Lagoon,* which is *infinitely* worse in every way than *Heaven's Gate,* but it does have something that they could sell, which is that subteens and teens take it very romantically. And so they put in about $15 million flogging this miserable movie, and selling it very shrewdly in terms of church groups and parents' groups, telling the parents that it's going to show their children wonderful, clean natural love. And damned if they didn't succeed so well, that a few months after I wrote a negative review (and just about everyone else did) I started to get letters from readers complaining that I had panned this beautiful experience which had meant so much to their family *(laughter)*. The power of advertising is enormous, and I think they might have gotten by with *Heaven's Gate* had they pushed it, had they opened it, say, the way they do with dogs in 1100 theatres, so word of mouth doesn't have time to spread *(laughter)*. They might have gotten something out of the first week at least, and maybe the second week. But they were dismayed because they could see the justice of what the reviewers were saying, that there was nothing there.

J-LG: But don't you feel as a writer in a magazine that you are part of the chain of the advertising business, and thus of the movie industry? How can you write in a little column like that between two advertisements? *(laughter/applause)*

PK: There are no ads there. I lost the movie advertising for the *New Yorker* many years ago.

J-LG: Not movie ads, but ads anyway.

PK: Well if you will look at the ads in the *New Yorker* they are all consumer products. That is to say, the company lost all the chemical companies when it published Rachel Carson's muckraking work. Every time they publish muckraking they lose a particular industry. There are some others like the tobacco industry, they won't take their advertising. There are enough shops, enough people selling expensive goods to keep that magazine editorially free. That's why it's the best magazine in the world *(applause)*. There are very few free ones.

J-LG: Even when I was writing in France, there was no advertising at all in the paper that I wrote in. You just said (when we were coming here in the car) that you had trouble because you were asked to cut two or three lines.

PK: But that's a space matter, it's not an advertising matter.

J-LG: Well, a space matter, what is it?

PK: There are make-up men. I'm writing for a weekly, for people who produce a very beautiful magazine. They didn't have 25 lines for me and so I had to trim, because of course the movie reviews and the other review columns are thrown in at the last minute, and the other things are set. If you do run long, you have to cut. So I was in a rush yesterday to trim the piece as I had to make the plane to get here. But at the *New Yorker* I have *never, ever,* been asked to change an opinion, or to do anything to oblige advertisers. And that is a rare experience for me, and for many other writers.

J-LG: Well look at the way the industry works. Even if you are not like a *Time* critic (because *Time* is in the movie business too), you are still part of the industry. Making a newspaper is part of the industry, it's part of the culture.

PK: Jean-Luc, your films attract educated, wealthy people. I mean, workers do not go to your films; that doesn't mean we reject your films because of the people who are in the audience. The more Marxist your films got, the more upper middle-class your audience became *(laughter).* But we don't say that that affects the quality of what you're doing. I am absolutely free as a critic to say what I believe. How much more freedom can a critic ask?

J-LG: Well, I think I have no freedom at all, and I wouldn't think of it that way.

PK: Oh, I think that's bull *(laughter).* You're free . . ., I mean, the movies you make are as good as you can make them, aren't they?

J-LG: Yes, sure, I'm free to fight.

PK: Well, that's it.

J-LG: But I think if American movies are not so good today, it's because there should be a different way of writing about them. I don't know if it's possible—from what you say it's not. You are not free, for example, to write regularly about an unknown movie. You would be fired by your editor. You are not free—let me put it that way. When I checked on the last two years of articles that you wrote in the *New Yorker* (I don't want to attack you personally), you tried to be different from the other ones to a certain point. You told me about *Kagemusha,* for example, that you tried to review it after everyone else had reviewed it. But why not two years after, why not two years before? Why don't you speak of a movie before it is completed? You are a movie critic. A movie critic is not just being a reviewer. You write about a Paramount picture when Paramount decided to open it. And so where is the freedom? *(applause)*

PK: Well, let's put it this way. I could write. . . .

J-LG: No, I don't want to attack you on that. I think it's because it isn't possible to write about an Italian picture the day Paramount or United Artists is opening *Heaven's Gate,* because then you would be talking about a picture that may never appear here.

PK: No, actually I can review any movie any time I want to. The editor would love it if I wrote about unknown movies or obscure movies because then there would be less correspondence attacking me *(laughter),* because nobody would have seen the picture. It is my choice to review what I review. I have a pretty solid idea of what movies people want to hear about, and, journalistically speaking, it is utter idiocy if you write about movies that the country cannot see. Eighty percent of the readership of the *New Yorker* is outside of New York City. I try to write about films that are at least in circulation or will be, so that there is a chance people will hear about them. When I write about something like *Used Cars,* I know that it's going to be gone in New York except for a tiny theater somewhere. But maybe people around the country will get a chance to see it or will even watch it on television. No, I think there is a lot more freedom. I think you want to see the system as being more oppressive than it is, which I think is perhaps one of the problems that the public has had with some of your recent work. You take such an all-out condemnatory point of view that there are no cracks where people can do anything.

J-LG: No, that's not my problem. My problem is very much related to the critics. I tried to open the picture (and with my next picture I will try again) in some other place, not in New York. All the exhibitors refused by saying "You must open it in New York and we will wait. What are they going to say in New York at *Time* or the *New Yorker* or places like that? If they say good things, we'll take it." For me, the real producer for my movies and for a lot of European movies is the same because here in America you don't very easily accept foreign products. And I'm not as good as Japanese car builders. . . . The real producer for me is not Barry Diller at Paramount, or someone else in another company, it's you, it's Vincent Canby, it's Andrew Sarris, it's people like that who make the. . . .

PK: I think our word is fairly benign, I think my colleagues are often overly generous with their praise rather than not, because readers think there is something the matter with you if you are always hard on movies or if you pan a lot. They think you're sick, or that the sickness is in you. But I don't think that you quite understand the problem. The reason people don't want to open a movie without New York reviews is simply that the people will not go to it in a community because they simply have not heard about it. They would rather stay at home watching television—it doesn't cost anything. When they go out to a movie, something has to lure them and if they haven't heard anything about a movie, if they haven't seen television commercials or heard reviews or seen reviews, they assume it's a nothing movie, it's a dog or they would have heard about it and they won't buy tickets. That's why a picture like *Smile* folded. *Smile, The Long Goodbye*—a lot of pictures have died because they opened without New York reviews. Some of those pictures I think could have done very well had they gotten the New York reviews. And you get wonderful New York reviews *(laughter)*.

J-LG: Not always *(laughter)*—this is an exaggeration. Because, especially in America, which is a big country, a large territory, the order to go and see something is coming from one tiny point. But this is not even twenty percent of the hundred percent of the reasons why movies are so bad.

PK: Well, I don't think that's quite true. In Washington, D.C. the critic there on the *Post* has a considerable influence. In Los Angeles there are critics with a lot of influence. I mean they make a *lot* of difference in certain communities.

J-LG: Yeah, but no. I mean, a picture would never open in New York because some Wichita critics have said. . . .

PK: No, no, it wouldn't, that's true.

J-LG: Well, this is something that will make the picture bad.

PK: No, but a picture can get bad reviews in New York and still become a success in any community where there is a really active critic on a power paper. And that has saved a number of movies that the New York critics have mauled. But I think you are negative from too many different directions. I think you want to see power centered where there isn't all that much power. The real power in movies is in the advertising, is in the marketing people who not only determine which movies get financed, but which movies they are going to sell. And they work this out well in advance of the picture being made. I write about a lot of movies that hardly anybody goes to see, because there is no really big scale television commercial advertising behind those movies. It's a very complex system, but there are ways to fight it. I mean, there is hope within it, and I think you somehow *want* to see it as totally wrong *(laughter)*.

Questions and Answers

Question: Mr. Godard, could you comment on the role of film in political change?

J-LG: I never believed in it. I don't think an image or a chain of images can change something directly. And I believe in it less and less because I think people are more interested in words than images. It could change, but I believe that people are afraid to see things—that they prefer to talk about things and see them after. . . . The image is like evidence in a courtroom. For me, making a movie is like bringing in evidence. If I bring in the wrong evidence, it can be discussed, but *words* have to be used to build new evidence. It's the same way a scientist works. I feel very close to scientists because we are both building approaches to things. That's why I'm not working in criticism anymore these days—practically— because *there* words always come first.

PK: I do think films can be political, but I don't think that Godard had the temperament to make films that were effectively political. If you look at someone like Pontecorvo, the *Battle of Algiers is* a politically effective film, whether you agree with his point of view or not. So in some ways is *Queimada! (Burn).* There are people who have the temperament, who are so convinced of what they're doing, that they do use films politically. But I think when Godard, because of the sophistication of his own questioning point of view, tried to make political films, they *were* all words, they were really lectures to the audience. And people rejected them because those films did not work on them emotionally the way, say, Eisenstein, or Pontecorvo, or some other directors do.

Q: Are you saying that films like *Sauve qui peut (la vie)* [*Every Man for Himself*] do not make any political statements, particularly feminist ones?

PK: Oh, the feminist statement in that I was ashamed of him for *(laughter).* In a work of such despairing content, I was ashamed that he had the scene of these two women smiling at each other, as if to say, "Ah, but women may be no better" or "are better." I mean that's like Ashley Montagu or somebody telling you that women are better than men, or more intelligent than men. That was the one scene that really rankled because it was too much, too much of making a little political point. And practically every movie has got that scene now. I mean, the women's "sisterhood scene" is the new cliché *(laughter/applause).*

Q: How much relative weight do you think American films give to narrative, image, rhythm, etc.? Specifically, what in your opinion is the role of the image as opposed to the story in American filmmaking?

J-LG: I never understood clearly what you Americans mean by narra-

tive or story. I was always accused of not having a story in my pictures
and I always thought that if ever there was a picture with a story it was
mine *(laughter)*. A criticism I would make of American critics is that they
talk too much about the characters and not about the movie itself. (. . .)

Q: What do you think of Michael Snow's films?

PK: (to Godard) Do you know his work? It's conceptual, minimalist
work . . . *(laughter)*. I don't mean that in a pejorative sense, some of it is
quite extraordinary. I have been on foundation committees where I voted
vigorously to give him support. I think his work has all sorts of potential
interest and all sorts of interest aesthetically. But he's really working in
an area that isn't the theatrical film. He is really working more like a
painter but working in the film medium. And his work is comparable to
some of the work of the minimalist painters. (. . .)

Q: (on criticism and on the film *Melvin and Howard*)

J-LG: To me, a good review, good criticism (whether it is in the
Cahiers du Cinéma or *Film Comment*) would be trying not to say "I
don't feel," "I don't see it the way you saw it," but, rather, "Let's see
it, let's bring in the evidence."

PK: I try to give the evidence of how I felt about a film. Why don't you
do a piece on it?

J-LG: No, because we can't do it just by talking, we can't. We have to
bring in the evidence. And maybe, to write. . . .

PK: I think you're seeing it as a different kind of movie from the movie
it is.

J-LG: What have we seen? We should look at it *(laughter)*. A real critic
would project it now.

PK: Not necessarily, that's a different kind of critic, okay?

J-LG: No, it's a necessity, it's not a question of different kinds of
critics, it's not an approach. If the doctor says to you when you are sick,
"Look, Ms. Kael, I don't *see* that you are sick, I don't *feel* it," well, you
would never be cured *(laughter/applause)*.

PK: Look, I mean criticism is not an exact medical science, or an exact
science of any kind.

J-LG: It should be.

PK: You've written a great deal of very fine criticism without doing it
that way.

J-LG: It should be, if not. . . .

PK: Oh, this is perversity again *(laughter/applause)*.

J-LG: No, is it perversity to use image and sound to talk about image
and sound? This is not perversity.

Q: I'd like to get back to the question of political films that we were

talking about before. You mentioned *Queimada!* and *Battle of Algiers*—
they are both very mythological . . . they tell things . . .

PK: *Battle of Algiers* is mythological?

Q: Well, in a certain sense, yes, everything is resolved. . . . It's easier
for you to relate to it whereas *Every Man for Himself* is a very political
film that deals with temporal sequences where you are forced to deal with
despair. The aesthetic despair is presented to you in such a way that you
have to be in it. In your position as a critic it's much easier for you to
relate to *Battle of Algiers* than. . . .

PK: No, because I reject *Battle of Algiers.*

Q: There's too much distance between you and the Swiss prostitute in
Every Man for Himself so you really can't appreciate it (laughter). . . .
Everyone seems to feel that the film was too negative when, in fact, the
film was very uplifting.

PK: I think for one thing the young man misunderstood what I was
saying. I was saying that I think that the *Battle of Algiers* is a politically
effective film. That does not mean that I like it. I think it did move
audiences politically, and that Godard's work moves them in much more
subtle and interesting and questioning and skeptical ways. And that is
why I felt he was not effective in his own terms. I mean when he was
talking about the camera being his *gun,* his weapon. . . .

J-LG: I never said that *(laughter/applause).*

PK: You see, I don't feel he ever was a political filmmaker in that sense.

J-LG: You can't kill anyone with a camera. I was always fighting with
militants or leftists about using the metaphor of a gun for a camera.

PK: But, I understood from a number of your films, particularly the
ones that followed *Weekend,* like *Wind from the East,* and a great many
of the films that were very didactic politically, that you were trying to use
film as a political weapon. Am I wrong?

J-LG: Not in that sense. I was trying, but I'm glad I was wrong. It took
me quite a lot of time to discover it and it was my way to do this leftist
trip, too. I'm glad that I went deep enough to see that there was no gun,
and that the real power was somewhere else. But I quite agree that I used
leftist speeches and things like that. I think a good example is *La
Chinoise.* It's a rather good picture, in the sense you say he's a "good
man" or he's a "good human being." It was made in 1967 before the
1968 events in France, before the Weathermen here, before the Baader-
Meinhof in Germany, or the Red Brigade in Italy. At the time, it was
hated by the left, who said, "These people are ridiculous." And today,
after seeing it fifteen years later, we discover that all those people, even

Bobby Sands a few days ago, are childish, and it's because they are childish that they are important people.

PK: Well, I hope you'll recall that I gave that a salute.

J-LG: Sure.

Q: (to Godard about his current philosophy)

J-LG: I have no philosophy, not today. To me, making a movie, it's like being a detective or a lawyer or a judge or a prosecutor bringing in evidence like in a court case, and trying to find out what it's about. (. . .) I remember about twenty years ago when I first came here with my first picture, I said, "It's a pity, especially in America, that movies and cinema are taught in schools." And now, after twenty years, it's become such an industry that I'm really sorry that I gave them the idea *(laughter/ applause)*. But they are doing something different from what I had in mind because they are teaching with words, not with images, or they project a movie and then talk about it.

PK: Well, I mean, you know there are a lot of different teachers too.

J-LG: This is what we are doing here. We are not doing criticism, we are just happy to talk to each other.

PK: Criticism is a very lonely work.

J-LG: Well, it shouldn't be. Because if the French New Wave was powerful, it was because it was only four people or four kids who were talking to each other. Every time there is a new movement in cinema here, like Coppola and Spielberg, or in Italy with Rossellini and Fellini—it only lasted two or three years. . . . The people involved were not yet established directors. They were not afraid to talk to each other about what they were doing. Today, they are afraid. Even critics don't talk to each other about movies. For us, when we wrote, it was very different. I was writing at the same time as François or Claude and Jacques, and we looked at films, and we disagreed and we discussed it together. It would be as if here you and Andrew Sarris *before* writing talked to each other. . . .

PK: Well, that would make things tough on the moviemakers.

J-LG: The tougher it is, the better *(applause)*.

PK: No, Jean-Luc, the way you were doing it when you were young is the way a lot of film critics still do it. On a lot of the underground papers they talk with their friends, and they do work that way. Once you're in a position on a large paper or magazine, if you did it that way, a picture might not stand a chance. Because if it were a group opinion, if it were a consensus judgment, that would be hell.

J-LG: In the long run, it would be better.

PK: Oh well, what can I say again? *(laughter)*

Q: (on how Godard makes his money)

J-LG: Well, I have a company I formed twenty years ago. There are two of us in the company (Sonimage), me and Anne-Marie Miéville. We tried to live together and we failed, so now we have two separate apartments. The apartments are three-room apartments or condominiums you call them here. They are very small. Since we live separately, we have two cars which belong to the company. She has a small car, and I have a bigger one *(laughter; Godard pulls a calculator out of his pocket).* I think we spend about, let me think, I have to think in Swiss francs and French francs and then in dollars. We spend about, I have to calculate *(laughter)*—I'm multiplying, I should divide *(laughter).* Each of us spends around $1500 a month. But the two of us own the company and we use the company's money as ours, so I am able, earning that amount of money a month, to come here at my own expense, to pay for the Concorde and to take a first class ticket on TWA *(laughter/applause).*

Q: (to Kael on the difference between film reviews and film criticism)

PK: I think reviewing and criticism are basically the same thing. Generally, if the critic isn't very good you call him a reviewer. Fifteen people can be in a room and look at a movie shot by shot and still interpret what they see with totally different values and with totally different judgments. Generally speaking, I think it's simply a difference of point of view there. Sometimes in our views, say on *Melvin and Howard* for example, it could be a cultural thing. I mean, we would probably disagree very sharply about a film that was specifically very French too. I don't think that analyzing a movie shot by shot is any more scientific than describing your emotions when you see it. There is no such thing as scientific criticism. Value judgments are not made on a scientific basis and there is no scientific criticism in any of the arts.

J-LG: I have a strong need in my work to be criticized and to know where I was wrong or right, but with evidence. I'm afraid to be the only judge of my own picture. I need to be criticized, but with good evidence. If I were to commit a crime I would need evidence from you proving whether or not I had a reason to commit the crime. I read the review you did of my last picture, but I don't care whether you like it or not, I want the evidence.

PK: Yes you do, come on *(laughter).*

J-LG: That's not true.

PK: Oh. . . .

J-LG: No, that's not true at all. I wish I were given more evidence from critics that would give me ideas for my next picture. I'm sorry, but from your review I couldn't get any ideas for my next picture *except* that I don't agree with Pauline and this is no help to me *(applause).*

PK: No, but look, I went through the movie and I was very specific about what I liked and didn't like. That, for me, is evidence. I mean not in a scientific sense, but it's critical evidence. You obviously don't regard that as evidence because you don't agree. There is no reason why you should feel you need to learn from critics. (. . .)

Q: Miss Kael, I'm sure you're aware that one of the major criticisms of your work is the growing concentration on violence and perversity, if you will. I, personally, would like to thank you for writing these reviews because they made films like those accessible to me. I would never have dreamt of going to a violent movie if I hadn't read your review first.

PK: What kind of game are you playing, Miss? *(laughter)* Which films that I have recommended have you gone to and how exactly have you reacted?

Q: *Dressed To Kill,* and I didn't watch half of it but I wouldn't have missed it. . . . Are there more violent films being made today or are you choosing to review only violent films?

PK: Actually, most of the films of violence are big commercial films, and I give very little space if any to them. I single out the ones that I think really need the violence or use it for an effect. I happen to think that *Dressed To Kill* is one of the wittiest suspense comedies ever made. And its violence—I think that issue has been blown up considerably. I think most suspense comedies do have a certain amount of bloody thrill in them. I mean, movies were attacked from the beginning of movies for sex and violence, and that issue is still with us. But there are a lot of movies where I think the violence is offensive. For example, in a movie like Clint Eastwood's *Magnum Force,* where I thought the only thing that people were sitting there waiting for was the next violent episode because there was nothing but passivity and boredom in between. I point out where I think violence serves a purpose, as in, say, *Taxi Driver.* I'm going to talk about that film as a violent work of art or as a violent work in certain terms where I think it's legitimate. But I by no means say all violence is swell. I'm the person in the theater who draws back from it often. But I try to distinguish because, well, at the moment, for example, there is an enormous campaign against movies based on the assassination attempt on the President. And instead of saying "Let's get rid of guns" the gun lobby is saying "Let's get rid of movies like *Taxi Driver,* let's crack down on the movie industry." Well of course the reason *Taxi Driver* is so close to that assassination is because it was based on the story of Arthur Bremer. I mean, Paul Schrader *took* the profile of Arthur

Bremer and it happens to fit a lot of assassins. And so naturally people are going to see the next assassin as in that profile. But I think you've got to make distinctions between different kinds of violence. Right now the women's movement in particular, has become rather holy as if there were no legitimate use for violence at all. And in that particular movie they have said that the Angie Dickinson character was killed as punishment for adultery, which really shows no understanding of the movie at all. I mean, what's funny, is that this poor, harmless woman, who's charming and whom you like, I mean what's funny in a very Hitchcockian sense, is the first time out of the box she goes and has some fun, she gets it *(laughter)*. And if you can't respond to it on that level, of its wit, then you're not seeing that movie, you're seeing the issue you went into the theater to see proved.

Q: (. . .) There are a lot of men running around killing women, thinking it's a very sexy thing to do. I think this is a very unhealthy view of sex.

PK: I'm always uneasy when that word health is invoked. I really think you're drawing very close connections there. I mean the movie is made in different terms than those in which some people are talking about it, and I think you have to see it in terms of a sex comedy, which is what it is. (. . .)

J-LG: I would like to talk about Scorsese, for a moment, and his fight against Kodak, about the fading of the color. I mean everybody complains about it. Well, first you can use another stock than Kodak. You can use Fuji, and if you don't want film stock, you can use video tape. Scorsese could shoot his picture on video tape. Tapes are made to last for at least 200 years. Nobody's obliging Martin to shoot on bad film stock. So why does he keep complaining? You can change it. For example, I like Kodak, I even thought of putting an ad in *Variety* thanking Kodak for making bad stock because I'm sure the color of my picture will fade and so maybe some people will order a new print *(laughter)*.

PK: Are you saying he should not put up a fight for decent color that will last?

J-LG: What do you call decent color?

PK: I mean the fact is that most Americans. . . . If you look at a 20th Century-Fox, a wide-screen movie of the fifties, it has faded to a pale blue.

J-LG: So what?

PK: Well there are a lot of us who would like to see movies in the condition they were made in.

J-LG: Okay, so beginning today or tomorrow, change stock. Do it on videodisc.

PK: But you cannot get the same effect in video that you can get with a camera.

J-LG: Of course you can, even much better.

PK: Well, I would doubt that a number of directors would agree with you. But the fact is he's putting up a fight to get good color stock on the market.

J-LG: They don't want to change, they just want to complain.

PK: Oh well *(laughter)*.

(inaudible comment from audience)

J-LG: It's possible, and there is something which is deeper. Why do we want our picture to last longer than we do ourselves? *(laughter)*

PK: I mean the color fades within a year or two. You can't even get a strong black contrast now that you can't get Technicolor.

J-LG: You can.

PK: The last Technicolor film was really *Godfather II*.

J-LG: Why don't they go back to Technicolor?

PK: Because the technicolor processing is not done in this country anymore.

J-LG: Why don't they do it again?

PK: Well that is what he's trying to get.

J-LG: No, he is trying to get other people to do it, but not he, himself, to do it. So it's too easy. These people like to complain a lot. I just wanted to say that in my opinion, why should we think that our pictures. . . . I mean, at least, when a woman is making a baby, she doesn't think that the baby should last for more than she will last herself. So why are we thinking our pictures should? When we see paintings today by Rembrandt, El Greco or Giotto, the color has nothing to do with what the color was at the time it was painted. Most of those pictures have been destroyed by time or other bad things which can happen to paintings. When they are restored, they are completely different.

PK: I think Scorsese has made the point very strongly that he wants to see the pictures of the past half century in the shape they were when they were made.

J-LG: Well if he wants to, he can. He just has to get together with other directors, or other cinematographers to rebuild Technicolor. Technicolor exists in China. If you don't want to do it here you can go to China.

PK: I think he's putting up a fight for that reason, to get it restored. But I do think you have to make a stink. An awful lot of people don't realize how color has faded. He has made people aware of that. People that go see something like that old war horse *Gone With the Wind,* have no idea that it's *nothing* like what the picture looked like.

J-LG: Yeah, but he's fighting in the wrong direction because he can order new positives—the negatives are quite good. You can see all my pictures, but you just have to order a new print. That's all you have to do. For the next hundred years you can see all my movies in very good color. You just have to order a new print. If you don't have the power to do it, who *does* have the power? This is the real question. It's easy to attack the Vice President of Transamerica, it's too easy.

Annals of Film Criticism: Pauline Kael

Kristine McKenna / 1982

From *The Los Angeles Reader* 3 September 1982: 1, 6–9, 18. ©
1982 by Kristine McKenna. Reprinted by permission.

Generally regarded as America's most influential film critic,
Pauline Kael, whose work appears in *The New Yorker,* is inargu-
ably the most controversial writer currently assessing movies.
She has been both praised and vilified for her prose style,
which is a distinctly American and quite sexy melange of slang,
common sense, humor, and knowledge, delivered in a rolling
conversational tone. Kael never hedges her bets and always
takes a strong stand on whatever she writes about, nor does she
back off from taking the unpopular position. Ever on guard
against cheap sentimentality and the obvious solution, she has
a tough intelligence and her vigilant pursuit of a cinema of risk
and vitality reveals a deep respect for both film maker and
audience. Kael's reviews encompass how movies affect us, how
we can learn from them, and what they say about us. But, most
important, she never fails to convey what's beautiful and fun
about movies. And that's why I—and probably a lot of other
people too—scan the contents pages of *The New Yorker* for
her name.

Kael hadn't given an interview in more than two years when
she responded to my request with a surprising yes. A year of
scheduling conflicts and postponements ensued after she ini-
tially agreed to talk with me. Kael suffered a serious back injury
last year and the bulk of what little energy she's had in recent
months has gone toward the completion of her eighth book,
5001 Nights at the Movies, which is a collection of the capsule
reviews she's written for *The New Yorker.* With the book gone
to press and scheduled for publication this fall, and with her
back on the mend, we finally arranged to meet.

Talking with Kael in her small, sunlit office at *The New
Yorker,* I found her to be an open, unpretentious, hip woman,
yet she has the sort of dignity that prevents one asking prying
personal questions. Her phone rang frequently during the course
of our conversation; the callers were usually friends, to whom
she spoke with great warmth and concern. She seems a generous
woman. The most striking thing about Kael, however, is her
tremendous enthusiasm and curiosity about anything and everything. No piece of the puzzle is too small to consider, because,

as she points out in her reviews, it all connects somewhere.
And, more often than with any other art form, it occasionally
all comes together at the movies.

Question: *Are you surprised at what you've achieved in life or did you*
feel from the time you were very young that you were a smart person
with something to say to the world?
   Answer: No, I didn't feel that way early in my life. I think my big
disappointment in life was realizing that there aren't that many brilliant,
gifted people. When I first came to New York and went to screenings, I'd
see all these well-dressed, handsome people and I'd think, "Oh my God,
they must know so much." Then when I'd attach names to those people,
I'd repeatedly find myself thinking, "Oh, that's that schmuck who writes
that awful stuff!" When I was a kid I thought there were a lot of brilliant
people who wrote dull stuff because they were corrupt, and it took me a
long time to realize that most of them just couldn't write much better.
God knows there *are* a lot of them who are corrupt and write what their
editors and advertisers want them to write, but there are also a great
many who can't do better.

When did you begin thinking about writing?
   It wasn't until I was out of college. I had professors who loved the
papers I wrote and would read them aloud in class. I'm a very fast writer
and they loved the turns of phrases and that kind of thing. A number of
them told me I should write but I never took that seriously because I'd
never met a person who was a writer and I thought of writers as being
more privileged people.

What's the earliest memory fixed in your mind?
   That's complicated because I'm not sure in some cases whether I
remember or I heard things from members of my family. I grew up on a
farm in California and I'm the youngest of a very large family so I've
heard a lot from my older brothers and sisters.

What's the first movie you recall as having an impact on you?
   The first movies I remember are the ones I saw while sitting in my
parents' laps. This was before baby-sitters so I got taken along to the
movies and I can remember images from certain silent films—*The Volga*
Boatman with William Boyd, *Ben-Hur* with Ramon Novarro. The funny
thing is my brothers and sisters don't remember them even though they
were considerably older.

Why do you think you responded to movies so strongly?
I don't know. Why can some kids get up and play the piano? I used to
have the same memory for fiction. Twenty years after reading *Remem-
brance of Things Past* I could've diagrammed the plot for you and told
you the course of each character. But that's gone now. I think specializ-
ing in movies has kept them closer in my mind than books.

*Have there been people who steered you in a particular direction as
a writer?*
No, I don't think I ever had much steering.

No mentors?
No [laughing], I think that whole mentor theory is a howl. Having a
child made a difference because it made me want to make something of
myself for my child's sake. If you have a sense of humor, you can spend
an awful lot of time out boozing with people and having a marvelous
time, particularly on the West Coast, which is heaven. I know so many
brilliant people in San Francisco whose lives just sort of disappeared out
from under them. But you know, trying to get your experience down on
paper is tremendous fun. I don't have a lot of patience with people who
tell me writing is agony. I know that it is for a lot of great writers so I
respect that, but still, I feel privileged to be able to make a living writing.
I've worked at everything else and I know how really rough and boring
most jobs are. I started working at sixteen and had every crummy job
you can imagine until I was forty-six.

Weren't you doing things like running revival movie houses?
Only for about five years and that too was incredibly hard work. I did
all the booking, supervising, advertising displays, program notes, hiring,
and firing—it was hellish work really. The theater phones were in my
home so I had all these lines constantly ringing.

Were you writing during that period?
I had been writing before and after that period but at that time all I did
was manage the theaters. Most jobs are so draining that you can't write
or do much of anything at night because you're so fed up and tired. Still,
most of the things in my first book were written at night after finishing
another job.

How do you see your writing evolving?
Finding my own voice was the toughest thing. It took me a long time to
get rid of the academic habits of writing like a good student with footnotes
and solemnity. I think Americans are often snowed by a certain kind of

British form that dominates the graduate schools. We're not really allowed to use colloquial American English; at least we weren't when I was in the philosophy department at Berkeley. I think what liberated me was writing about movies. Because movies were not taken that seriously, I was able to try to develop my own way of writing about them. I wanted to be accurate to the movie experience and not write about them in the phony, moralistic terms that so many people use, but to capture the excitement I felt when I saw a good movie. I don't want to tell you that it's worthwhile or good for you; I want to convey what it really was that I responded to. Sometimes I feel that I get it but a lot of the time I feel that I haven't been able to do the movie justice. The most exciting times for me are when I can be absolutely truthful to how I felt about a movie and get it on paper.

Where were you writing prior to The New Yorker?

Life magazine, *McCall's, Holiday, Vogue, The New Republic.* Mr. Shawn (editor of *The New Yorker*) had been reading me and liked what I was doing and he published a few of my pieces in the magazine before I started as a regular critic.

Had you found your style by the time your reviews began appearing in The New Yorker?

No. My writing may have been somewhat snappier earlier, but I think my best work is in the pieces I've done for *The New Yorker* that are reprinted in *Deeper into Movies,* and especially in *Reeling* and *When the Lights Go Down.*

Do you have structured writing habits?

I write with a pencil on whatever paper is nearest at hand. I like yellow legal pads but if there are none around I use anything that's cheap to write on. I can write at any point when other things are out of the way. I don't have barriers or blocks and I'm eager to get at it.

Twenty-five years of crummy jobs must've given you a different perspective on writing.

Yes. For one thing, I love being able to work at home. I hate getting dressed up and going to an office. It's wonderful to wear a pair of jeans and slop around in an old shirt, and go down to the kitchen and fix yourself something and take it back to your desk. It's a good, relaxed feeling to be able to work on your own time.

What do you have on the walls of your home?

Loads of paintings—there's stuff on every available wall. My daughter's a painter and so are a lot of my friends on the West Coast. I have paintings by Jess, and a piano that he painted, many paintings by a West Coast painter named Harry Jacobus, a lot of my daughter's things, and a lot of sketches and drawings.

You commute into New York from Massachusetts so I assume you're not a die-hard New Yorker.

No, I've never loved New York, perhaps because San Francisco is too much in my bones. I like aspects of New York but I find it too noisy and aggressive. Despite my tone in print, I'm not a very aggressive person and I find it hard to deal with being pushed around.

Do people tend to distill movies down to a message or moral as opposed to experiencing them the way they would, say, a Beethoven symphony?

It depends on the movie. A lot of people think Costa-Gavras's *Missing* is a great film because they like its message. If you don't like it, they see you as a reactionary who's pro what the government is doing in El Salvador. I think in a sense the film is intended to have that effect and people aren't misreading it, but they're also not judging it as a film. Although I panned Costa-Gavras's previous movie, *Special Section,* which dealt with the courts in France during the Nazi period, nobody wrote to complain. But since writing that I didn't think *Missing* was very well done, I've been inundated with letters, primarily from people who think I disagree with its message.

Do people seek out films that confirm previously held beliefs?

Often they do. I think they're pleased when a film confirms their beliefs and often think it's a great film for that reason.

Performance artist Laurie Anderson recently commented, "Politics and art simply can't be connected. What if someone wrote an incredibly beautiful opera praising Reagan's policy on gun control? It fulfilled all your requirements for art but repelled you politically. The two issues just can't be connected." Do you agree?

I like her work quite a lot by the way—her video tapes are wonderful. Politics and art do seem to be connected for a lot of people, although, of course, it all depends on how you define politics. I think people who try to use art for political purposes generally produce bad art, but again, these things are hard to separate. An artist's whole feeling about life, and that includes his political views, comes out in the best movies. I agree with Laurie Anderson that it's a mistake to *demand* of an artist that his work be political, but at the same time, when you see *her* work you know that she's not a conservative person.

Do movies shape a culture's values or merely reflect already existing ones?

Both. *The Wild One, On the Waterfront, Rebel Without a Cause*—films like these formulated what people were beginning to feel during particular periods. A lot of kids told me, "God, that was the story of my life" after seeing *Easy Rider*. It summarized the emotions that were welling up in them and *then* it became the story of their lives. That was also true for a lot of people with Brando and *The Wild One*. The negativism about American life, the rejection of middle-class values and materialism—that movie formulated those attitudes for people. Boys from about eighteen to twenty-two often see a new movie hero as a statement of how they feel. I think a lot of kids felt that way about John Travolta in *Saturday Night Fever*.

Is it neurotic to project yourself into a movie to that degree?

No. I think all art helps you to see yourself and your own values more critically. If you get hung up on seeing yourself as a particular movie star and never develop beyond it, that can be a form of narcissism.

Do movies distort our sense of reality and give us false expectations of life?

Certain kinds of dreaming away at the movies might lead a person to have false expectations of what the future is going to be like for him, but there's much less of that than there used to be with movies. It's true that people went to fairy-tale movies in the thirties, but we can't tell how many of them believed in those movies, or needed that reverie to get through the hell of the next day. I don't think we should be too quick to condemn movies for what happens to people.

Have movies shown you things you feel they had no right to show you?

There are movies that are so grossly done that it's not really *what* they've shown me, but the way and the reasons why they did—which is often just to get a reaction and get everybody hot and bothered. In *Victor/Victoria* there's a row of chorus girls in a Chicago nightclub, which I thought was a really gross view of women's bodies. It's designed to make people feel "hip hip hooray" and the audience does applaud it, yet it's a very crude view of women. But that scene might have been done satirically and with great charm by a more sensitive director. It all comes down to how talented the artist is, and what he's expressing either deliberately or unintentionally.

Does the public encourage taste and sensitivity?

In the case of *Victor/Victoria* the audience is certainly applauding gross

qualities. I don't know . . . it's such a touchy thing . . . but I do think that
television has been a desensitizing medium and certain movies have
certainly not sensitized people. You could almost say that great works do
and crummy works don't.

What's your idea of an immoral movie?
I'm awfully reluctant to call anyone immoral. There are scenes in
movies that I feel work up the audience's appetite for certain kinds of
gross action, movies where the audience is so bored by the stuff in-
between that the only reason they're sitting there is to watch the next
massacre. Those movies are highly dubious morally but often they simply
reflect the lack of talent of the person who made the movie. The only way
he could get you involved was to whip up some killings. It's very difficult
to talk in moral terms when you're dealing with incompetents.

Are there taboos in movies?
People are always looking for a taboo so they can make a movie to
knock it down! I don't know that there are any strong taboos in movies
other than that you don't see real sex scenes in big studio movies. Things
are handled very discreetly because they don't want to bring down any
court trouble. Since there is no real national ruling on this subject, any
and every community can sue and make releasing a movie a real night-
mare. The studios are also still careful about miscegenation. I know of
people who've had projects where they wanted to use black actors and
actresses and the studios have said no, partly because of the foreign
market—there are countries that won't buy the picture or run it on
television. Then there are subjects that are almost taboo. People don't
really want to make sports films because with the exception of Japan,
which is hooked on baseball and made *The Bad News Bears* movies
lucrative, most of the world is not interested in American sports such as
football. But these are commercial factors rather than taboos.

*You commented in one of your books that "the best movies generally
have at least an 'R' rating." Why is that?*
Because "PG" and "G" movies tend to be conceived of as family
entertainment and family entertainment has always been blanded-out pap
designed not to offend anybody. Most "PG" movies tend to be like
television prestige movies and they bore kids. They're about how somebody triumphed over an illness, or how an athlete who was injured came
back. They're inspirational, which often means saccharine and tedious
and I think they're often bad for kids because anything bland and boring
makes them lethargic and they use their minds less. The best movies for

kids that I know of are classic adventure movies like *The Crimson Pirate* or *The Adventures of Robin Hood,* which have some zing and zest to them.

A West Coast critic recently said that "in the last few years Kael has become increasingly fascinated by the erotics of movies." Is that an accurate observation?

That has become part of the subject matter of movies and, in trying to capture truthfully what the experience of a movie is, I think I have got into that more. I think part of the reason that my writing is better in the three more recent books is because movies have become more personal and explicitly erotic.

What movie tricks are you consistently a sucker for?

I'm sure there are some that I fall for, but tricks generally get worn out. I'm pretty hardheaded and I've been looking at a lot of movies for a long time.

Musical theorist Brian Eno recently commented that one of the unique things about movies is the way they allow you to monitor changes within yourself; if you see a movie, then see it again ten years later and respond to it quite differently, you're given a clear diagram of how you've changed. How often do you find that your evaluation of a film changes drastically over a period of years?

Not often because I get into movies fairly intensively when I write about them, and also because my work didn't start being read until I was somewhat late in life, and that makes a difference. If I had started publishing movie reviews when I was twenty-five and then seen the same pictures when I was thirty-five, I might have responded differently. But starting as a paid critic in my late forties, I was seeing things from a fairly long point of view. Eno's comment is generally true though. Kids have told me they saw *L'Avventura* when they were teenagers and hated it but when they saw it ten years later they really responded to it. A great many people who said they didn't know what I was talking about when I wrote about *Last Tango in Paris* said they'd gone back to it years later and it got to them.

Are visuals apt to upstage narrative or philosophy in a film?

For an artist everything is integrated. Narrative comes to you via visuals and philosophy is in every image. Sometimes a critic may have to separate those things in order to discuss the content of a film, but with any good film maker those things are integrated. It's only with the bums that you see a message tacked onto boring commercial visuals.

How quickly does visual language evolve? What I mean by that is, say, if someone saw a tree at the turn of the century they might've recognized it as a source of fruit and shade, whereas we in 1982 might register something along the lines of endangered ecology.

But people at the turn of the century also saw a tree as a purely visual entity. Shaker drawings depicting trees of life present a tree in design and aesthetic terms as well as the bountifulness of nature, continuity, and whatnot.

So you don't think visual language and symbols make abrupt shifts in meaning?

It all depends on the culture, but generally I don't think you can talk in too-pat terms about visual language because people are so different. For example, I have a visual memory of words and I'm almost embarrassed at how quickly I can spot an error on a page, and I'm able to do that not because I know rules of punctuation and spelling, but because I remember the way words look. I can also fairly exactly describe scenes in movies I saw a long time ago, but I don't have that memory for basketball or hockey. I think a lot of it depends on your emotional involvement. Because they affect me in a lot of ways, words and movies stay with me while a basketball game doesn't, even though I like basketball.

Are there specific issues that are best addressed in film?

No, I wouldn't say that. The best movies are made by people who want to make a particular film because the subject means something special to them.

Which is more powerful: the tools available to the film maker or the previously held ideas and experiences of the viewer? Whose will is apt to reign?

It's a tug of war, although sometimes film audiences are very passive. Younger movie goers who have watched a lot of television seem to be more passive than previous generations of movie goers. In previous generations kids went to movies once a week. The Saturday afternoon they spent at the movies was the only experience of that kind that they had and they often spent the rest of the week talking about the movie with other kids and they developed critical and emotional responses to it. Kids now watch television and when the program's over, or even in the middle, they turn to the next one. There's always more television going on on other channels so they never really talk about what they've seen in the same way. It isn't an intense experience that stays with them and they're less likely to develop critical reactions.

How much of the power of movies can be attributed to scale? If television were as big as movies would the experience be similar?

Not if it were continuous, with the distractions of phone calls, talking and so forth. The thing about a movie is you go in and it is not interrupted. It *is* big up there, it's the only thing you're seeing in a darkened room, you paid money to see it and you want to see it. You're irritated if people are talking and you're concentrating on it, whereas television really is a piece of furniture that you watch on and off.

Do you watch television?

Some. I have two sets, one in the living room and one in the kitchen. I love to cook and while I prepare dinner I watch the news. If there's someone on *The Dick Cavett Show* who interests me I'll watch that but I can't do nothing and watch television. If I have mending to do I'll do that during the Cavett show, or often I'll read while I watch television because most of what's on can be taken in with half an ear. To get back to what we were talking about earlier: Fortunately, a lot of kids who were at one point really sucked into the box, oblivious to everything else around them, have thrown it off. They become teenagers and want to go out with other kids and television becomes a drag. I think the healthiest kids are the ones who get weaned away from television when adolescence sets in. The really scary people are the ones who, once they have kids, just stay home and watch television using the excuse that movies are violent and dirty, which is nonsense. People who don't go to movies are always complaining about how violent and dirty they are.

Do you think man is, in fact, becoming more violent or is the media simply amplifying that aspect of his nature more dramatically than it has in the past?

The cities are deteriorating, the ghettos are in monstrous shape, and all you have to do is walk around New York City to see that it has the capability of breaking into violence at any point. But I don't think that man in the abstract is becoming more violent. Under certain circumstances people reach a boiling point. You see workers on the television news saying things like "if I can't feed my family I'll go out and rob," but that doesn't mean that person has become a violent beast or that this generation is any different.

Then the only difference now is that the television is bringing that worker's angry face into our homes?

The only way that television enters into this is by showing so much material wealth. Television—and TV commercials especially—tends to make people who don't have anything angry, and it makes them want those things and want them immediately. Television doesn't point out how hard some of the people who have those things may have struggled to get them.

What's the most widely held misconception about movies?

Right now, it's that they're in a bad period. I don't think they are, although certain big American movies have reached a kind of stasis. By turning movies into toys, *Star Wars* has had a bad effect on the executives. They want hits of that magnitude and they're afraid of adult subject matter or anything witty. And the fact is that people are not going to see some of the best pictures. Of course, I don't write about everything, but I've had something worth talking about in just about every column lately. When there are unusual, wonderful movies such as *Atlantic City, Diner,* and *My Dinner with André,* it's amazing how many people think there's nothing to see.

Can the public be "sold" on a bad movie if the promotional budget is big enough?

Yes, definitely, if the subject matter of the movie appeals to people or it has stars they want to see, or if it's promoted relentlessly. Many movies fail simply because the companies don't back them with big marketing campaigns.

Why was a movie like Pennies from Heaven, *which was very easy to like and featured a star the public is quite enamored with, allowed to die on the vine?*

Because some of the executives and the marketing division didn't believe in it. It's an absolutely wonderful movie that needed a chance but they dropped it because movie executives don't like to be identified with a film that isn't doing really well. Instead of getting behind it, they allow it to die. Sometimes if the head of a company is high on a film, the studio will work hard to promote it and actually put it over. *The Blue Lagoon* began very badly but the marketing men pushed it hard because it was a favorite of the head of the company and it eventually became a box-office success. Then there are films the companies have a cinch with such as *On Golden Pond.* You couldn't turn around without seeing Jane Fonda promoting it, plus it had the additional hook of "if you've ever loved Henry Fonda, you'll go see this movie." *On Golden Pond* is safe, can be summarized in a thirty-second commercial, and can't offend anyone— except independent, tough-minded people. But the studios tend to pull back on a picture that's in any way difficult. *Personal Best* is a lovely film and it hasn't had anything like the promotion it should be having.

It's a popular theory that an artist must be in some kind of conflict or turmoil to do good work. Do you think there's any truth to that?

No. I think the chances are that an artist of any depth has already been through a lot of turmoil and probably needs a little peace to do the work. People say look at the hell Dostoevski went through, but who knows what he might've done had he had a little security.

How important is music in movies? Can a great score salvage an otherwise mediocre film?

It certainly can. It can't make it a great movie but it can get it by. I've also seen movies that were so full of hype that they diminished the quality of what you were seeing. I saw *Taxi Driver* before Scorsese added the score and I thought it was better. The score he used is so hyperbolic that in various places it demeans what's on the screen.

Did punk affect movies?

I would say that punk is very much a part of the style of Jean-Jacques Beineix's film *Diva*.

What sort of music do you like?

Everything from Monteverdi to Gang of Four.

How can one recognize a revolutionary film? Is it apt to be a commercial failure?

Revolutionary is a tricky word but there are films where you instinctively know something new is being done. When I first saw *McCabe & Mrs. Miller*, it was one of the surprising experiences of my life. I could hardly talk when it was over because I knew I'd seen something that pulled you in a different way emotionally. The same thing was true with Godard's *Weekend*. Films like that don't come along very often and they're almost what you live for as a critic.

When was the last one you can recall?

There have been films that brought something new into movies even if they weren't great. *Saturday Night Fever* wasn't a great picture but it had a new spirit. There's a kind of elation in seeing something you've recognized around you but that nobody's been able to put on the screen before, and Travolta did embody something up there.

What other writers do you admire?

I admire a lot of Mailer. When he's in top form I think he speaks to the way a great many of us feel. I regret a lot of what he's interested in and has spent time on and wish he were interested in the things I'd like him to be interested in, but there it is, that's what he's doing! And there are stories. Saul Bellow's "A Silver Dish" was wonderful. Updike's story "Separating" that appeared in *The New Yorker* a few years ago and is part of *Too Far to Go,* which is now being released to theaters, was wonderful. You read a story like that and it stays with you. It's like a movie, there in your head all the time. There are so many good writers in this country—I'm mentioning the obvious talents.

How about other critics?

I'm not as interested in reading movie critics as I am in reading critics in other areas. I've been at this a long time and also, by the time I've done my review and their reviews are coming out, I'm finished with that film and on to something else.

What critics in other areas do you enjoy?

I wish there were more literary critics who were substantial. I do like Jim Wolcott's work a lot; he writes on movies for *The Texas Monthly,* on books for *Esquire,* on television for *The Village Voice,* and he has tremendous wit, flair, and a gift for language. It's exciting to watch someone that young—he's still in his twenties—develop.

Is a film critic's primary obligation to the art of film or to the film-going public?

Each critic has to answer that for himself, but for me it's to the art of film, because if critics don't support some of the new work there won't be any new work. If a person is doing something new and the public rejects it, it's pretty rough on him. But if even the press rejects it, if there's nobody out there who sees what he's getting at, then he's really alone and is apt to lose confidence in himself. The artist has to feel that there's someone somewhere who understands what he's doing.

Should a critic approach a film with the degree of knowledge of the average film goer or is it his responsibility to know more?

You do approach it like anybody else in that you go in hoping for a good movie but you're also going to know more inevitably, if you do your work with any diligence and/or intelligence. For one thing, you know what the directors, writers, actors, and key members of the crew have done previously. But the average movie goer is a fairly well-educated person who goes to a lot of movies and often knows those things too. Of course, there are the people who go to two or three movies a year, who turn out for the new *Rocky* or *On Golden Pond,* but the real movie goers have a pretty good understanding of the careers of people.

Still, inevitably a critic sees more, and probably does some thinking in the course of writing a review.

How much do you rely on your intuition in your evaluation of a film?
Completely, but my intuition is based on all I've learned. The only criticism in any of the arts that's worth anything is based on instinctive responses. I think anybody who tries to apply a yardstick or theory in evaluating art is going to do something very limited and valueless.

Would you say that the more we're able to intellectualize a work of art the less power it has?
No, I think some people intellectualize pretty instinctively! Some people love to intellectualize to the point that their emotions assume an intellectual guise.

Are there specific ground rules you try to abide by in reviewing a film?
I try not to give the plot away, particularly if it's a suspense film of any kind. I don't tell the jokes of a movie. I think that's a cheap way for critics to turn themselves into humorists. If it's a small picture and I think it's going to be a flop, I avoid writing about it. I try not to pan the same person over and over again but sometimes the same people keep having big hits and you have to write about them. I didn't write about the last two Truffaut films because I'd already panned him a number of times. I thought *The Woman Next Door* little better than a television movie and *The Last Metro* an embarrassment, a lukewarm nothing of a movie, but I probably should have written about them because they were enormously successful. I think people go to Truffaut for a certain kind of safety and I'm amazed at how many people liked those two movies.

You once said, "There are movies where you feel that what the movie is about is underneath the screen, it isn't on the image at all, but you can't write about that because that isn't what the artist meant to be dealing with and it's unfair to deal with these things unless the artist acknowledges it." Do you feel you must review a film according to the parameters set by the artist?
No. What I meant there was, for example, there are movies where the content seems to be homosexual but that isn't what the movie is dealing with. The movie may even be anti-homosexual yet the whole emphasis of it is homosexual, and you can't deal with that directly in your review without suggesting that the director or the writer is homosexual. This is a problem, particularly with English films; the emotions often seem concealed and you feel a kind of turgid pressure within the emotional scenes.

What prevents you from addressing those issues?
A certain amount of respect for people's feelings about the matters that
they conceal. Sometimes I know things about actors that relate to why
they've done a role a certain way but I wouldn't go into that because I
wouldn't want people to do that with me. These are human beings.
They're not just images on the screen and they haven't totally abandoned
their rights to privacy just because they want to make movies or be
in them.

*How powerful are critics? For instance, do you think the critics'
trashing of* One from the Heart *played a role in the ruination of Zoetrope?*
No, I think hardly anybody was going to see that movie, that's all.
When a movie gets bad reviews, the critics are often blamed for killing it,
but usually the movie simply isn't drawing an audience. Coppola was
doing all the promotion in the world but he really didn't have enough to
sell. And in the case of *Heaven's Gate,* the film had exquisite cinematog-
raphy, and Cimino does show moviemaking talent, but there's not one
single scene in the film that makes good sense or involves you dramatically. There's nothing in it for an audience, except perhaps a very
paranoid audience that wants to believe that that's an accurate view of
American life. On the other hand, I do think critics can help small
movies. If they support a movie strongly enough, critics can get the ball
rolling and get the studio to put in some advertising money. But if the
studio doesn't put in some money, the critics can't make it a hit. Then
again, on certain big films the critics don't make any difference. I know
that when I pan a film like *The Towering Inferno* it will still gross millions,
but I still want to say why I think it's a bummer.

Is film criticism an art form comparable to the novel or short story?
Those are arbitrary and silly distinctions, sort of like worrying about
whether somebody's a critic or a reviewer. Who cares?

Is there any aspect of movie making that you'd like to be involved with?
Not really. I had the opportunity last year when I was in Hollywood
and I still have several standing offers. Perhaps I don't have the patience
or—any longer—the energy required for film making, but I prefer writing
reviews. Nobody else will say exactly what I'm saying and I want to take
my chance and say it.

Why do you think your reviews arouse so much controversy?
You'd have to answer that—I can't.

What would you like to change about your life at this point?

I wish I'd been able to get into print earlier and not wasted so much of my life in grueling, dirty, back-breaking work because I lost so much physical energy at that. The big drawback to my job now is that I simply don't have the physical strength to do as much as I'd like to do. I had extraordinary energy when I was in my twenties, and in my thirties too, but it was thrown away on crummy jobs.

What's the difference between an artist and an entertainer?

All art is entertaining, depending on how educated you are. If you're educated enough, you enjoy Shakespeare; but if you aren't and don't have an instinct for it, you may find him tedious work rather than entertainment. There are entertainers who are not artists, but then there are also the pop singers who reach a level where they become artists. But these are just hairsplitting gradations. If art isn't entertainment then what is it? Punishment?

Did She Lose It at the Movies?

Sam Staggs / 1983

From *Mandate* May 1983: 10–13, 29, 80. Reprinted by permission. Originally published with a lengthier opening commentary by Mr. Staggs.

Like most interviews, this one required numerous telephone conversations, changes of plans, verifications of facts. During all the flurry, I remembered my first encounter with Pauline: a telephone conversation in 1970. I had expected a brassy, metallic voice to crackle over the wire: the press had portrayed her as a scold. Instead, she sounded like Marilyn Monroe, if Marilyn hadn't been shy and insecure. A breathy voice, sweet but firm, sexy, cultured, with more than a little show biz and perfect California enunciation. Her talk was full of Forties slang and the kind of four-letter words you find in *Mandate*. ("Oh, shit" and "Oh, fuck" pop up rhythmically.) After a ten-minute chat I felt frightfully excited, as though I had talked to a star: as indeed I had.

Part of Kael's appeal to gay men (she has always carried on a love/hate affair with her gay legions) comes from her greater-than-human quality. She's a brainy one-woman show, she's Garbo, she's Callas, she's Garland, she's Judy Holliday, she's Auntie Mame. Gays do like their quality, whether it's opera, movie stars, sweaters, or witty writers, and reading Pauline is better than reading Dorothy Parker. Her books resound with wisecracks; like the bitchiest queen in gay mythology, she has a sharp remark about everything. She is a star: when she's on and at her best she absorbs all the attention, all the love, all the hate. She is the ultimate Fag Hag, with every positive and negative nuance the term carries with it.

Mandate: Your new book, *5001 Nights at the Movies,* has several thousand annotations but not a word about the greatest trash movie ever filmed: the 1959 version of *Imitation of Life* starring Lana Turner and Sandra Dee. Can it be that you don't appreciate this *chef-d'oeuvre?*

Kael: I almost choked on the lump in my throat when Susan Kohner showed up for her black mother's funeral, and at the same time I was laughing. I don't know how I overlooked that one; it'll get in if I have a chance to do an expanded edition.

Is it the greatest trash movie ever? It's certainly one of the great tear-

91

jerkers. But the competition is keen in trash. How about Helen Gahagan and Randolph Scott in *She,* or Maria Montez in *Cobra Woman* (cherished by Gore Vidal), or another Lana Turner stunner, *The Prodigal.*

Mandate: Oh yes, many little boys who saw *The Prodigal* in 1955 grew up to be the drag queens of the Sixties and Seventies because of Lana's costumes. You refer, in *5001 Nights,* to your next collection of reviews from *The New Yorker,* even though it hasn't been published yet. When will it come out?

Kael: It's called *Taking It All In;* it's going to press this month, and it's scheduled to be out in February, 1984. It takes that long nowadays for a book to get published.

Mandate: What else do you do besides writing movie reviews and bringing them out in collections? You have a great amount of energy—this is apparent from spending five minutes with you. Do you cook and clean? Do you spend lots of time socializing?

Kael: Of course I cook and clean and I haul groceries and struggle with storm windows and do all the other things, but most of the energy goes into the writing. I used to have just about unlimited energy to draw upon; I could stay up all night and whirl through the day. Now that I'm in my sixties I have to store the energy up. I don't have the reserves to call upon. If I see a mess of people, I can't just sit down and write when they leave. And if I speak at a college, I'm too drained to write the next day.

Mandate: You spend most of your time at home in Massachusetts now. Why did you leave New York?

Kael: Pretty much for the reason above. I'm naturally gregarious as all hell; living in the country calms me down. And there were all the other reasons: in the country I can have a house and spread papers out; I don't have to clear the work away in order to set the table for dinner. Everything seems simpler when you get outside New York City. I don't feel as frantically rushed for time. Of course, part of this also comes from my decision to turn in a piece every other week instead of every week, as I used to. I know that it's less effective journalistically, because the reviews often come out later than readers would like. But I feel less of a hack this way—I can ignore most of the pictures that it would just be a grind to write about.

Mandate: Rumors continue to circulate that you plan to retire soon. I hope this isn't true. Will you comment?

Kael: I'm still having a good time reviewing—there are movies that give me a chance to think about things I haven't written about before. And when I went out to Hollywood in 1979, thinking that I might retire from writing, I discovered that I missed it. It was as if I weren't operating on all cylinders. I'd like to go on for another few years; I feel that way especially when I see something I really love and it gets panned by most of the press. Sometimes when I read the pans of movies like *Pennies from Heaven* or *The Devil's Playground* or *Come Back to the 5 & Dime Jimmy Dean, Jimmy Dean,* I feel just as bewildered as I did years ago when I read the pans of *Jules and Jim* or *Yojimbo.* And when I write I don't feel any older—it's when I read it over that I can see the hardening of the syntax, and see that the sentences move along the same way they've been going for a lot of years. My rhythms, unfortunately, stay the same. A friend told me that he was reading my column in *The New Yorker* to his wife when she was in the hospital the day after she had her baby. The doctor came in behind him, didn't see what he was reading, but said, "I can tell from the way this rolls on it's Pauline Kael."

Mandate: What is the first movie you remember seeing? How vividly do you recall it?

Kael: I'm not sure which was first, but I remember images from movies that I saw in the early and mid-Twenties when I was held on my parents' laps, such as the silent features that starred Bebe Daniels as a daredevil, and, of course, Ramon Novarro in *Ben-Hur,* and the other spectacles of the era. I was able to tag along with my older brothers and sisters until I could go to the movies on my own, with other kids. That was when I was about eight.

How vividly do I recall those movies? Well, certainly more vividly than my brothers and sisters did, because years afterward when I reminded them of incidents in pictures they'd taken me to, they had no recollection of them. And when I've seen one of those pictures again, I always know what's coming in the next scenes. My memory for actual events in family life during those years isn't nearly as good.

Mandate: Were you a Depression-era Valley Girl, or were you more serious-minded. I read in *Current Biography* (1974) that you majored in philosophy at Berkeley. This seems an unlikely field for someone with a ready put-down for people who get too lofty in their thinking or their writing. How did you escape the over-seriousness that philosophy students often contract (and seldom lose)?

Kael: I was neither or, rather, both. The youngest in a large family has a lot of advantages: you pick up a fair amount of knowledge from your older siblings, and your parents don't worry too much about you. And I think my parents and siblings liked me, because I was quick to understand things, and I was funny—I mean I could make them laugh. I can remember members of the family asking me to repeat gags I'd pulled on them when we had company.

As for majoring in philosophy at Berkeley: I think it's because I have that grounding that I can't take loftiness and systems of aesthetics as seriously as, say, some movie critics do. It's also why I can't take too seriously the advice I'm often given that I should write a book about film aesthetics. What do people think I've been doing in my reviews?

How did I escape over-seriousness—by which I guess you mean the solemnity of a horse's ass? Is it maybe a gift of nature? I laugh very easily, especially at my own idiocies.

Mandate: You have had a variety of jobs: sewing, managing two art-film houses in Berkeley, and having Sonja Henie's make-up tested on your skin before it was applied to hers. How did you get *that* job? What else have you done along the way before you became a full-time movie critic?

Kael: Since I didn't start making my living primarily as a critic until I was about forty-six or forty-seven, and, even when, a few years later, I was taken on at *The New Yorker* I was employed only six months of the year until 1980, I've done more than my share of knocking around. I think the Sonja Henie thing came about when I was working for a chemist who prepared special make-up for performers and he, noticing that I had what he called "extreme Nordic skin," thought I was an ideal guinea pig for the make-up that Sonja Henie, who was one of his customers, needed for her ice shows. (I must have been twenty or twenty-one at the time.) She would come in (sometimes with Eleanor Holm) and inspect the cream on my arms. I don't believe she ever spoke a word to me; she would talk to the chemist while fingering the patches on my arms. (I probably presented my arms as if they were pieces of furniture to be inspected.)

Other jobs: well, if you want to write, it's probably best to have some money, or failing that, a lot of skills. I had no money, but I discovered I could fake my way into jobs and then learn how to do them very fast. I still write with a pencil—I don't type and I don't drive (largely because I just didn't have the dough for a typewriter or a car, and then I just got used to life without typing or driving). But I've cooked for a living and been a seamstress, written travel reports about places I've never been to, written instructions for do-it-yourself kits for things I've never put together, written advertising copy, ghosted books, taken care of small children, and almost anything else you can think of. Except, I've never been a waitress and I only lasted two and a half days as a bookkeeper. I used to be able to stay awake when everyone else fell asleep, but put a ledger in front of me and I nod out instantly.

Mandate: Various other critics have attacked you rather viciously in print, e.g., John Simon, Richard Gilman, Renata Adler, Andrew Sarris. Why do you think you provoke such strong reactions?

Kael: Your guesses are as good as mine, and I'm not crazy enough to put mine in print.

Mandate: Ordinary readers often react just as strongly, people with no personal axe to grind and no weekly columns to fill with controversial copy. I myself have taken part in some vehement pro-vs.-con Pauline Kael debates with friends and colleagues. In the early Seventies I had a boyfriend who disparaged your writing, and to the bitter end of our brief affair we argued over your kind of movie analysis—the all-encompassing sort that covers the whole range of society reflected in films, versus the narrow formalistic and *auteur* brands of criticism. Was I right in giving up my trick to defend you?

Kael: If you refer to him as a trick, I guess you were right to give him up.

Mandate: Seriously, though, why do you hit so many nerves among the common readers? Why do you stir up such antagonism as well as such passionate devotion?

Kael: In my writing, I was trying to get at what I actually responded to at the movies, and I couldn't do it in formal, scholarly language. I worked to loosen my style—to get away from the term-paper pomposity that we learn at college. I wanted the sentences to breathe, to have the sound of a human voice. I began, for example, to interject remarks—interrupting a train of thought, just as we do when we talk, and then picking it up again. And when I began to feel the freedom to write as easily as I spoke, the writing itelf became pleasurable.

Maybe part of the resentment I stir up among critics who suffer when they write is that they can tell I'm having a good time. My guess is that just as my slangy colloquial style appeals to some readers because it sometimes enables me to get right at what I think the emotional substance of a movie is, it turns off other readers, who prefer more literary, distanced criticism. For example, I'm frequently disparaged as "opinion-ated"—I think what this comes down to is that often I don't share in the consensus that builds up on certain movies. Sometimes, it builds up even before the critics have seen a picture, as it did on *Sophie's Choice*—I suspect that a lot of readers are snowed by big themes and advance articles in the *New York Times*. And then, if they read me making fun of the picture, they're outraged and think I'm irresponsible, and especially so because I don't couch my review in the language that has come to be equated with "objectivity."

Mandate: What accounts for your large following among gay men?

They took you up long ago almost the way they adopted Judy Garland, Barbra Streisand, and Bette Midler as patron saints.

Kael: If that's true, I'd like to think that it's a tribute to the taste of gay men.

Mandate: When I told one of my colleagues at *Mandate* that I was going to interview you, he said, "Why her? She's a homophobe." I don't think you are homophobic, but unfortunately some gays have come to believe that you are. Some writers in the gay press—David Rothenberg in *New York Native,* for example—regularly group you with anti-gay critics like John Simon and those who write for the *New York Daily News* and the *New York Post.* Some people even consider you somewhere between the Jerry Falwell/Anita Bryant redneck queer baiters and the Norman Podhoretz/Midge Decter intellectual fascists. Now I have known you for over a decade and I don't believe you are really anti-gay. Can we clear up these awful misunderstandings once and for all?

Kael: I think that the homophobe talk is just craziness. I don't see how anybody who took the trouble to check out what I've actually written about movies with homosexual elements in them could believe that stuff. I mean movies such as *Victim* back in the early Sixties, or, more recently a film such as *Pixote.* And over the years I've consistently pointed out how homosexual men were used as convenient villains in movies such as *The Laughing Policeman* and Clint Eastwood's *Magnum Force, The Enforcer,* and *The Eiger Sanction.* Look at my review of *The Enforcer* in *When the Lights Go Down* and then look up the picture's other reviews; did anyone else bother pointing out that Eastwood yells "You fucking fruit" as he kills the rotten enemy of society?

Stuart Byron kicked off this homophobe rumor by a piece in the *Village Voice* in 1981—the November 11–17 issue. Take a look at his interpretation of what I wrote about *The Sergeant,* and then take a look at what I actually wrote about how playing a homosexual seemed to paralyze Rod Steiger as an actor—it's in *Going Steady.* Some of what Byron based his case on is a howl. Apparently back in the late Sixties he was talking to me somewhere about what a fine movie Hitchcock's *Topaz* was and I said, "Oh, but you're a Hitchcock queen." He said "the implication was clear. Because I was gay, my opinion of Hitchcock—my opinion of anything—was suspect." Well, I grew up in San Francisco, where if I saw a girlfriend who was hooked on coffee, I might say, "Oh, you're a coffee queen." The term had spread from the gay world, of course, but my remark to Byron was just like saying, "Oh, but you're a Hitchcock freak." Jesus, did you ever *see Topaz?* You needed some way to break off a conversation with anybody who wanted to tell you it was wonderful. Byron also perpetuates the line that Andrew Sarris has been using for years, that I somehow "implied" that he and his fellow "action film" enthusiasts—the auteurists—were homosexual. I don't think that ever occurred to me. What I was talking about was my impression that action films were so male centered that they didn't appeal to women nearly as much as they do to men.

Mandate: I must confess, Pauline, that I've never quite forgiven you for your 1981 review of *Rich and Famous,* in which you said: *"Rich and Famous* isn't camp, exactly; it's more like a homosexual fantasy. [Jacqueline] Bisset's affairs, with their masochistic overtones, are creepy, because they don't seem like what a woman would get into. And Bergen is used almost as if she were a big, goosey female impersonator. Directed by George Cukor, this movie has an unflagging pace, but it's full of scenes that don't play, and often you can't even tell what tone was hoped for . . . it's a tawdry self-parody." Many other gay men feel as I do. That review angered me so much that I threw *The New Yorker* across the room. I felt that our cause—the gay cause, and consequently a chunk of our lives—had been mocked by the greatest living writer on movies. Why were you so intemperate in your language? Why did you bring a homosexual analogy into a review of a film that was boringly straight? I might have understood somewhat if you had made similar statements about *La Cage aux Folles,* but I've never had any inkling as to why you wrote what you did. Vito Russo had an explanation of sorts in *American Film* for September, 1982. He wrote: *"Rich and Famous* had a promiscuous heroine (the Jacqueline Bisset character) and got attacked for it, notably by Pauline Kael, who attributed the promiscuity of a heterosexual character, a woman, to a homosexual sensibility, as though straight women have never been promiscuous or been given the permission to be promiscuous. So when George Cukor created one for the first time, Kael said they shouldn't be like that; it's homosexuals, they're the ones who are promiscuous." For me and for the others who were offended by the *Rich and Famous* review, please give an explanation.

Kael: I think you're misreading me. We see the picture very differently: you see it as "boringly straight." I see it as a picture with what is now called a closeted sensibility. The erotic passages simply didn't feel convincing to me as heterosexual, but surely it's not anti-gay to point out that the nuances of male-male and male-female pick-ups and seductions are somewhat different? My point about the telephone scene ["Bisset . . . is in New York for a few days . . . and a young man of twenty-two . . . is in her room interviewing her for *Rolling Stone.* She gets a phone call, and while she's on the phone he stands with his back to the camera, and the focus is held snugly on his bluejeaned rear. (Are we in the audience supposed to be turned on *for* her?'')—*Editor's addition*] was very simple: the character played by Jacqueline Bisset is being turned on by what she can't see. Usually in a movie when we see someone falling for a man or a woman, we see from the same point of view as the one who's doing the swooning. In this scene in *Rich and Famous,* the point of view seems to be screwed up. We're looking at a voluptuous shot of the young man's bluejeaned rear while watching the woman get heated by it—but she's facing the wrong way.

My only quarrel with homosexuals is with those few writers, such as Stuart Byron, who use techniques of intimidation, such as in his publishing these remarks: ''Here's hoping that we will not have to suffer through her reviews of *Taxi zum Klo, Making Love,* or *Partners.*'' And also these remarks: ''. . . there have been times when I've felt like throwing her into the back room of the Mine Shaft or onto the dance floor of the Saint so that she could see the evidence of post-Stonewall self-acceptance.'' If the Mine Shaft and the Saint are Byron's idea of gay liberation and self-acceptance, it's clear that we don't see eye to eye. I'm a little shocked at the violence in Byron's tone and in the tone of several other writers who have picked up on his article. I try, as a reviewer, to write freely and unself-consciously; this kind of bombast makes that even tougher. Once these things were published, I started getting hate mail from men who said they were gay—some of them said they had always liked my reviews before they learned I was a homophobe. It's painful to think that they don't trust their own feelings about my writing—that they believe I harbor ugly feelings about them, simply on the basis of someone else's say-so.

I don't believe that the overt or honest expression of a homosexual theme has ever offended me in any way; it's only the covert that I've kidded—and never, I hope, as a hanging judge.

Passion of a Critic: Kael on Mediocrity, Risk and American Movies

Michael Sragow / 1985

From *The San Francisco Examiner* 18 December 1985: E1, E5. Reprinted by permission.

Ever since I got over the idea that a good reviewer is someone you always agree with, Pauline Kael has been my ideal as a movie critic. Writing in the *New Yorker* week after week for 18 years, she's displayed the most reliable taste buds in the business, along with a knack for spotting incipient talent that verges on the sibylline.

But that's not what makes her essential, which is the passion and intellectual commitment and aesthetic excitement that she conveys in her writing. Even when I object to 80 percent of her criticism of *Heart Like a Wheel* or her praise of *Indiana Jones and the Temple of Doom,* I still admire the beautifully felt-out way she expresses her point of view.

State of the Art, her 10th book, is also her best in the 10 years since she came out with *Reeling.* (It's a William Abrahams Book for E. P. Dutton, available in hardcover for $22.50, in paperback for $12.95.)

For reasons of publishing economics—her collections were becoming too big and thus too expensive—it covers two years (June 1983 to July 1985) instead of her usual three. And it features none of her famous overview pieces on the intersection of art and industry or on careers like Cary Grant's and Orson Welles'.

She explains why in the interview below, which she gave at the Clift Hotel while touring for her book two weeks ago.

Her criticism here has a wonderful concentration—even, at times, a contemplative calm. In one essay after another, she combines her extraordinary alertness to the film at hand with a vast breadth of reference, a free-ranging wit and sometimes breathtaking descriptive prose.

The table of contents may list the movies she covers in her columns, but that doesn't do justice to the variety of topics she covers in passing.

At the beginning of her *Terms of Endearment* review, for example, you can find the best appreciation of half-hour series on TV anywhere. Once again, she's nonpareil at delineating acting styles, whether Steve Martin's or Meryl Streep's, and directing styles, too, whether David Lean's or Satyajit Ray's. And her reading of *A Passage to India* offers an original interpretation of E. M. Forster's strengths and failings that sweeps away dusty schoolbook preconceptions.

Kael has been a consistent enemy of academics' deadening effects—particularly the tendency to base opinions on classical authority. But the best way I can explain the special strength of her reviewing is to quote that master of journalistic criticism, William Hazlitt:

"In art, in taste, in life, in speech, you decide from feeling, and not from reason: that is, from the impression of a number of things on the mind, which impression is true and well-founded, though you may not be able to analyze or account for it in the several particulars . . . Many are too refined to be all distinctly recollected, but they do not therefore operate the less powerfully."

Kael would probably agree with Hazlitt's aesthetic. Afterwards, though, she analyzes and accounts for all the particulars, and recollects distinctly. It's her combination of extra-sensory perceptions and intellectual checks and balances that makes her a formidable and, yes, an enduring critic.

Question: Why is there no big umbrella essay in this book, as there is in *Taking It All In* and *When the Lights Go Down?*

Answer: In the beginning of the review of *Raiders of the Lost Ark,* I did a piece on the management people taking over the decisions about which movies should be made. That was four or five years ago, but it's still the most recent and awful development I've covered.

The only new wrinkle is that the young moviemakers who really are in a powerful enough position to do something have gone in the direction of making old-fashioned movies for kids. It's certainly true for Lucas and what he's produced, but it's also become urgently true for Spielberg, that the movies he sponsors rip off his own work. And he doesn't seem to realize that he's cheapening his own imagination that way.

Q: Have you seen *Amazing Stories?*

A: Yes, I have. There was a comedy, one I quite liked, called *Mummy, Daddy.* I also watched that hour-long one that Spielberg directed about two months ago, *The Mission.* It was like a World War II movie. I thought of *A Guy Named Joe* and all those awful World War II movies that Spielberg has gotten hooked on. And it was absolutely brilliant technically.

It's very funny—I stood in front of the set staring at it, because I knew if I sat down I wouldn't be able to sustain any interest in it because it was so stupid. But standing right in front of the set, it was technically so brilliant that I just looked at it shot by shot.

Also, the kid was so much like Richard Dreyfuss in *Close Encounters.* It's as if Spielberg wants this slightly stocky, infantile kid image, that he's in love with that image, and he sees something noble and saintly in it.

Q: I like a lot of Spielberg and Lucas movies. But when I was trying to think of when movies hit this awful plateau, I came up with 1977—the year *Star Wars* came out.

A: I had hoped with *The Goonies* that audiences would really start falling off to the point where those two guys would be forced to grow up. But it's still the dominant thing in American movies, and it's so convictionless, so empty. You see *One Magic Christmas,* and it's imitating some flop movies of the '50s, and it has nothing fresh, nothing that pertains to this period.

Q: At a time when movies seem to be sinking into a morass, how do you keep your equilibrium?

A: There are always the small movies from left field that keep surprising you. The *Songwriter* that turns up, or even *Pee Wee's Big Adventure,* or *The Re-Animator.* And then there are the good movies the studios and distributors somehow never really promote, pictures like *Heartbreakers* and *Dreamchild,* which, of course, is a lovely film.

The amazing thing is that the movies that are most successful now are often the most mediocre. Advertising has become so overwhelming, we're so inundated with it, that most people never hear about the oddball good little movies that show up. And they go to *Rambo* and *Rocky IV* and the pictures that get the biggest campaigns. Then that process keeps going because then the newspapers have all their follow-up stories from this great hit, and everybody feels they have to see it because so many other people are seeing it.

I thought the early '70s was a great period in American movies—the period when Scorsese and Coppola and De Palma and Altman were breaking through. It was a great period also because the audience began to respond to the new excitement in movies.

By any expectations that we might have formulated in the late '60s or very early '70s, the kids who grew up as part of the movie generation would be dashing to movies like *Under Fire* and *Shoot the Moon* and *The Right Stuff.* But they aren't. There was a good public response to *Stop Making Sense,* but probably not nearly as widespread as it should have been in terms of that movie's vitality.

The movie generation kids who still go to movies have settled into seeing polite, gentle foreign films, films that seem to satisfy their need for a movie that looked or felt artistic in some way. It's very hard to get that old film generation out to see *Dreamchild,* or even to get them to see *Sweet Dreams,* which has some American kind of vitality.

It's more difficult to get an audience for high-spirited, energetic movies like *Songwriter* than for something like *Blood Simple* or *Desperately Seeking Susan*—films that really have no particular charge except they sort of tie in with the mood of the moment.

Q: What kind of mood do they tie into specifically?

A: They're yuppie movies, in a way. *After Hours,* in particular, is a movie that you feel yuppies can get excited about. It has this emphasis on technique as the whole thing, and on everything that's popular in graphics and advertising at the moment. It has a kind of freaky quality to it. And it's not really about anything, and that, too, makes it seem more of the moment. It ties in very closely with *Bright Lights, Big City,* a novel I have no great respect for.

Q: An extraordinary number of the best foreign films in the book seem to be, actually, just very vivid story films of a kind one used to associate with American movies, like the uncut *The Leopard* or even *Bizet's Carmen.*

A: And *The Shooting Party.* That's really a surprising beauty of a film. I think it might have drawn a much, much larger audience if the press had treated it better. I don't know why so many critics emphasized that it wasn't as good as *The Rules of the Game.* That's like saying if any play isn't as good as Shakespeare, there's no use seeing it. Obviously, *The Shooting Party* doesn't have the formal excitement of the Renoir film, but I think it's one of the half dozen best films that have opened here this past year.

Q: I think a lot of your best writing is in your reviews of *A Passage to India* and *The Bostonians,* where your literary readings of the original works are very rich and exciting. Did you feel a certain relief just in being able to grapple with the subjects?

A: I certainly felt that with *The Bostonians,* because it's a novel that's been so often misinterpreted. And in order to show what the movie missed and why the movie didn't work, I wanted to get a chance to point out what I think the book is about.

And I loved writing about Henry James, whose work I know terribly well. I've always laughed at myself—I'm such a James fanatic, or was, at least, for a long period, that the book I took to the hospital when I was having a baby was James' *Notes of a Son and Brother,* because it was the only James I hadn't read at that point.

Q: It also seemed to be one of the few chances you had to write about complex issues, like the whole power relationship between men and women.

A: That was possible a few years back in movies, writing about *Get Out Your Handkerchiefs*. The movies I really love are the ones that give me a chance to get into areas that I haven't got into before. That's part of the fun of criticism.

It's something that many people on the outside don't seem to realize. They think of criticism simply as judgment. They don't think of it as exploration of themes or performances, or of making connections and flashes of perception and jumping ahead sometimes to see what the director is trying to get at even if he doesn't get it. It becomes a kind of intuitive process. If I outlined a review, I'd never write it, because the fun for me is discovering the connections as I write.

Q: What other movies were most fun to write about in this collection?

A: *Prizzi's Honor, The Home and the World, The Makioka Sisters. Pee Wee's Big Adventure* was no great test, but it was fun to try to suggest what makes this odd-ball movie really charming.

Q: The book's introduction is brief, but it does summarize a few things very completely—like people now wondering how movie critics can sit through all this stuff.

A: Up to the last few years, people who met me almost always said, "God, you have the best job in the world; you get to see the movies." Now people express sympathy, because they've seen enough bummers to know what sitting through bummers day after day is like.

Q: Have movies gone back to the '50s?

A: When I was first getting published, in the '50s, there was a kind of idiot smile over the culture we used to talk about: the kind of blandness that came out in pictures like the Bing Crosby *White Christmas,* which I remember reviewing on the radio, on Pacifica, and just detesting. Then it became the biggest box office film of the year. Now it's talked about as if it were an honorable movie.

It's amazing that today's movies are actually imitating that same kind of bland good will and dreariness—that kind of falsity in the whole culture which you felt the '60s had wiped away. It did not seem possible that movie heroes would come back draped in the flag, but the billboards for *Rocky IV* show the flag there with Stallone, and the billboards for the new Al Pacino film, *Revolution,* show him with an American flag behind his head. We're getting the same kind of God, mother and country routine.

We're getting an awful lot of these family-oriented pictures, as if the only thing that mattered was for the family to be together. It becomes the holy family in a picture like *Target*. It's kind of amazing to have Arthur Penn make a picture like that when he's the man who, in *Bonnie and Clyde*, first cracked open American movies, in the spirit that was later realized by Scorsese and Coppola and so many others.

Q: What are some of the other good films that got away from the audience?

A: I thought *Secret Honor* was one of Altman's best. Mazursky still comes through—he did it for me with *Moscow on the Hudson*. I liked *Dreamscape*—that had a young director, Joseph Ruben. It was a nice little thriller and had a very good performance by Dennis Quaid, probably the best role he's had, except in *The Right Stuff*.

Quaid's best work hasn't reached a mass audience, and so he doesn't get talked about as if he were a movie star in the way that somebody like Steve Guttenberg does because he was in *Cocoon*. That happens to so many good people, though.

I mean, the actress that I write about more in this book practically than any other is Diane Keaton, because she was absolutely marvelous in a couple of movies that didn't make it. And you just don't hear her talked about with the excitement that you hear about, say, Kathleen Turner. I like Kathleen Turner, and I think she's a charming comedienne. But Diane Keaton has something very special, and of the period, while Kathleen Turner is sort of an eternal movie type, just a bigger version of it and probably more talented than a lot of them.

It's amazing, though, how many good women there are. I long to see Pamela Reed in more roles, and Diana Scarwid, and Christine Lahti, Judith Ivey, Maria Conchita Alonso, Kathleen Quinlan, Lesley Anne Warren, Ellen Barkin, Amy Irving, Rae Dawn Chong . . . (sigh).

Q: What else do you long to see?

A: More yuppie movies like *Lost in America*—that was an anti-yuppie yuppie movie.

Kael & Demme: Meeting of Two American Film Heavies

Rob Nelson / 1988

From *The Badger Herald* [University of Wisconsin—Madison] 9 September 1988:4–5. Reprinted by permission.

Getting film critic Pauline Kael and film director Jonathan Demme together to discuss the state of the art of filmmaking, and Demme's in particular, was something akin to "uniting the dog catcher and the dog." That's the way Bruce Jenkins, Director of Film and Video at the Walker Art Center in Minneapolis, phrased it before introducing his guests at a symposium held at the Walker late last month. "But if you're going to invite a dog catcher," Jenkins said, "you might as well get the best."

Indeed, Pauline Kael is widely respected within the field of film criticism. She has been writing for *The New Yorker* for twenty years, and has had ten successful and acclaimed books of her reviews published, including the classics *I Lost It at the Movies, Kiss Kiss Bang Bang, When the Lights Go Down* and her most recent *State of the Art.* A collection of the last three years of her work at *The New Yorker,* tentatively titled *Hooked,* is scheduled to be out before year's end.

Cherished by countless movie buffs and despised by almost as many others, Kael is at very least an original, deeply opinionated and passionate about the movies. A year away from age 70, she is still writing for *The New Yorker* and has lost very little, if any, of her vast knowledge of film, her acutely discerning eye, and her scathing wit. She adores adoring movies (the titles of her books illuminate her obsessive, incestuous relationship with film), but finds that amidst the Hollywood of the 1980's, a good film is almost as rare as true love.

There are those few exceptions, though; the movies she appreciates she defends vehemently. Among these are the films of Jonathan Demme, including *Handle with Care, Melvin and Howard, Stop Making Sense, Someting Wild,* and his latest, the recently released *Married to the Mob.* Her influential and zealous support of Demme has, from the beginning, been inextricably linked to his success. When Kael's exaltant review of his 1977 *Handle with Care* ("It could be that *Handle with Care* is almost too likable a movie . . . it's comic style has the light touch of thirties Renoir—who would have thought there could be such a thing as redneck grace?'') included a formal damnation of Paramount for lopping off the film's original ending without Demme's consent, the studio quickly restored the film for a subsequent re-release.

Demme revealed that he has been equally interested in Kael's work. "If you're a filmmaker, you read what Pauline Kael says about you, and you read it in a certain way. I've had my mind changed on several occasions by her. She has a point of view, an artistry that's extraordinary for a film enthusiast [to read]. When *The New Yorker* comes out and you see that, by God, she likes your movie, it's a spectacular feeling, and you read it over and over. When she doesn't like your movie, you read that one only once.''

Demme is still affected by Kael's opinion of his work. In one of the more inspired moments of the evening, when Kael casually mentioned that she thought *Married to the Mob* was "a wonderful movie," Demme promptly stood up, threw his hands in the air and shouted, "Yeah!"

Seated with Demme at a small table on stage just to the right of a movie screen (which would be used to show Kael's selected clips from Demme's films), Kael began the evening's conversation by summarizing her affection for the director's work. "What I love about Jonathan Demme is that he searches for the poetry in the tacky, the everyday. I value that much more highly than the so-called tasteful movies people make. It takes more courage to be as unhighfalutin and democratic as he. And movies are, or were intended to be ever since they were first shown, a democratic art form.''

Demme, an energetically impulsive speaker by contrast to Kael's mannered reserve, responded with the first of his typically cryptic self-analyses: "I've been lucky enough to have been invited into a lot of different houses, and I guess I developed an eye for kitsch, to use your word, Pauline. The way I've applied that to movies is you try to get a good cast, a good script, and you don't screw it up.''

After viewing the high school reunion scene from *Something Wild,* Kael described the Demme trademark of a mesmerizingly chaotic mise-en-scene. "I love the cluttered, messy screen in your movies. They're wonderfully busy.'' Demme: "I think that's one of the things I learned from Roger Corman (the infamous B-movie producer of the '60s and '70s who sponsored the first directing efforts of Coppola and Scorsese, among others). "When I first started working with him he took me out to lunch, sat me down and said, 'Okay, Jonathan, we've got an hour. The most important thing to remember is that this is a visual medium, first and foremost. The eye is the primary organ, and if you can't keep the eye stimulated you're not going to keep the brain stimulated.'

"Working with Roger was just a great experience. It was like a big school. It was every bit as valuable as going to film school, only you were getting paid, not the other way around."

When the floor was opened for questions, an elderly man said he liked *Something Wild*'s first hour, but then felt violated by the violence in the film's second half. (The man was referring to the dark, Hitchcockian turn the formerly lighthearted comedy takes when Audrey's high school sweetheart Ray begins to terrorize Charlie). "In *Something Wild* I was trying to show that if you behave violently, you will taste violence," Demme responded. "That people were distressed by the film was distressing for me, you know? And I feel there are definite signals in the first half of the movie that the characters had better straighten up or else."

Kael elaborated: "Part of what is wonderful about Scorsese's earlier work [Demme had earlier mentioned Scorsese as his favorite director] like *Mean Streets* and *Taxi Driver* is that it does upset you, and it doesn't apologize. I don't think the violence in *Something Wild* is gratuitous, and I think it's absolutely crucial to the movie. Without that second half the movie would make no sense."

Kael and Demme are asked to name their favorite movies. After eluding the question a bit, Kael manages to name D. W. Griffith's *Intolerance* as a film she can always enjoy. Demme says that if pressed, he would choose Alain Resnais' 1967 documentary *Far from Vietnam*. "To me, that film is proof that movies can effect a positive change, even if it's only in one person."

"Most of what's been playing in theaters lately is dead," Kael said. "Of recent films there's been *The Unbearable Lightness of Being,* a movie that speaks to you in a different way than anything else I've ever seen. And *The Dead*. It's amazing that Houston was able to conjure such a powerful film so near the end of life. And that's about it. And Jonathan's film. But most of it is just awful.

"As a critic, I hate it much more than anyone else can. The major studios' films are generally so much worse now. Most of what's out isn't worth seeing. And having to write about this stuff, you feel degraded. It's occupying your head and it has no right to be there."

Kaeleidoscope

Ray Sawhill and Polly Frost / 1989

From *Interview* April 1989: 98–101, 130. *Kaeleidoscope* by Ray Sawhill and Polly Frost, originally published in **INTERVIEW** Magazine, Brant Publications, April 1989.

Pauline Kael's writing has been riling people since she published her first movie review in the early 1950s. The way she made sexual awareness and boldness contribute to a kind of heightened intelligence upset people—and may still. As a critic and a journalist, she combines a knack for what "works" in a theatrical sense with an analytical mind and a performer's spirit. Her first collection, *I Lost It at the Movies* (1965), was one of the landmarks of '60s nonfiction. Since then she's had an enormous influence on how popular culture is thought and written about (and she sometimes takes the rap for the sins of her imitators).

Kael's work is exciting in the way Norman Mailer's or Tom Wolfe's or Ryszard Kapuscinski's is. You come away buzzing; you take it personally—in ways you're not used to taking nonfiction. ("Why doesn't she like Tarkovsky's or Sirk's films as much as I do?") Her reviews are so persuasive that when you don't agree with her you can go around for days arguing with her in your head.

Kael was born in 1919, the fifth and youngest child of immigrants from Warsaw who ran a farm in Petaluma, California, north of San Francisco. The family moved to the city when Pauline was eight. At the University of California at Berkeley she majored in philosophy. Before being able to earn a living as a writer she worked as a seamstress, a cook, and a ghostwriter of travel books, among other jobs, supporting herself and her daughter, Gina, while turning out film criticism and broadcasting reviews on Berkeley's Pacifica radio station. From 1955 to 1960 she managed the Berkeley Cinema Guild and Studio, the first twin cinema in the country. After *I Lost It at the Movies* she began publishing in mass-circulation magazines. Since 1968 she has written for *The New Yorker,* except for a break in 1979, when she spent five months working for Paramount in Hollywood. Her latest volume, *Hooked* (Dutton), has just been published and includes reviews of films by Jonathan Demme, Pedro Almodóvar, John Waters, and Philip Kaufman.

Kael has given her house in the Berkshires a sensuality you don't expect from a writer. You walk into it and think visual artist or musician, not writer. It's a big, old, turreted place she bought years ago, when it was sagging and rotting. She and her daughter repaired it and opened it up, baring the woodwork. Art hangs on nearly all the walls—much of it by her daughter, most of the rest by friends. Kael has an instinctive feel for the placement of things; every object in the house seems to be something she responded to immediately. She often has music playing—a broad range, from Branford Marsalis to the counter-tenor Russell Oberlin. The day we stopped by, it was Aretha Franklin, her six-year-old grandson Willie's current favorite. After a visit from her daughter and grandson we sat by the fireplace while snow piled up outside.

Ray Sawhill: Which of the other arts has it been most important to you to follow?

Pauline Kael: When I began writing about films I was almost equally interested in jazz, which I followed through much of my life. I used to be able to tell you who played what instrument on just about every jazz record that ever came out.

I was very lucky to grow up in San Francisco, because although I had no money things were cheap. You could go to the Broadway plays that came out there; you could see almost anything for fifty cents. And there were kids' rates for concerts. So I had a terrific introduction to theater and music.

I was terribly interested in fiction. And in theater. And opera. And in painting. *[laughs]* I've had to narrow my interests, because you can't raise a child or be involved in taking care of a house and do everything you want to do in your life. Certain things have gone by the boards simply because of the time and energy it took to live and to write.

Polly Frost: Did you play jazz at some point?

PK: Oh, I stopped doing that fairly early. I was a young teenager when I played in a girls' jazz band. I played classical music mostly. I used to go hear Papa Hertz—Alfred Hertz—conduct every week. But my tastes ran very heavily to jazz.

PF: I can see you coming to writing from a jazz background—the use of words in a different way and the rhythms. Did jazz influence the way you write at all?

PK: If so, indirectly. I do tend to riff. I've got a lot of parentheses in there. *[laughs]*

RS: The spontaneity, too.

PK: Well, I *want* that. I want what I do to move along by hidden themes. I rarely try to think anything out ahead of time. I want it, paragraph by paragraph through the whole structure, to surprise me. But I want the *fun* of writing. I don't want to take the juice out of that.

RS: Your writing has a conversational tone, and yet it has a freedom that people don't have in conversation. How consciously have you pursued that?

PK: *Very* consciously. People often think I'm saying things inadvertently, and it amuses the hell out of me. They think that I don't know what I'm saying. Mainly I've been trying for speed and clarity, trying to write the way I talk.

When I started writing for magazines in the '50s I was dissatisfied with the studied, academic tone of my first pieces. I hated fancy writing, and I tried to write as simply as possible. I was conscious of the fact that I was writing about a popular art form. I don't think I would have written in the same way if I had been writing about classical music. How can you deal with movies truthfully, in terms of your responses, if you don't use contractions, if you don't use "you" instead of "one"? I mean, I'm not a goddamned Englishman. I don't say, "One likes this movie very much." *[laughs]* I was trying for the freedom of an American talking about movies, but it took me awhile. What broke me loose from academic writing was that I wrote a lot of advertising copy anonymously—and unsigned notes for the theaters I managed. Writing in an unsigned form frees you of the inhibitions of academic writing. I was just trying to reach the public as directly as possible. And I found that I was doing it more naturally. It's mainly a kind of courage that you need in order to write the way you think instead of writing the way you've been taught.

RS: Were there critics who excited you?

PK: A lot of writers and artists excited me. There were movie critics that I liked a lot—James Agee more than anyone else, I guess. But I never thought of Agee as a role model; I simply liked reading him. I disagreed with him a lot, but I loved the passion of his language. He got exercised about movies in the more personal writing he did for *The Nation,* where he expressed real rage if he didn't like something. It seemed to me the way we actually react to movies. We don't react in cultivated terms; we come out and say, "I hated that piece of. . . ."

RS: Did you read people like Shaw or Lionel Trilling or R. P. Blackmur with pleasure?

PK: Oh, sure, I read them all. I read Blackmur with a great deal of pleasure. I probably identified more with him than with any other critic. I can't explain that to you now, but Blackmur, when I first read him, just struck some chord with me, and I read all the authors he talked about.

I was living with a young poet named Robert Horan at that time. And we were reading Blackmur together and being excited about him. For several years Horan and I discovered books of poetry and jazz musicians and other artists together. We read Dylan Thomas' first teenage book of poetry together, Horan reading the poems aloud to me. And it was sort of Eureka! This is the new work we've been waiting for! We experienced a lot of things together like that. We would spend our Saturdays going to art shows together. And we had a very, very close relationship in the arts. We would argue viciously when we disagreed about something. It was tremendous fun. We were both young and a little bit crazy, in the sense that practical things didn't matter the way matters of the mind did—matters of mind and emotion.

You make discoveries in the arts with other people. Robert Duncan was a very good friend of mine, and we explored a lot of things together. We had our biggest talkfests in the late '30s. Later, when we were on different sides of the country, we would write letters to each other. We would read the same books and exchange impressions and ideas. And then we would get together somewhere and talk for forty-eight hours straight. *[laughs]*

RS: You once told me that you'd read everything Henry James published.

PK: My James kick came a little bit later. When I went to the hospital to give birth to my daughter in the late '40s I was just reading *Notes of a Son and Brother,* which was the last volume to complete whatever was available in James.

PF: Do you tend to binge on writers?

PK: I tend, when I get interested in a writer, to read everything, though there are writers that I like a lot, like Dickens, that I still haven't gotten through. But most writers—you know, if I started Firbank I would read everything by Firbank. When I started Dorothy Richardson's *Pilgrimage* I read from beginning to end, volume after volume. I love getting immersed in a sensibility.

RS: Is that true of all the arts, or does it mainly hold for reading?

PK: It mainly holds for reading. You learn funny things about it. For example, you're reading everything by Virginia Woolf, and you adore *The Waves* and *Mrs. Dalloway* and this one and that one, but that damn *The Years. . . .* Something is wrong; it's dreary. But usually you read a book by someone, and you get really involved, and you just keep going, book after book. And then you feel you've got that writer; you know him—there he is.

But I wouldn't want you to think that at the time I was reading, say, Melville or James I wasn't also being a foolish woman—or a foolish girl, really. I mean, I was crazy about Jack Teagarden's singing. *[laughs]* He's somebody you probably have never heard of—a trombonist. Just a particular style of singing. Every once in a while I'll catch him on the radio when they're playing old music, and I'll think, Oh, that's how to do it. You don't need a voice; you just sing. And I was always wild about Harry Ritz's dancing; I thought it was in a class of its own.

PF: I've heard that during your freshman year at Berkeley you went out dancing every night.

PK: I love dancing.

PF: What was the dancing-and-music scene like then?

PK: Well, it was all in San Francisco and Oakland—Turk Murphy, Bunk Johnson . . . a lot of terrific jazz in the Bay Area. And somehow or other I went out every night.

PF: How'd you get your studying in philosophy done?

PK: I'm a fast take. *[laughs]* The professors in the Berkeley Philosophy Department wanted me to go on and teach phenomenology, but I got a little tired of it around that point. The idea was for me to take a Ph.D. in philosophy and a law degree at the same time, but I decided I'd had it and kicked up my heels some more instead.

PF: What kind of dancing did you do?

PK: Oh, to Dixieland and Chicago-style jazz in the '40s, and before that to a lot of Glenn Miller and Guy Lombardo at the San Francisco hotels, because that was the big-band era—this was '36 to '40, my college years. All the big pop bands were playing at hotels then. And every night you could go dancing at some shebang. Sometimes it would be to Woody Herman, and that would be great.

RS: How many hours of sleep could you get by on at that point?

PK: Four or five. If you wanted pleasure enough, you'd cut down on sleep, because that's the only thing you can cut down on. *[laughs]*

RS: Was this partly being off on your own?

PK: No. I was also a serious student, and I was working as a teaching assistant and reader at Berkeley. I was correcting papers for seven courses a semester and going half blind. But I was spending an awful lot of time in conversation and dancing, too. And going to a lot of movies.

PF: At what age did you feel the urge to write?

PK: Well, writing criticism came relatively late, much later than for most of my friends. It was the orgy of all the talk with Robert Horan at college that somehow finally got me out of the notion I had of going to law school. I suddenly couldn't face law school and all that dry material when I was getting so excited by everything else. I wrote some pieces with Horan—essays. They were quite funny, but nobody published them. Maybe they were overwitty, because the two of us would build on each other's jokes, and they just got wilder and wilder.

I got interested in playwriting after college and wrote plays fairly intensively for a number of years but was very discouraged at the difficulty of getting them on. Stanford was going to put one on; they had it in rehearsal. But the students decided they wanted to do something of Giraudoux's instead—they wanted clowns and jugglers. So I didn't get anywhere. But I actually think I was not too bad. *[laughs]*

RS: What sorts of plays were they—comedies?

PK: No, they weren't comedies, I'm afraid. Damn, they should have been. There was probably too much soul-wrestling. Maybe that's one of the reasons I'm not more impressed by Ingmar Bergman. I did my own share of soul-wrestling, and it's not too tough to do.

When I started doing movie pieces, all this interest in the arts clicked together, as if I'd found my medium. And maybe because I didn't take it too seriously it was easier for me to find my voice and my tone; I wasn't inhibited the way I was in other art forms. Writing about movies, you could be playful, you could be colloquial, you could be American. Whereas writing plays, you were struggling to express yourself, and it was altogether more painful and less entertaining for other people.

PF: What about your radio work?

PK: Well, that was in the '50s, after I'd published a few movie pieces. Weldon Kees, who was a well-known poet and man around the arts at the time—and a good friend—had a struggling radio show on a commercial station in the Bay Area, and he asked me on as a guest. Later the Pacifica radio people asked if I'd like to record some pieces I'd written. And then they asked me if I'd like to review regularly. It was hell in some ways because I didn't have any money and they didn't pay at all. They didn't even pay my way into the movies.

So I was doing a weekly show for no money. I had a small child, and it was very rough. I had a loyal following in the Bay Area, with people buying my tapes and talking about them, but I didn't get any work on the East Coast out of it.

PF: Was it a shock to move from San Francisco, with all of its sensual pleasures, to New York?

PK: Well, I was in New York briefly during the early '40s. A lot of people that I met in that period took me to amazing things. Gian-Carlo Menotti took me to the Met for the first time, and it was Ezio Pinza in *Don Giovanni*. I saw Marlon Brando in *Truckline Cafe*. I had some great experiences. And I had absurd experiences: Samuel Barber took me to Radio City Music Hall for the first time, and we saw *Mrs. Miniver*! *[laughs]* It was ghastly, and we sat there staring at each other in horror.

PF: You lived in New York for a couple of years?

PK: I lived in New York for about three years, and then I went back to the West Coast until 1965, when I published *I Lost It at the Movies* and came East to write for *Life* and other magazines. And in '65 it took a lot of writing to pay the rent. That year I was on a plane, going to give a lecture, and a husband and wife were sitting across the aisle from me. She was reading me in *Mademoiselle* and he was reading me in *Holiday*, and then they swapped magazines. It was very cheering, but it was also sort of scary, because I was writing in half a dozen magazines in the same month.

RS: How have your work habits changed over the years?

PK: Well, I don't work all night anymore. During my early years at *The New Yorker*, when I was writing long pieces every week, I would often stay up all night to finish something for the deadline day. And I would see very beautiful dawns. But also you get a sinking feeling in the pit of your stomach as you stagger toward your bed. *[laughs]* Then the phone starts ringing three hours later. And people who phone you in the morning just laugh when you say, "I just got to bed." They think you're some lazy bum.

Mainly I get to work earlier in the day now. It used to be that, writing weekly, I was rushing to movies. And sometimes I didn't find the movie I wanted to write about till the night before the copy was due, so I just splattered it out. In many ways, that's the truest reaction you'll ever get. But even so, I can't do that anymore. I can't use the words that come to me most readily, because those phrases have become stale. So now if friends use a good term in describing a movie, I say, "Can I use that?" Because I think, Gee, it's different from what I would say—that's great.

RS: Do you have any regrets about your career or about your writing over the years? Do you wish you had started earlier or had gone about things differently?

PK: Oh, well, I *did* start fairly early; I just didn't have a livelihood to sustain it. I published my first pieces before I managed theaters. But I had to manage theaters to make a living, and do programming for colleges and a lot of other jobs. By the time I got hired at *The New Yorker* I was almost 50. And so, yes, I regret all the years and energy that went into crummy jobs and trying to sustain life. On the other hand I probably gained a certain amount of experience and breadth from them. But there's no question in my own mind that I could have done more as a writer had I gotten an earlier start, when I had all that crazy energy.

RS: Do movies stand in a different relation to the culture as a whole now?

PK: Yes, I think they do. In the '60s and '70s movies played an adversarial role in the culture. And a lot of middle-aged and elderly people were very offended when they went to the movies. The language was freer than they liked. There was an easy-going, comic attitude toward American patriotism, a more easygoing attitude toward sex relations. The older people stayed away from a lot of movies, and when they did go they often claimed they didn't understand them, because movies moved faster and were more elliptical. So movies became sort of the enemy. Now they are definitely not the enemy. I wish they were.

PF: When I was in college my friends and I would go to movie marathons—we'd go to see five Kurosawa films. Kids don't seem to do that now.

PK: Now they see things on VCRs, but they're probably not having orgies of Kurosawa. *[laughs]* There are people who use VCRs well. But it isn't the same thing as sharing that excitement with an audience. There's no way of discussing a film when it's not affecting the whole culture at the same time. That was always part of the excitement of movies. You went to a restaurant and you'd hear everybody in the next booth talking about the same movie you'd seen two days before, which you'd been arguing about. And with VCRs movies don't stay in your mind the same way. You need the big screen.

PF: How has your reviewing changed over the years?

PK: I felt an excitement about writing about movies, particularly in the late '60s and the first half of the '70s—the period when Altman made one terrific movie after another, when Coppola and Scorsese and De Palma were doing sensational work, when Bertolucci was coming through. The movies fed my senses then. I had the feeling that all I was trying to do was keep up with what was going on in movies.

The director I left out just now was, of course, Godard. It was Godard who got me hired at *The New Yorker,* indirectly. William Shawn, who had seen some of the Godard films and realized that something new was going on in them, read me in *The New Republic,* where I expressed my excitement about them, and wanted me in *The New Yorker*.

RS: Imagine that William Shawn was interested in Godard films!

PK: It's wonderful, isn't it? Shawn had a vast interest in what was going on in the arts. And when he saw something going on he reacted with great intensity.

Godard represented the big turning point in '60s movies. While college students were talking about Bergman the new voice was Godard. I felt tremendous excitement at almost every Godard film right up through *Weekend.*

There are still movies that come along where you feel something's going on with the individual artist. Blier's *Get Out Your Handkerchiefs* was exciting to write about. So was *The Unbearable Lightness of Being.* But when Coppola and Altman and Scorsese were breaking through, they spoke to what was going on in the country. And so the act of writing criticism wasn't just talking about whether the movie was any good. You were talking about what the movie meant, how you felt about it, what it stood for.

In general I'm looking for something that shows some talent, some freshness. You can see what I mean by analogy to literature. Suppose you were one of the first people who read *Middlemarch*—you'd want to tell people about it. That's how I felt about *McCabe & Mrs. Miller* and *Nashville* and *Godfather II.* I wanted to say, "Look what's going on here!" That doesn't happen much right now in movies. There's something rather paralyzing in the culture.

PF: You've spoken in the past about a particular kind of excitement that you can get from a good American film.

PK: Well, I respond to American films when they're good in a way that's much more direct than the way I respond to foreign films. It makes sense that we want films that represent American culture, especially since it has a kind of crazy energy. There's a particular kind of humor and a speed that we get in a good American film. You get it in, say, *The Lady Eve,* the Preston Sturges comedy. I've never seen a European comedy that gave me the kind of buzz that *The Lady Eve* did when I first saw it.

American movies are pop for us in a way that foreign films rarely are. That's the fun of Almodóvar; he has that pop element in his work, because he's so influenced by American movies.

PF: I know you enjoy Almodóvar's films. Did you enjoy the work of Charles Ludlam?

PK: I *loved* Charles Ludlam. I once took Claude Jutra, the French Canadian director, down to the Ridiculous Theatrical Company. And Claude said, "*This* is theater." And he had tears streaming out of his eyes, he laughed so hard. I loved Charles Ludlam's shows, and I thought there was a real craft and polish and crazy elegance in what he was doing. And, of course, it's like Almodóvar. Almodóvar has the resources of movies, but he basically has that feeling for a company, too. It's a wonderful kind of theater because you can do mad, excessive things and the audience digs it because they've grown up on the same cultural references you have.

RS: You always seem to be able to enjoy the campier sides of show business and art.

PK: It's a basic element in any theatrical art. It's so vital to theater, that campiness. Maybe being able to make fun of what you're doing is so much a part of the sophistication of theater and movies. It's what's fun in something like *Tequila Sunrise*. There's just enough. . . .

RS: Overripeness?

PK: Overripeness, sure. People want to regard that as decadence. As if any mention of Charles Ludlam were a tribute to trivia. A lot of people don't really get it. Or they think you're making some bow to the gay readership. And it's not that. It's subversive—in the sense of making fun of dull, proper values. And it's much wider than the gay readership.

Part of the fun for many of us—you see it now if you look at old movies of the '30s—is that extravagance of gesture, doing things to excess. Every emotion is made bright. And it helps us satirize ourselves, helps put our own emotions in perspective, because they are so overdramatized. I think that growing up at the movies you get a sense of perspective on yourself through the campiness of what you enjoy.

I don't think I could have a close friend who didn't respond to the craziness of certain kinds of theatrical art, who didn't enjoy that kind of ripeness. I've generally become friends with people because we laughed at the same things. And we're laughing at ourselves, at our responsiveness to this phenomenon.

It's a way, also, of not taking the arts too seriously. It's one of the things that I've tried to write about and that readers get most indignant about, because they feel you're not being a cultivated, serious person if you talk about your pleasure at silliness, at lushness. But if I see a *Jean de Florette,* I *die* with boredom. I can't sit there and watch Gérard Depardieu playing a hunchback and not have people realize how ridiculous it is to have a tall hunchback. That's the kind of thing Charles Ludlam played to supreme extravagance. When I was a child I loved John Barrymore because of his buffoonery. He was always making fun of himself.

PF: So it's safe to say that you don't go to the movies for self-improvement?

PK: Self-improvement and art don't really belong together. If art opens your eyes and opens your senses that's something else. I do think that a great movie makes you experience things more intensely. But that intense thing often comes to you via extravagance.

RS: Since the Bertolucci-Blier years, the *Last Tango, Get Out Your Handkerchiefs* years. . . .

PK: I wouldn't put those in the same class. I think *Last Tango* really is extraordinary and stands by itself, even in terms of Bertolucci's work. In the same way that Godard and Altman each burned up the screen for a period, with a whole series of movies, I think Bertolucci did it faster. *Before the Revolution, The Conformist, Last Tango*—nothing he's done since has had that kind of lush excitement, or the total involvement, or the freedom. *The Last Emperor* has a kind of simple flow to it, but the passion seems to be missing.

PF: It must be hard to sustain the kind of energy that went into those early films.

PK: Well, filmmaking is peculiarly a burning-out medium. I think it takes so much out of you because you can express so much of yourself. There are very few directors who haven't burned out.

Peckinpah kept going longer than most. Of course, he didn't live very long, really, but there was a crazy excitement burning in that man. He was the least theoretical of them all, and I think that accounts for it. He often thought that he was saying things in movies that weren't what he was expressing at all. What came through were his feelings, not the meanings he intended to put there. He became rather spiteful in many ways, but he was an amazingly gifted man. It was a great pity that because of the violence in some of his movies he became a figure that the American press loved to jeer at. And he played along with that, in a way. But, you know, you can become perverse if you're treated stupidly enough for a long time and hampered in doing what you want to do. It doesn't take much to get hold of a pencil. But people who really want to work in movies, and who are as passionately addicted to it as Peckinpah, are in a terrible position. They're at the mercy of a lot of people who basically hate them.

PF: You knew Peckinpah. How good was he at making enemies?

PK: He would spot the weakness in people and really twist the knife. On the other hand he was generous, wonderful. He was a very civilized man in many ways and an utter monster in other ways. And those things are not unusual in a movie director.

RS: A moviegoer interested in movies for their erotic possibilities can find himself looking in odd directions these days, like Diane Keaton's performance in *The Good Mother*.

PK: Well, Diane Keaton is one of the rare actresses who've had one role after another that was sexual. Debra Winger has brought sexual elements into her performances in some movies, too. And Jessica Lange. I think those three are the best young actresses on the American screen. They're the ones whose work I go to see with the most excitement. Keaton astonishes me, because in movie after movie she does daring sexual, revealing things. And then she'll do something that's unbelievably inventive, like her performance in *Crimes of the Heart*. And in *The Good*

Mother she goes totally out on a limb. She's probably the finest young American actress we've got. But then Debra Winger or Jessica Lange will come along and do something, and I'll say *she's* the finest. *[laughs]*

But Michelle Pfeiffer really is extraordinary, too. She's so crystalline in her beauty, she's such a vision, that people may not recognize what a talented actress she is. I loved her in *Natica Jackson,* that little film she did on television from a John O'Hara story.

PF: What did you learn during your stay in Hollywood in 1979?

PK: I learned how many good scripts there were that weren't going to be made or were going to be made in such a distorted form that no one would ever know how good they'd been. For myself I learned how much fun it was *not* to have deadlines and to spend time with young writers. And I learned how scared people were of me. People treated me as if I were a high priestess!

But I began to miss writing. I got the sense that my mind was going to sleep. Because you would talk to a writer about his script, or a director about his plans, and you would have to say the same thing the next day because they get so obsessed and nervous and tense that nothing fully sinks in. And you just keep repeating yourself.

Of course, when I talk about the good scripts going begging it has to be understood that my idea of a wonderful script doesn't necessarily mean a script that would please the public. I can't pretend that the pictures I like are hits. A great many of them are not. Some of the pictures I've loved the most in the last decade have been only marginal successes or box-office disasters—*Shoot the Moon, Melvin and Howard, Citizens Band, Pennies from Heaven. . . .* These pictures failed. Yet there's some glory for the executives in having done them.

PF: You once wrote that lousy movies left you with an appetite for facts and information and real people and real events.

PK: Yes. Every once in a while there's a film like *Thy Kingdom Come,* and there's a purity in the excitement you feel, because you're seeing the complexities of people's emotions—the people who get caught up in the fundamentalist movements. What you rarely get from a documentary is the aesthetic kick or the pop kick that you also go to movies for. Unless it's a very great documentary, like, say, Kon Ichikawa's *Tokyo Olympiad,* it may not have much in the way of aesthetic dimensions. Or, if it does, as in *The Thin Blue Line,* possibly you resent them—at least I did. It's a beautifully made film, but the beautifully made element in it works against the subject. You feel the director is aestheticizing a factual situation instead of approaching it more simply. There's something morally offensive in that approach, I think.

PF: Are you a news watcher?

PK: Yes, I'm a news freak. I catch the 6:30 news on one network and the 7 o'clock on another. I watch CNN hearings. I love watching news. Or else I'm obsessed with it—I don't know which.

RS: I have trouble getting through the way the news is presented. Do you fight that?

PK: Oh, sure, it's a parody, the way they all say the most obvious things, when what you see in a few seconds of footage contradicts what they're telling you. It's quite incredible to hear the vacuous lines that come out of the news readers' mouths.

PF: Is that part of the fascination for you?

PK: Yeah, because you're watching these people crippling and strangling the news, and when they do have a great event and can't miss with it—when it's an earthquake or something of that sort—each network will concentrate on the same pathetic figures. They manage to pull your emotional strings so blatantly that you want to smack them one. Except for *Wiseguy,* which I really enjoy, and *L.A. Law* sometimes, I can't watch series television. But I can watch the news endlessly, because there's always enough new happening to keep me fixated, and there's always this rage at the way it's presented.

RS: Can movies be made now with the kind of honesty of De Palma's *Blow Out?*

PK: Well, the box-office failure of *Blow Out* was, I think, a tragedy for De Palma and for John Travolta—it's just about the best work each of them has ever done. But it probably served as a warning to some of the people who might have wanted to do something politically sophisticated. It's as if people get penalized for sophistication. I think that's true of Altman—he got ornery. Like Peckinpah, Altman became difficult to deal with, but at the same time the man is a genius, and he came through with a string of the greatest films ever made in this country, so you'd think people would put up with his orneriness. The studio executives don't mind somebody ornery if he's a mediocrity, because they understand the terms in which he's functioning.

PF: I find *The Untouchables* depressing, because it's as if De Palma acceded to the Reagan era's nostalgia for heroes, whereas *Blow Out* was a personally felt expression of what's going on in this country.

PK: I think De Palma's script for *Blow Out* is infinitely superior to the David Mamet script for *The Untouchables.* The script for *The Untouchables* is square. But, on the other hand, that squareness did make it possible for De Palma to reach a big audience, and he did direct it marvelously. De Palma's a ranking American director who had never been given his due. Just in human terms you have to be glad when somebody good comes to the fore. People don't sell out or give in to the system or anything like that quite as simply as we thought when we were kids.

PF: Are there movies that you really can't justify enjoying or writing about?

PK: Damn it, if I enjoy it, it seems to me I'd better be able to write about it. It would be dishonest to enjoy something and not admit it. If you laugh all the way through a comedy and then write a pan, something is wrong with you. You have to be able to believe in yourself enough to be truthful about how you react.

PF: Should everyone trust their instincts?

PK: I can't speak for everybody on that; I think a lot of people have lousy instincts. *[laughs]* But to be a critic it sure helps to be able to trust your instincts. What else have you got? If you don't trust your instincts maybe you're in the wrong profession.

RS: Couldn't somebody argue that the other thing you have is your tastes?

PK: But tastes become instinctive. Your instincts aren't something apart from your knowledge and your education and your tastes. Your instincts are everything you know acting together immediately, viscerally.

PF: Is it possible that a critic could not have great taste and still show us something about the medium?

PK: Yes, there are critics whose judgments are way off but whose perceptions of a movie are quite stunning. I'll read a review and think the person is blind to what the narrative is doing, but he'll describe certain details and I'll think, Gee, I took that in and yet I didn't fully register what it meant. In many ways the perceptions and the observations are more important than the judgments. We read critics for the perceptions, for what they tell us that we didn't fully grasp when we saw the work. The judgments we can usually make for ourselves.

The Pearls of Pauline

Mark Feeney / 1989

From *The Boston Globe Magazine* 11 June 1989: 18–19, 47–54.
Reprinted courtesy of *The Boston Globe*.

"I don't have the memory for my own life that I have for movies and books," Pauline Kael says. "People tell me about things I did—or things that I said—years ago, and I don't know what they're talking about. But I do remember movies of that period." She laughs as she says this.

It would be disappointing if she said anything else. For no one quite loves movies as Pauline Kael does, or so loathes the bad ones. No one else has written about them as acutely, as provocatively, as intensely. As movie critic for *The New Yorker* she has made more enemies, influenced more writers, and delighted more readers than anyone else who has made a career of looking at images moving on a screen. James Agee may remain the patron saint of American movie criticism, but at this point in her career it's hard to deny that Pauline Kael is the greatest movie critic America has produced.

This year marks the second in a trio of milestones. In 1988 Kael celebrated her 20th anniversary at *The New Yorker*. On June 19 she turns 70. And next year is the 25th anniversary of her first book, the one with the title—mingling ardor, innuendo, and rue—that still captures the essence of her writing, *I Lost It at the Movies*. (Her 11th book, *Hooked,* a collection of reviews, was published in April.)

On a sunny afternoon in Kael's turn-of-the-century house in the Berkshires, this 5-foot tall figure in Nikes and Pendleton is about as intimidating as any other devoted grandmother. (Kael proudly points out pictures of her 7-year-old grandson, William, in his Superman suit.) Her quavery voice, logs crackling in the fireplace, and a scattering of toys on the coffee table complete a scene out of Norman Rockwell.

But then there are the anomalies—a copy of *Variety* on the kitchen table, stacks of current books in nearly every room, a pile of what appear to be film scripts on a shelf in the dining room, a throaty laugh a torch singer might envy—to suggest that, yes, this is the same woman for whom George Lucas named the villainous General Kael in his $40 million production *Willow*.

Long ago Kael earned the sincerest tribute our culture has to give,

122

first-name familiarity; and for anyone who loves movies, the name
Pauline can mean but one person. What other critic can say with a shrug,
"I keep hearing about [Hollywood] people who have to call their analysts
immediately or take to their beds after they read my review—it both
makes you laugh and it makes you wince"?

Legends grow up around her. "I've read in print that I edited [Martin]
Scorsese's *New York, New York*—I mean, it's preposterous" she ex-
claims. As if on cue, the phone rings soon after; it's *Premiere,* the film
magazine, wanting to verify that she made a cameo appearance in Woody
Allen's *Stardust Memories* (she didn't). Her stint as a producer in
Hollywood in 1979 still excites gossip. Then there are the controversies
surrounding her. Perhaps the best known are Kael's 1975 review of a
rough cut of Robert Altman's *Nashville,* which appeared several months
before the film's theatrical release, and Renata Adler's celebrated 1980
attack on her in *The New York Review of Books* (Adler declared Kael's
work "piece by piece, line by line, and without interruption, worthless").

"I can't think of many people who are, not indifferent, but *disinterested,*" a nationally known reviewer says on the subject of Kael. Preferring anonymity, he pauses to think of a colleague with a nonpartisan
view. "You know her famous enemies, and you know her powerful
friends . . ." His voice trails off, as if to indicate how few others
that leaves.

David Thomson, the author of *A Biographical Dictionary of Film,*
admires Kael—with reservations. "She gave film criticism its power and
position more than anyone, without question," he admits. Yet two
aspects of her work trouble him. "I wonder that someone with her range
of knowledge and intellectual curiosity has not extended her work into
books," rather than just reviewing and collections of reviews, he says.
And, "So far as I know, she has never publicly changed her mind on a
film she's written about. I do think, psychologically, that that point goes
deep into her. It is her incapacity to admit doubt or a change of mind
that, well, it is the thing about her I find most daunting."

John Gregory Dunne, the novelist and screen-writer, has memorably
argued the case against Kael. "At times she seems less like a critic than
a den mother," he once wrote, "swatting her favorites gently when they
get out of line, lavishing them with attention, smothering them with
superlatives for their successes." Indeed, "reading her on film is like
reading [the crackpot Soviet biologist T.D.] Lysenko on genetics—
fascinating, unless you know something about genetics," he wrote. "The
Rosetta Stone of her work is 'Raising Kane' (Kael's essay on the making
of Orson Welles' *Citizen Kane*) . . . which reads as if it were not so much

written as chattered in a movie scene by one of those film buffs who has
seen everything and understood nothing.''

Kael's admirers and detractors agree on one thing: her methodol-
ogy—or rather its absence. She refuses to tie herself to any theory or
aesthetic of cinema. The very term "cinema" irritates Kael; she writes
about "movies." "It's fun to be able to react to what's new and see, you
know, the changes as they come up," she says. "That's really the
running aesthetics of movies so far as I'm concerned." She belongs to a
line of American writers whose most notable exponents include Thoreau,
Mencken, Dwight Macdonald, and Randall Jarrell: All slightly cranky
and thoroughly combative, they refused to join any school other than that
created by their own enthusiasms and the love of expressing complex
thought in deceptively simple prose.

"I think that Pauline has been underrated as a writer, really, has not
gotten sufficient recognition *as a writer*," suggests Roy Blount Jr., the
humorist and a neighbor of Kael's. "She has risen to what is the
distinctive American writer's challenge, which is to create an eloquent
prose style that derives from American speech. I think that lots of her
reviews have been extraordinary essays that stand as essays independent
of the movies.''

Few critics in this century have better—or more aggressively—
exemplified T. S. Eliot's dictum. "The only method is to be very intelligent." Instinctive, impulsive, idiosyncratic, her method is her madness
for movies. Anyone who has read even a little Kael knows that she pours
herself into her writing. "When you read most critics, you know they
don't care one way or the other," she laments. "If you read the reviews
in the papers like *The New York Times* or most papers, you feel they
could argue pro or con a book or a movie . . . . It's very rare you get a
really committed voice saying, this is how I feel about something. It's
almost as if they would disqualify themselves; they wouldn't be thought
'objective,' whatever that damn thing is.''

What's up on the screen she takes personally. Kael's immediacy of
response has produced some of her most outrageous writing, as well as
some of her finest. The touchstone for Kaelian excess remains her 1972
review of Bernardo Bertolucci's *Last Tango in Paris*. "Bertolucci and
Brando have altered the face of an art form," she announced, calling
Last Tango's premiere "a landmark in movie history comparable to May
29, 1913—the night *Le Sacre du Printemps* was first performed—in music
history." She still stands by that assessment, though it has come to look
less and less tenable.

The movie touched a nerve in Kael, a nerve that (even admirers concede) readily responds to sex and violence on the screen. She has championed graphic directors such as Sam Peckinpah, Brian De Palma, and the Martin Scorsese of *Mean Streets* and *Taxi Driver* (while also excoriating such explicit films as *A Clockwork Orange* and *The Exorcist*). Kael would contend that the visceral elements those film makers brought to the fore are central to why we go to movies. As she noted in explaining the title of her second book, *Kiss Kiss Bang Bang,* those words "are perhaps the briefest statement imaginable of the basic appeal of movies." To disregard that appeal is not just dishonest, one could argue, but also to miss much of the pleasure movies can give.

To convey her responses to such an elemental art form, Kael arrived at a singularly effective prose style: slangy, conversational, rigorously unpretentious. "I have tried to write about movies in the language that's appropriate to them," she says. To see how successful she's been, all one has to do is read other critics. Pick any random half-dozen (and not just movie critics), and at least one or two will be children of Kael's. Their emulation demonstrates Kael's achievement in two ways: Their numbers show the powerful pull of her style; their inferior practice of that style suggests her still-unrivaled mastery of it.

"It distresses me, the number of people who write like me," Kael says. "People in general seem to assume I must be flattered by it, or that I somehow encourage it. I have nothing to do with it, and it's like a succubus. It's awful to open something up hoping to read something and [instead] find your own thoughts being echoed. And sometimes your own thoughts of many years ago that you wrote about a totally different picture are being used to apply to something they don't *apply* to!"

That famous Kael style—like a string of firecrackers going off on the Fourth of July—would seem as easily attained as putting match to fuse. Its apparent ease is the product of strenuous effort. William Whitworth, now editor of *The Atlantic,* edited Kael's copy at *The New Yorker* during the late '70s. He calls Kael "just the hardest-working writer that you can imagine, and incredibly demanding of herself. She would worry about a specific word, a specific line, whether it did just what she wanted it to, whether it had any life, whether it was funny, and on and on. It was really something to watch that and, in a small way, to get to participate in it," he says. "To share those sessions with her, thinking aloud about this and that, and see what is, in my opinion, one of *the* great talents—one of the greatest stylists in critical writing in journalism, certainly in my professional lifetime—to see that talent at work was a wonderful experience, as far as I'm concerned."

Even more than the seductive style, Kael's stance toward movies—and culture generally—has contributed to her powerful impact. She absorbed the best of those critics who preceded her: the seriousness of Macdonald and Robert Warshow, the intensity and wit of Agee, the unbuttoned style of Otis Ferguson, the iconoclasm of Manny Farber. And, going beyond what any of them had done, she managed to encompass the dizzying spectrum of an art form that could run from Hollywood schlock to high art. (Every now and then the schlock turns out better than the art.) What all the raciness and wisecracks and scrappiness can obscure is the astonishing range of a critic who, as conversant with Jean Renoir as with Richard Pryor, refuses to vulgarize the one or patronize the other.

Greil Marcus is best known as a rock critic, but he has also written extensively on books, movies, art, and politics. He says of Kael, "She showed us what criticism could be, what the possibilities were in terms of writing about popular culture. What sorts of limits didn't have to be paid any attention to."

A friend of Kael's, Marcus speaks also as someone profoundly shaped not just by her work but by her example: "You don't have to just stick to a movie. You can just use everything you've got. It was really thrilling to come across writing that was so voracious and so ambitious, that had so much life in it and such a complete absence of pretense. I guess she was the first critic I ever read that made me feel like I was engaged in a conversation with her. I certainly never would have become a critic if it wasn't for her—and that was long, long before I ever met her."

What Kael once attributed to the best films of the early '70s, "a new open-minded interest in examining American experience," informs all her work. Few writers came better equipped to exploit the mixing of high and low, the explosion of energy and general opening up of new avenues that the late '60s and early '70s witnessed. And among those so qualified, perhaps none was better suited to keep some perspective on the revolution in the culture. Kael was, after all, almost 50 before settling in at *The New Yorker,* with a widely varied personal and professional background to draw upon.

"A bookish girl from a bookish family," as she once described herself to Studs Terkel, Kael was born in Petaluma, California, in 1919, the youngest of five children. Both her parents had emigrated from Poland, and Isaac Kael succeeded well enough in business to be able to retire in his early 40s. "He was sort of a gentleman farmer in the sense that he really didn't know anything about it and he boned up on it. I mean, that isn't supposed to work, but it did," his daughter says with a laugh.

The Depression forced the family to sell the farm and move south to San Francisco. With the exception of a few years during the '40s, Kael would live in the Bay Area for the next four decades. "No, I'm really a San Franciscan," she concedes. "It's just a fluke that I'm a San Franciscan stranded in the Berkshires."

Kael entered the University of California at Berkeley in 1936, majoring in philosophy. ("It's very hard to know how you get from philosophy to movie reviewing. Don't ask me!") She recalls, "It was a good time in terms of political ferment, but it was also a time that was *very* hard financially—it was very rough—and nobody seemed to have very much money."

Though there had been expectations of law school or a teaching career, Kael instead went to New York with a friend, the poet Robert Horan. "Guys in uniform would follow any girl down the street, and if you said no, they'd say, what are we fighting for! It was pretty funny. It was a good, hectic time; the war vitalized the city," she says. "I was involved with friends, involved with the arts. I was going to everything. I was there for about three years. It seems so long ago now. But it was exciting."

The unconventional life Kael led in New York continued when she returned to the Bay Area three years later. "I was there, of course, during the Beat period, and knew all those people," Kael says. She tried her hand at writing plays and making experimental films. She reviewed movies on Pacifica radio. "She was a big hit," remembers *Film Quarterly* editor Ernest Callenbach. "She even then had the same kind of snap to her stuff that she deployed later in *The New Yorker*."

She married and divorced three times. To support herself and her daughter, Gina, born in 1948, Kael worked at a variety of jobs: advertising copywriter, bookstore clerk, cook, seamstress, textbook writer, and, the most notable, managing America's first twin movie house.

Film critics are often called frustrated film makers. They might be better understood as heightened filmgoers. In that sense, the time Kael spent running the Berkeley Cinema Guild and Studio from 1955 to 1960 was an invaluable—and unique—preparation for her reviewing career.

"The Cinema Guild was the first good repertory cinema in America," says Tom Luddy, now a producer at Francis Ford Coppola's Zoetrope Studios. "It had a kind of critical approach and published program notes. It had an informed, educated repertory policy." Kael's innovative programming made the theaters a Bay Area institution. In those days, Luddy adds, "everybody had the Berkeley Cinema Guild schedule on their refrigerator door."

The work was "all consuming," Kael says—she did everything from changing the displays to answering the phones—but its rewards were considerable.

"People really loved the good stuff. I got audiences to come to movies like *Unfaithfully Yours,* which had never drawn anywhere in the country before," she says. "And I played *Touch of Evil* about every three months and packed the place with it before anybody else in the country had heard of *Touch of Evil.* I played the early Bergman films long before they were being played at Harvard or other places. It was fun; it was exciting turning up things and drawing an audience to see them."

Away from the theaters, Ernest Callenbach says, "she ran a kind of afternoon and evening salon in her house, where she would pad around the house in slippers, as I recall, with a glass of bourbon and ice in her hand, holding forth, and a miscellaneous selection of fans and hangers-on who would hang around and chat with her about movies—the topic was almost inevitably and always movies. As you know, she wields a mean wisecrack, and it was always a very entertaining time."

Many of those wisecracks found their way into Kael's writing. Her first review, of Chaplin's *Limelight,* appeared in 1953 in a small journal. Over the next dozen years she published a wide variety of work in quarterlies and obscure film journals and as anonymous program notes. Kael has claimed that her first 10 years of writing netted her all of $2,000. That would change in 1965, though, with the publication of her first book.

"I remember precisely when I was struck," says William Abrahams, who has edited all of Kael's books. "She had three or four reviews in a piece about movies in *Partisan Review.* And I thought it was *marvelous.* I mean, nobody else had ever written about movies like that! She made it terribly interesting to read, and it was very exciting. Of course, I had no idea who she was. So I simply wrote and said, 'Do you have any more?' " She did, and Abrahams recalls their first meeting, which took place in Boston, "vividly."

"The switchboard called on the given day and said, 'There is a Miss Kael here for you.' I came downstairs, and, of course, I hadn't the faintest notion of what . . . you know, sometimes you form an opinion, but what can you say on the basis of having read a piece of movie criticism?

"Anyway, there was this woman who was even shorter than I am—and I'm short!—I think that's why we took to each other so immediately: We were on eye level.

"Then we went off to have lunch at the Ritz. It was *wonderful. . . .* Believe me, she was a very outspoken, remarkable woman then," he says. "This was 1964, and her style was totally surprising then—not what you heard at *The Atlantic Monthly,* let me put it *that* way . . . and I don't think you heard it in the Ritz dining room, certainly! I was just delighted and agog and terrifically taken with the way she talked. It was so honest and straightforward and no holds barred. She was very, very candid and, clearly, said what she wanted to say.

"In the course of the lunch—I think at that point we had already more or less agreed that we were indeed going to do a book—I said, the only thing that is missing, we don't seem to have a title for this book. And I've always wondered whether she really meant it when she said, 'Well, we can call it *I Lost It at the Movies.'* Of course, I thought that was sublime!"

The book was a sensation and secured Kael's reputation. She moved to New York and free-lanced for *Life, Vogue,* and *Mademoiselle.* A reviewing job at *McCall's* in 1966 ended, notoriously, when she called *The Sound of Music* "The Sound of Money." Nor did a stint at *The New Republic* end amicably ("the readers were so used to Stanley Kauff-mann," Kael notes, "they thought there was something berserk about my having a personal voice as a critic"). Kael's career had reached an impasse: The more highly regarded she became, the more jobs she lost.

If life were like the movies, the solution would have been simple: The prettiest girl marries the handsomest boy. Which is what happened. The best magazine in America asked the best movie critic to join its staff. "A woman friend of mine, when I was debating whether to take the offer from *The New Yorker* back in late '67, she said, 'Take it.' . . . I said that I didn't know I'd be appropriate to the pages of *The New Yorker,* and she said, 'Do it. If you write for *The New Republic* and my mother reads it, that's just your opinion. But if you write for *The New Yorker,* that's *IT,'* and we both laughed." Mismatched though the patrician *New Yorker* and pugnacious Kael may have seemed, the marriage turned out to have been made in magazine heaven. It was Fred Astaire and Ginger Rogers all over again: The magazine gave her class, she gave it sex appeal.

Every other week Kael spends 3 1/2 days in New York. "I go into the city and see about six movies for each one that I decide to write about," she says. "I waste a lot of time seeing things that aren't worth talking about. I generally have 10 to 15 movies, at least, backlogged in my head before I sit down to write about one."

The review written, she harbors no illusions about its impact: "The movie critic has an effect on the smaller movie, or the foreign film, or the new film. We can keep certain directors working if enough of us praise their work: the movie companies will listen to that. But I think very few of us have major power. It's true, a *Times* review, if it's negative enough, can hurt a small-budget movie, but it doesn't hurt a big one.

"I don't have to worry about that," she says. "I can, maybe, do some good for the egos of the people involved in the movie. And I can get a small number of people to go see it, and maybe have some influence on some other critic. But that's *nothing* compared to the power of TV ads for a movie and the power the movie company itself has."

Until 1979, Kael reviewed weekly for *The New Yorker* from September through March (Penelope Gilliatt took the other half of the year). Since 1980 her reviews have appeared biweekly. An intervening sabbatical included five months in Hollywood working as an "executive consultant" at Paramount Pictures. ("All it did was give me a better sense, really, of how many terrific scripts there were that were never going to get made or just going to get ruined. . . . I also had a very good time!") While some readers detect a falling-off in her work since her return, that work retains Kael's unmistakable stamp. This summer she goes on sabbatical again, for three months, to update her collection of capsule reviews, *5001 Nights at the Movies*.

Movies today, Kael thinks, are a far cry from what they were during the palmy days of the 1970s. Besides the obvious changes in moviegoing, ranging from the VCR ("it's cheap, it's easy," she admits) to the multiplex theater (which she likens to "a latrine"), the very climate for movies has changed.

"There *was* an excitement culturally in the '70s and [to] writing about those pictures as they came out. Pictures like, well, when *Weekend* came out—the whole series of Godard movies culminating in *Weekend*. And the whole series of Altman movies. And the *Godfather* pictures coming out in the middle of all that!

"Something was happening in American life, but something marvelous was also happening to American movies," she says. "I think it's the greatest period American movies have ever had. I mean, people can talk all they want to about 1939. Those are pretty stale movies compared to what went on in the '70s.

"You know, they talk about the golden age of the cinema as if it took place in the late '30s or in the '40s. There was nothing personal and exciting in most of those movies. They were machine-tooled. They were a lot of fun. But except for Preston Sturges and a few fluky individualists, they just didn't have the personal voice of the movies of the '70s."

She elaborates: "No, there are individual movies that are wonderful now. There are some marvelous movie makers and marvelous movies now. But they don't tend to reflect the culture or to speak for the culture as directly. And I don't think they change *us* as much. They just don't have the effect on us. For one thing, the interesting movies are not talked about in the same way they were talked about then.''

When asked if that is a function of the medium, the culture, or both, she replies, ''It's both, it's both. Movie makers in the '70s felt they were doing something exciting, something very personal. I think the whole drug problem, success, the end of the Vietnam War, everything changed so much in the society that it's no wonder the movie makers lost their confidence. So the same people who were doing daring and exciting work in the '70s are doing much more conventional work now.

''I mean, it's a blessing to see Scorsese come back with 'Life Lessons' in *New York Stories* because it shows a new kind of confidence and happiness in him,'' she says. ''He's working in the medium more confidently than he has for a while. And you feel, 'This is terrific.' It's not *Mean Streets* or *Taxi Driver,* but at least he's in good shape. So many of the wonderful directors are not in good shape—or, like Hal Ashby, are dead. It's awful to think the man who made *Shampoo* and a lot of those terrific movies is gone already. And so many of the other directors seem burned out, or they can't quite get their bearings again.''

What has shaped American movies more than anything else in this decade has been the Lucas-Spielberg combine. Such films as the *Star Wars* trilogy and *E.T.* have set box office records and profoundly altered Hollywood. Kael's feelings are decidedly mixed:

''I think Spielberg is a great movie maker—or a *terrific* movie maker— but his sensibility is all-American boy by now. And the subjects of his movies are not exciting in the way movies were in the '70s. In craftsman terms he's as good as anybody. But he doesn't have the personal voice—the personal voice he *did* have he showed in *E.T.* and *Close Encounters of the Third Kind;* those are terrific movies. But he's foundering. You don't know why he makes the movies he makes, really, except he's looking for subjects. You feel that on the screen, and it just doesn't work for you.

''Lucas I don't think is a great movie maker. But the cumulative effect of the *Star Wars* trilogy has been devastating to the American movie companies and to American movies. Because the fact those movies made so much money and were so successful and could be marketed all over the world makes it that much more difficult for somebody to do something very personal and expressive.

''And he doesn't seem to understand the influence he's had; he's just trying to repeat his successes,'' she says. ''So that with the Disney/ Touchstone people just trying to get basic, all-American, home-run movies—you know, huge hits—and with the influence of the *Star Wars* trilogy, movies have had some serious blows. Those factors changed movies from what we were excited by in the '70s to something rather standard and shameless. There is a *shamelessness* to pictures. . . . I mean, I never thought in the '70s you could regress in the society the way these people are, and I *never* thought it could be accepted. So maybe there'll be another shift in the '90s, maybe people will become hip again. Right now they're not very hip.''

A few new (or relatively new) film makers do excite Kael, such as Jonathan Demme and Pedro Almodóvar. As do some unlikelier figures. "I do think that, as I indicated in *Hooked,* part of what's keeping movies alive is all these clowns who've come from *Saturday Night Live* and *SCTV* who are *terrific,*" she says. "I mean, you can't get away from it. When you can see Bette Midler, people are willing to see her even in a second-rate movie. Or Lily Tomlin. Or that marvelous Catherine O'Hara in *Beetlejuice.* And they'll go to the movie because Steve Martin is in it. Or Bill Murray. Or Michael Keaton. There are so many terrific performers—Robin Williams is enough to sustain you through a lousy movie.''

That raises an obvious question for someone who sees so many movies a year, and has done so for decades now. William Abrahams insists that "the spirit is as strong as ever," but Kael acknowledges, "I'm more impatient with certain movies. I just don't want to be *bothered* by movies that don't have any really aesthetic, psychological, or social dimension. . . . I very often skip movies, even movies that have a pretty big box office and that people might want to read a review of, because I feel, 'I just can't go through this kind of thing again'; it's like 50 movies I've already written about. I think, well, if the reader doesn't know what I think of *that,* then there's no point in saying what I think about it anyway!''

By now she's laughing. She's gotten a second wind. She knows perfectly well that so long as there's the promise of something new, something good, coming soon to a theater near her, she'll be there, and if she's there, she'll be writing about what she's seen. That's what Pauline Kael found when she lost it at the movies, and she's never held back from the consequences.

"By temperament, I'm not a holder-back. No, these things are so much a matter of temperament. And, my God, I've lived this long and gotten by with saying what I wanted to, it'd be kind of silly if I started holding back now.''

Pauline Kael's Last Picture Show

Allen Barra / 1991

From *The San Francisco Bay Guardian* 28 August 1991: 29–31.
(c) 1991 by Allen Barra. Reprinted by permission

Pauline Kael has spent the last three decades raising hell. She has punctured myths, skewered icons, and deflated some of the movie industry's largest egos, all the while celebrating what other critics dismissed— the new, the dangerous, the irreverent.

She wasn't the critic who got quoted the most, but she was the critic who mattered the most. When history adds it all up, she may well have been the only film critic of her time to have mattered at all.

Then, a couple of months ago, a few short, unceremonious sentences in *The New Yorker* announced that Kael was giving up regular film criticism. Colleagues and former foes alike lined up to pay tribute. Some of the "tributes," like Tom Carson's in *Entertainment Weekly* and John Powers' in the *L.A. Weekly,* were poison-pen letters disguised as valentines; Kael had savaged a lot of films that other critics had championed, and this was their last chance at a payback.

Most, however, ran from the affectionate to the outright sentimental. It was not that Kael had suddenly become beloved, or even popular—for years she has drawn nearly as many reviews as the movies she has written about. But many in her trade seemed to feel that the time had come to acknowledge the influence Kael has had on the tastes and sensibilities of a generation of movie reviewers—and by extension, moviegoers. Overnight, Kael went from being a center of controversy to an object of reverence.

"We were very lucky to have someone of her ability as a critic of influence," said David Chasman, a film producer, as if in eulogy. "Some of the more exciting things in movies over the last 25 years wouldn't have been noticed if not for her."

Clive James, the normally acerbic British critic, says she is "clearly the most significant critic in the English language since Shaw."

Kael, now past 70, has not actually retired. She'll continue to write about movies, though she won't be reviewing them. And reports that she has retreated to her three-story Napa Valley-style home in the Berkshires are greatly exaggerated. She's been living and writing there for more than

133

20 years, making biweekly forays by taxi into Manhattan to see films, theater, and opera, or to attend an occasional critics' gathering. The trips will now become less frequent, which suits her fine—regardless of the name of the magazine with which she will always be associated, she has never liked Manhattan.

Though Kael may be considered the most influential American critic to write on any art form—Edmund Wilson and H. L. Mencken come to mind, but Kael has probably reached more readers than both of them combined—she has never had the power of TV reviewers like Gene Siskel and Roger Ebert, Gene Shalit, or Rex Reed, who are as much personalities as they are critics, and who can make even bad films commercially successful. Kael's influence, on the other hand, has been on the audience of cognoscenti. She helped create a vanguard that was receptive to the best new work.

She sighs wearily when her visitor reads from an article in *Newsweek* saying her tastes have often been out of synch with the public's; that "the overkill in her scorn for *Dances with Wolves* seems in direct proportion to its popularity."

"When," she asks, "were my tastes *ever* in synch with the public?" (She lost a reviewing job in 1965 for panning several popular films, among them *The Sound of Music,* which she called "sugar-coated lies for the masses.")

"I was always championing films like Robert Altman's *The Long Goodbye,* which nobody went to see. Geez, it's depressing after all these years to find that some people think a critic's job is to be in synch with popular taste." She sighs again. "It's depressing how many *critics* think that's a critic's job."

For that matter, Kael's tastes have often been out of synch with other critics and writers as well, some of whom have launched literary broadsides against her, adding to the Kael mythology. In a 1980 attack, Renata Adler, writing in *The New York Review of Books,* accused Kael of writing jazzy, slang-laced prose that relied on mere intuition and suffered from an irreverence for art.

To the first charge Kael pleads guilty: "I've always been attacked as 'impressionistic.' That means I don't have a sufficient respect for film theory." To the second charge, she also pleads guilty: "I *do* have an irreverent attitude toward art."

And for 30 years, Andrew Sarris, the former *Village Voice* critic who now writes for *The New York Observer,* has been attacking Kael, whose famous 1963 essay "Circles and Squares" dealt Sarris' reputation a blow from which it has never recovered. During the last decade alone, Sarris shot at Kael from no fewer than four different publications. Though it has gone down in film-critic lore as the Sarris-Kael Feud, the fact is that Kael has never replied to any of Sarris' jabs. "I said what I had to say about his theory 28 years ago," is her final reply on the subject. "I've always been a little surprised he took it so personally."

On the other side have been the famous "Paulettes"—the legion of young male critics who are said to ape Kael's styles and tastes. She prefers not to discuss any of the accused for fear of "putting a stigma on them." She adds, "This Paulette stuff is kind of like McCarthyism—once you're accused, you're on the defensive, you have to keep explaining that you're not one, even though there's no evidence that you ever were one."

The Myth of the Paulettes is so pervasive that it binds together writers like *Vanity Fair*'s James Wolcott and *The New Yorker*'s Terrence Rafferty (Kael's successor), whose styles (Wolcott is rich and wordy, Rafferty somewhat austere) don't even resemble each other, let alone Kael's. "And what if I have influenced other critics?" Kael says. "I've never understood why that's supposed to be so evil."

The Village Voice's Sebastian Dangerfield may have an explanation: "Look at any list of Kael's enemies and detractors and you'll see more conformity than you'll ever see among the so-called Paulettes. Add up all of the writers that Kael's influence is supposed to be the strongest on, and what do you see? An absence of theoretical jargon and political agendas. *That's* why her enemies are so paranoid about the existence of something called 'Paulettes.' Anyway, if Kael's influence is so strong, why does most movie criticism suck?"

Kael has never spent a lot of time hanging out with other film critics. "I'm always amazed," says Michael Sragow, a friend of Kael's and a fellow critic (for the *San Francisco Examiner*), "when someone writes that Pauline has spent her professional life 'writing about film.' I don't think film as such really interests her that much. Just look at the content in her work—it's obvious that she saw film criticism as the best way of writing about everything that ever piqued her interest, from Tolstoy to country music to politics."

Why, then, give up what has been for her the perfect job at the perfect place? Could it be that, as she wrote 25 years ago, the best movie critics "can no longer bear the many tedious movies for the few good moments and the tiny shocks of recognition?" Had she predicted her own burnout? The question draws a laugh, then a response: "Let's call it a combination of health [she doesn't elaborate] and the lack of interesting new things about. I don't want to become a hack."

There isn't much danger of that. One doesn't talk with her long without sensing that "terrible strength" her friends invariably speak of—the astonishing intelligence and drive that took a single woman in her 40s raising a daughter to the absolute peak of an area of letters that was as male-dominated as the movie industry itself.

She works and lives in a home that brings a little of her native Northern California into the rocky New England landscape. It contains nearly as many rooms as an inn, and each one has enough books to stock a wing of a small-town library. Her record collection is eclectic: albums by Prince and Led Zeppelin, opera, classic jazz (in her youth she played violin in an all-girl jazz band). She writes in a bright room on the second floor that has one of her few concessions to the world of the '90s magazine business, a fax machine purchased for her by her admirers last year. There, too, is a wide writing table, on which she wrote by hand the most famous and most passionate essays and reviews in American film criticism—some of which remain as controversial as the movies themselves.

Kael has never tempered her opinions, but her voice has a lovely lyrical quality to it that gains a lilt when she's on a roll, talking about her favorite subject. During the past couple of years there has been less and less of a lilt when discussing movies.

For Kael, the energy has been steadily leaking out of American movies since the mid-'70s, a time when the impetus of the counterculture was waning and what had been optimistically called "the Film Generation" was turning into what Kael has called "the *Masterpiece Theater* generation."

"I think it's nutty," she says, "when writers talk of the '40s as being a 'Golden Age.' Start with, say, *Bonnie and Clyde* in 1967, which I think is the film that really fired up a lot of film enthusiasts [and which was the subject of one of her landmark essays in *The New Yorker*], and look at the truly great films that came out over the next seven or eight years, films by Robert Altman and [Francis Ford] Coppola and Scorsese and Brian De Palma, and you'll see a depth and richness that American movies never had before. I really think—I'm just pulling a phrase out here, but I think it applies—there's a *grown-up* quality to those films that the earlier Hollywood films had lacked."

Since then she has seen only isolated instances of that spark. "Altman is still capable of outstanding work, as he showed in *Vincent and Theo,* but does anyone really see in *The Color of Money* or even *GoodFellas* the kind of passion and precision that Scorsese showed in *Mean Streets* or *Taxi Driver*? The only improvements have been in technique, and technique isn't why we loved those films in the first place."

Kael has even been disappointed in the most recent of her favorite '80s directors, Jonathan Demme. She was not overwhelmed by Demme's long-awaited commercial breakthrough, *The Silence of the Lambs:* "He picks the right strings all right, but the film has no soul. It's pulp material treated as art, and I think that's a bit of a fraud. I like my pulp treated more like pulp, as in *The Grifters.*"

She dismisses *Dances with Wolves* as "ludicrous, as phony as the phoniest of old Hollywood westerns. God, it's really ridiculous. Hollywood has been 'fair to the Indians' since the silent films, and every few years someone comes along and makes money off of audience sympathy." Of Kevin Costner, the movie's producer/director/star, Kael wrote in her review: "This epic was made by a bland megalomaniac . . . the Indians . . . should have named him 'Plays with Camera.' " (It should come as no surprise that Kael ridicules the predictability of the Oscars, which celebrated Costner and *Dances*. "I laughed my way through them this year," she said.)

She scorns the current crop of big directors like Oliver Stone. "He's a pounder," she said. "His only technique is to bang the viewer over the head until he gives in. There isn't an ounce of variety or nuance in his work."

The irony, she says, is that the sluggishness of American movies comes at a time when acting has never been better. "I've seen just about all the important stuff since the silents, and I can't ever recall a time when there have been so many good actors around. Most of the time, it's the actors and not the directors that get you through these movies." The lilt returns to her voice. Give her a few minutes to remember and she'll rattle off clusters of names like machine-gun bursts: "Michael Keaton, Steve Martin, Bette Midler, Wesley Snipes, Andre Bravener, John Cusack, Morris Day, Pat Hingle, Dianne Wiest, Annie Potts, Tim Robbins, Mare Winningham, Christopher Walken—oh, my, there are so many good ones today. Let's see . . . Jeff Goldblum, Pamela Reed, Margaret Whitton, Judith Ivey, Anjelica Huston, John Glover, Bruce Davison, Keith Carradine, Julie Kavner—there's so many good actors out there, they just aren't making good films to put them all in.

"Martin Short, Andrea Martin, Catherine O'Hara, all the *SCTV* people. Improvisational comedy has probably accounted for more good acting over the last 15 years or so than any other single factor. I think Phil Hartman and Jan Hooks on *Saturday Night Live* are two of the best comic actors I've ever seen. I think Judy Davis, the Australian star, is a great actress. Michelle Pfeiffer—I don't recall any leading lady of the past who was so beautiful and such a fine actress. I guess she's so beautiful that a lot of critics don't see how good she is. Mel Gibson also fits into that category."

Free-associating with Kael can be great fun. Ring off the names of a few actors and she'll almost always have a fully formed opinion. Daniel Day-Lewis? "When you consider how much Day-Lewis has already done and how young he is, his potential seems terrifying." Joan Cusack? "I loved her in *Working Girl;* she was the best thing in the movie. You could see the audience was responding to her. Why she doesn't get cast in some lead parts is a mystery to me."

Morgan Freeman? "Well, I'm on record saying he might be the best American actor. It's ironic that he's now become a star for one of his weaker roles [*Driving Miss Daisy*]." Beverly D'Angelo? "She's a wonderful actress and a delightful comedian. She's really a symbol of what's wrong with movies right now, that a woman so beautiful and talented can't seem to get lead roles. It's rough for a woman. She's been around for a while, so they just don't think of her. But she's gorgeous and so much fun to watch. Every time I see a movie with some bland new actress who *People* or *Entertainment Weekly* calls 'Hollywood's hottest new star' I think, 'How much more interesting that part would have been if Beverly D'Angelo had played it.' "

Robert De Niro? "I don't think he's really been a great actor for a few years now, but he gets all this reverential treatment." Tom Cruise? Kevin Costner? "I think Costner was good in *Bull Durham;* he was sexy and relaxed, and his blandness was well-used in *The Untouchables.* But for the most part he's dull and not very surprising. I'd really be surprised if he can sustain this current wave of popularity; he really doesn't have much in the way of resources to draw upon. Cruise, at best, is two-dimensional. I think Jeff Bridges and Kurt Russell are much more fun to watch."

All right, so how come the best magazines run all these features on Cruise, Costner, and Andie MacDowell and never anything on D'Angelo and Cusack? "I suppose because there's really no place for young writers to go who really want to do serious writing about movies and actors. All these god-awful movie magazines—*Premiere, American Film, Entertainment Weekly,* I think I'd even put *Vanity Fair* in this category—they seem to be run by star-struck editors who get hung up on a few people and they don't care or perhaps they don't even know that these people aren't doing any interesting work.

"Madonna was interesting for a while, but since she hit the mainstream, she's gotten rather dull. She just hasn't done enough interesting work to justify all those magazine covers; all the stories reveal are editors' obsession with her. I mean, really, there's an astonishing amount of ink being wasted on someone who basically just inspires a lot of trivial fantasies.''

According to Kael, the new movie-fixated slicks have driven the old movie rags like *Photoplay* and *Silver Screen* off the market. ''Basically, they were written for working people who wanted to fantasize about the lives of the stars. The new, slick rags, are written for an educated, much more sophisticated reader who wants to fantasize being a screenwriter or director. I really don't think that's much of an advance. Young writers need to get into print, so they serve the function of poorly paid PR people for the studios. And the magazines don't want critical stuff, or they'd lose their access to the studios and the stars.

''It all gives the impression that there's enormous interest in a medium that in fact is not really thriving. Let me add that this is all happening at a time when criticism has never been better—I mean the general level of newspaper and magazine criticism, not the TV stuff, which is basically there to plug the movies. There's no one on TV who warns the public about all the crap out there.''

It's a tough job, but now somebody else will have to do it. This September will mark the publication of Kael's tenth and final collection of reviews—you could add up the published work of all other active American film critics and not approach that total. And as you read this, the final edition of the Rolls Royce of movie guides, her *5001 Nights at the Movies,* with more than 800 new titles, is in the stores.

But after a few months off, it will be time for Pauline Kael to get into a taxi, ride down to New York and go to the movies.

Pauline Kael: The Critic Wore Cowboy Boots

Marc Smirnoff / 1992

From *The Oxford American* Spring 1992: 40–51. Reprinted by permission. Originally published with a brief introductory essay by Mr. Smirnoff.

Oxford American: In which way do movies most often fail?

Pauline Kael: Well, it's so often almost impossible for writers and directors to get financing for any kind of vision they might have that they often compromise at just about every level. The book *The Devil's Candy* [by Julie Salamon] about the making of *The Bonfire of the Vanities* is awfully good because it shows you how the executives made the decisions that destroyed the movie and they did it trying not to be irresponsible, trying to be responsible to the money people. And the director, Brian De Palma, himself trying to be responsible and having had a couple of failures so he no longer had confidence in his own vision, went along with the executives and tried to be a reasonable man, and all the meaning was gradually drained out of the material, decision by decision. And that often happens on pictures. When you talk to a director afterwards, he'll tell you how, step by step, everything went out of the original idea. On the other hand, a lot of directors never have an idea. They were hired to fulfill this idea that the executives have. You know, the executives will get some idea that something should be made on a subject that's hot, and they'll commission writers who'll be rewritten endlessly, and the director will take the project and often there is just nothing there. Sometimes you'll read a script, and you can't believe that that's actually going to be made because you've read dozens of scripts that were good that nobody will make, and this absolutely empty dog will go into production partly because some actor said, Yes.

OA: Why is there a lack of innovative movies?

Kael: You can feel a resentment in people, and you see it in the press. It's as if they thought that any sort of experimentation was an insult to them, and if you look at the stuff that gets praised in the press, it's very discouraging because you know that somebody who tried to do something different is going to get panned.

I feel no affinity to most of the pictures that are big box-office winners.

I mean I didn't even go see *Terminator II*. *Terminator I* was enough—it was already a remake of a section of *Westworld*. If you go see, what was it? *Backdraft,* you think, this is inconceivable! It's just a dressed-up version of the old James Cagney-Pat O'Brien stuff that was mildly entertaining in the thirties. And it's done so heavily now with such elaborate special effects that all the fun it once had is drained away. It's not a great period for movies. The only real surprises, I think have been those things that come out of places like Ireland, like *My Left Foot* and *Eat the Peach,* which was a lovely little film that hardly anybody saw, or England, where *Mona Lisa* was made by an Irishman. There are surprises, like Mike Leigh's English movies, but from this culture the surprises have been, well, I'd say, the most interesting film I've seen this year is one that premiered on television: the one called *Hearts of Darkness: A Filmmaker's Apocalypse*. It's about Francis Ford Coppola and the making of *Apocalypse Now*. It's fascinating because it's about what happens to a director in the course of making an epic, and it's about the manic-depressive cycles that Coppola went through making that picture. And it's extraordinary because it is a truthful view of filmmaking. Most of it was shot and recorded by Eleanor Coppola at the time in the Philippines, and she got fabulous material. I don't know if the young filmmakers who put it together and also added the interviews of the later material, fully recognized what that film revealed. But it's a very scary, funny, remarkable movie. In many ways it's far more interesting than *Apocalypse Now* was. It really is something.

OA: What direction are movies going?

Kael: I don't think anybody knows. It's a mess, and you just hope that there will be some brilliant new people setting new directions, and that maybe somebody will go to the movies they make because sometimes brilliant people set new directions and nobody follows them. Ten or fifteen years ago I would have had a thought about that, but everything's gone so backwards in moviemaking. Techniques seem more backward. Now you're overjoyed if you get a halfway decent storyline. You no longer ask for innovation much because you just don't get it. Things seemed to be really innovative in the seventies. In the eighties there were some wonderful movies but they just weren't innovative, so you can't guess on direction. Oh, it would be easy to say, they'll come from third world countries, but I sort of doubt it. Some wonderful work came from Australia and New Zealand, but there aren't populations big enough to sustain major moviemaking there, and so those directors come to Hollywood, and most of them are caught in the same traps, and even when their movies are awfully good they often don't succeed. Fred Schepisi, who did *The Chant of Jimmie Blacksmith* and a lot of other terrific movies, has not had a major hit in Hollywood. *The Russia House*, which should have been successful, wasn't. In some ways, it was Sean Connery's best performance, and Michelle Pfeiffer was lovely in it. It had a nifty Tom Stoppard screenplay, and it was very cleverly done, but the audience didn't go to it.

OA: There sure are a lot of gangster pictures being made.

Kael: Yeah, there are. That's because it's an easy subject to sell to the third world countries and to sell all over the world. Gangster pictures barely even need subtitles. They can be easily dubbed for Europe and Asia and South America and everywhere. They have such a natural appeal to sub-literate cultures. It seems awful to say, but some of our greatest directors work in genres that are really beneath their intelligence because there is an audience out there for them. And right now Americans are behaving like sub-literate audiences. That's what they want to be. If you made something like *The Terminator*, you know you can sell it all over the world. If you make *The Russia House*, it's going to take a very sophisticated audience to react to it.

OA: In the eighty-five movies you review in *Movie Love*, I counted thirty-three, if I am right, that you found enjoyable or better. That sounds like a respectably high figure. Was it a rich period for movies?

Kael: No, it was not a rich period, but it was rich in fine acting. I think so many people ignore the great acting in movies and this has been a terrific period. I don't think American acting has ever been better than it is now. And you can go to a movie that doesn't show much innovative filmmaking and still see, say, a great performance by Jessica Lange or Debra Winger or, say, Daniel Day-Lewis. It makes the movie worth seeing, but there's no point pretending that it's great movie art. It's great acting that's on the screen. And a lot of it is from the comedians who developed in television—men like Bill Murray and Robin Williams have been bringing something new to the American screen: a funny, kind of hip personality that they adapt to their roles.

OA: And Tom Hanks?

Kael: Oh, yeah, Tom Hanks and Michael Keaton. There are a lot of them, fewer women than men, but there is, or was, Bette Midler. And there are people who haven't quite loomed up the way they may, but who, in small roles, like Catherine O'Hara, do stuff you've never seen before, like what she did in *Beetlejuice*. I mean, she's an amazement. I loved what Robin Williams did in *The Fisher King* which came out after the period I reviewed in the book. Have you seen it? The acting in it is really extraordinary. Almost everybody in the picture does well: Jeff

Bridges and Michael Jeter and particularly Amanda Plummer, and Mercedes Ruehl, who gives a kind of physicality to her role that I don't think I've ever seen on the screen before. And Robin Williams may be playing the holy fool, which he's played before and which I found tiresome in *Awakenings,* but in *The Fisher King* I thought he was really great. I saw a movie last night that has an extraordinary performance—*Frankie and Johnny.* Michelle Pfeiffer is just astounding in some scenes. She's so beautiful that I think people don't want to recognize her full talent. She's an amazing little actress.

OA: You say Debra Winger "is one of the two or three finest (and most fearless) screen actresses we've got." Who are the others?

Kael: Oh, two or three. That's always dangerous because you wind up with four or five. Diane Keaton, Jessica Lange, and Anjelica Huston. And Michelle Pfeiffer is turning into one of them. There are others who when they get the chance can be. I mean, Christine Lahti, isn't quite up there because she hasn't had the roles. She's awfully good, and whenever Kate Nelligan gets the chance, she's quite something. Annette Bening is someone who does things that are surprising. I think there are probably more than two or three, but right up there at the peak, I would say, would be Debra Winger and Diane Keaton and Jessica Lange. Did you see *Crimes of the Heart*? There's another case of a movie where the substance has a lot of mediocrity, but it had three performances by Diane Keaton, Jessica Lange, and Sissy Spacek that could not have been improved on. They really did something—they convinced you they were sisters.

OA: Who are the best actors?

Kael: That's tougher. They're a more dispersed group. Even though the roles in recent years have been much more men's starring roles, they've not been very interesting roles, whereas the women, although they've not been in as dominating positions, have had more of a chance to show what's in them. Who are the men? You can't ignore Jack Nicholson, Nick Nolte, Tim Robbins, and Warren Beatty and some of the big stars. But the more interesting ones, I think, would be people like Michael Keaton and Tom Hanks and, I'd say, Bill Murray, who every time I see him astounds me, and I put Robin Williams there and . . . who are the other men? It's hard to think offhand. Steve Martin in comedy. I don't like him when he does serious acting, but in comedy or in *Pennies from Heaven.* What he did in *Pennies from Heaven* was quite extraordinary and Bernadette Peters, what she did in that was pretty extraordinary too.

OA: With all these great actors around, America has chosen Kevin
Costner as its current favorite. What kind of actor is he?

Kael: He wasn't bad in *Bull Durham*. Maybe with a script and a
director he can show something, but there is a basic emptiness in his
work and I think it's his lack of a voice which showed particularly in
Robin Hood. In a period movie you need a voice because you're automat-
ically going to be compared to people who have a certain amount of
flourish, and when he's up there with Morgan Freeman, who has a great
voice and great presence, and with Alan Rickman, who has a terrific
voice and has a style, suddenly Kevin Costner is just a vacuum on the
screen. I should have included Morgan Freeman on the list of great
actors. He's right up there. Sometimes he's done work in those bad
movies that leaves you breathless, particularly something like *Street
Smart*. He played a pimp in it and he was just the most scary, brilliant
pimp you've ever seen. Sometimes Denzel Washington is right up there
too. A lot depends on the role.

OA: Has watching actors so much ever helped you in real life? Can you
tell when people are lying?

Kael: No, acting is different. No, I don't think in real life I'm any better
judge than anybody else is. I think we're all suckers in real life.

OA: Of the movies you reviewed in the new book you seemed most
impressed by *Casualties of War*. Almost three years have gone by since
it was released. Do you still think so highly of it?

Kael: Oh yeah. I do have friends who are very hip about movies who
don't like *Casualties of War,* who feel that it's done on too grand a scale,
that it has too monumental a feeling. I think it's one of the films that
tragically didn't reach much of an audience when it opened in theaters
and it will never be that good on VCR because the action is spread out
over a very wide terrain and there's no way to see the full film on VCR.
So in some ways De Palma has lost twice. I think he has had a really
brutalized career because his greatest work hasn't reached an audience. I
think *Blow Out* is just an extraordinary movie and hardly anybody saw it
when it opened, and by the same token John Travolta lost out because
people simply didn't see some of his best performances. His work in
Blow Out is first rate, and then to see him made fun of as if he was not a
really first-rate actor is very sad. I don't know what can be done about
that. The terrible thing about a popular art form is that if it doesn't reach
an audience the first time around, it's pretty damn hard. I've heard the
television news saying to tune in at a certain hour and they would tell us
what are the big new hit movies. They didn't say what are the good new

movies. A man who produces a good movie that isn't a hit is a clown by ordinary standards and he's going to be made fun of by everybody.

OA: A profile of Sean Penn in *American Film* magazine says that in *Casualties of War* "he is completely miscast and he has even a worse New York accent than Uma Thurman in *Henry and June*." How wrong is this view?

Kael: On both counts. I thought Uma Thurman was wonderful in *Henry and June*. Accents don't worry me that much. I thought Sean Penn was absolutely splendid in *Casualties of War*. I think he's a much underrated actor, and it's a pity that he keeps making announcements that he wants to direct instead of act because he has done phenomenal work as an actor. Some of the scenes in *Casualties of War*—his shaving scene near the beginning—were original and moving in ways you don't expect a young actor to come up with.

OA: I'm still trying to figure out why you let *The Untouchables* off so easily. In an interview you called the script "square." Then you said: "On the other hand that squareness did make it possible for De Palma to reach a big audience"—is that a rare copout?

Kael: I treated it as a commercial movie. I didn't think it was a movie in the class of *Blow Out,* and I said so, but I thought for the kind of movie it was, it worked well. Sean Connery, in particular, is fun to watch. And at that point, even though Kevin Costner seemed a blank, he seemed sort of a plausible blank. . . . David Mamet is just incredibly overrated and his screenplay has a dead quality about it. I think the picture got overvalued but I still enjoyed it. It was an entertaining film even though I didn't think it was great De Palma. When you think about it afterwards, it's Costner who bugs you. But I think it's the way the role was written and conceived. The character is such a dumbo. I mean, I don't think that's particularly Costner's fault because he showed in *Bull Durham* that he could read a line if he was given a line to read, but his scenes in *The Untouchables* with his wife were deadly. My God!

OA: I liked *Blood Simple* a whole bunch and I know you did not like it—

Kael: I didn't, but I really liked *Raising Arizona*. I was quite shocked at *Miller's Crossing* and even more shocked by *Barton Fink*. It seems to me a misconception at almost every level. It's a terrible picture. The Coen brothers' sense of style is so limiting too. Very strange, arrogant conception of the past. An appalling movie. I thought the roles played by John Turturro in both *Miller's Crossing* and *Barton Fink* were deeply offensive. I mean the idea of representing someone like Clifford Odets as a stupid man, almost retarded, is quite bewildering. I think I hated just about everything about that movie although I thought John Mahoney looked like William Faulkner and brought a certain elegance to his opening scene. And I loved Judy Davis. I think she's one of the actresses I would list with the women I listed before. I think she's absolutely marvelous but she didn't get much of a chance in that movie.

OA: One of the things I found pleasing about *The Fabulous Baker Boys* was that we did not have to watch Jeff Bridges and Michelle Pfeiffer having sex. The audience was permitted to understand that the two made love as most people do—in bed without their clothes. Are too many sex scenes put into movies out of a knee-jerk response to pandering and selling out?

Kael: I think they're put into movies out of the feeling that people will put down the movie if it doesn't have them, and I agree with you they have become extremely banal. For a number of years the couples rolled over each other endlessly, and now, I mean, the scenes work so hard to try to give you some new angle, and they're just not very good. There just isn't much way to photograph those scenes and do anything with them. I don't know whether, if they went all the way, whether they'd be any better. I doubt it. We're so aware that we're watching actors playing lovers that it's very uncomfortable. I find it tedious. I saw a movie the other day with such a long love scene that I could feel the audience getting bored during it. And I'm sure that the filmmakers thought they were being honest. It's in *The Prince of Tides,* and suddenly, after a certain number of scenes, there's a culminating love scene between Nick Nolte and Barbra Streisand and it's the most boring scene in the movie.

OA: Those scenes all look the same.

Kael: It might be better if they kept their clothes on. We could at least get some texture from the clothing.

OA: Well, that's what they did in *Baker Boys,* and it seems to me it just kept you on the edge all the time.

Kael: That's a wonderful movie. It wasn't a success which is very mysterious. Sometimes movies which you would think would be big box-office successes just don't attract the wide audiences, either because of the way they're promoted or because the audience is just drawn to *Terminator* and *Lethal Weapon* and doesn't relate to the nuances of something like *Married to the Mob* or *The Fabulous Baker Boys.* I just assumed *Married to the Mob* would be a big success because it's such a charming comedy, and it seemed like popular movie making, but there was nobody there, and when I saw *Frankie and Johnny,* which isn't nearly as good as those movies, but still has a moderate appeal, I was quite surprised. There were six people in the theater. It's almost a miracle when a movie that really has charm like *Beetlejuice* draws an audience.

It becomes a fluke when a film that really has any originality wins an audience. I thought it was amazing that *Drugstore Cowboy* did as well as it did, and it by no means was a big success. It's bewildering. It's as if there was some way you were going to be penalized for doing something halfway intelligent. It's scary, isn't it?

OA: At least three movies based on books by William Faulkner— *Intruder in the Dust, The Reivers,* and *The Long Hot Summer*—are all pretty good. Does that mean that Faulkner has been treated well by Hollywood?

Kael: Not really. They've been changed enormously. I think *Intruder in the Dust* was the most faithful one and of course he was present during the making of that. The others had been pretty well turned into very different material from what he had in mind. But he hasn't fared as badly as some people. Hemingway has probably been done worse even though Hemingway has been filmed much more than Faulkner. In many ways the closest to Faulkner's spirit to get on screen is in something like *Thieves Like Us* which isn't Faulkner at all. It's the Altman Southern film that's just beautifully made and it has something of a Faulkner spirit to it.

OA: What kind of effect have VCRs had on Hollywood?

Kael: You simply don't get the full picture, and you don't get the size and intensity. You lose all the detail if you look at a movie that is particularly visual—a movie by a great film director on a big screen—and then look at it on television. You almost want to weep because it's just no longer the great movie you saw. What you're getting is essentially the narrative and the acting but you're losing almost everything else and you're losing the emotional resonances which come from the full image. It's heartbreaking to think of the work of the greatest directors being known by people only from television images. On the other hand, I've exposed my grandson to the early films on VCR because that's the only way he's going to see them. I didn't want him to feel that *Home Alone* was the only kind of movie there was, so he has seen Buster Keaton and the Sabu version of *The Thief of Baghdad* and *The Crimson Pirate,* the Burt Lancaster film, and dozens of adventure classics and early comedies. The only way I could make it possible for him to see them was on a VCR. So it's better than nothing. It's certainly better than nothing. But the tragedy is that people aren't going to theaters often when a terrific movie opens like, say, *Enemies* or *The Unbearable Lightness of Being,* because they feel they'll catch up with it on VCR later. If your standard of a good movie is, say, *The Terminator* there's no particular reason to see it on a big screen. You can get the same kind of dumb kicks at home and have a beer with your friends at the same time. But this may change.

You can't be too long in the face about it. Things may change in a couple of years. A couple of big movies may make the difference—you can't tell in a popular art form. Things change very quickly. I could never have predicted that the audiences who seemed so hip in the seventies would accept the kind of movies they accepted in the eighties. It still bewilders me that people who really enjoyed *The Godfather* movies and Brian De Palma's *Dressed to Kill* and a lot of very hip movies by Altman, could then accept what they accepted later on. I didn't think that there was a way that the culture would go back. We've had a strange cultural regression and it's dumbfounding. I could not have believed the people would accept the Gulf War the way it was accepted and the same kind of thing has happened at the movies.

OA: Where do you find the MTV influence on movies?

Kael: It's in movie editing a lot, in showing off. It's in sort of empty cuts. MTV doesn't have much to offer movies, but you do see a lot of fast cutting in movies as if they were afraid of boring the MTV generation. But the MTV generation I think is bored by MTV.

OA: Most soundtracks sound hideous, what's wrong with them?

Kael: You mean because they're loud and vulgar, and the music is appalling? Well, the music is used to pad out the meaning of the movie, and it's used to goose up the movie, to give it a kick that it didn't have. Every once in a while you'll get an interesting soundtrack. There have been a couple in recent years. The sound was quite marvelous on Altman's *Vincent and Theo,* and there was a fascinating soundtrack by Peter Gabriel for Scorsese's *Christ* movie. These are about the only two really interesting soundtracks I can think of. That's pretty incredible, isn't it? Godard did wonderful work with sound, and it looked as if he was going to revolutionize the way people treated sound in movies, and now it's going back to the most conventional kind of padded out stuff. Now they're not even doing rock very much. Now it's an attempt to reprise the old banal orchestral violin score in the big emotional moment. It's really an insult to the audience, but the audience basically doesn't know it's insulted. I shouldn't put it that way. Let me put it: The audience may even enjoy being insulted.

OA: The *Star Wars* soundtrack set us back.

Kael: *Star Wars* set us back in a lot of ways. Even though I thought the second film in the trilogy was really quite good, as a commercial phenomenon it set us back. And the *Indiana Jones* movie added to that even though I like the second one of that series also, but what they represented in terms of moviemaking was that the studios realized that the audiences didn't mind being treated like kids at a Saturday afternoon serial.

OA: As a fan of musicals, how do you view the state of movie musicals? What was the last good one?

Kael: It's an almost nonexistent genre now. I'd say the last really spectacular musical is the MGM *Pennies from Heaven*. I couldn't believe it when I saw the reviews panning that movie. It's very sad that Herbert Ross having done that amazing movie, should have gone back to making stuff like *Steel Magnolias* and made money at it, when he failed commercially with *Pennies from Heaven*. It is hard to know how people can do things that are ambitious or large spirited when their worst works succeed and their best work fails. But there have been movies that you couldn't really call musicals like *The Rose,* the Bette Midler film. There have been movies that used a lot of music and some of them have been pretty good, but it has not been a popular form. I can't believe it in some ways. I can't believe Aretha Franklin was used so sparingly. Except for *The Blues Brothers* she never really got a chance to show on screen what she could do. There have been so many tremendous performers who just haven't had a chance to be part of a great musical conception.

OA: What about James Brown in a musical?

Kael: Oh sure, it seems unbelievable that a great American art form that seemed to have every opportunity to expand and to adapt with the times got lost and buried. The whole age of rock is not represented by a single important movie.

OA: I'm quite interested in your five months of employment in Hollywood in 1979.

Kael: Well, it actually went very well. I had a very good time. The papers were determined to make it sound, and the magazines were determined to make it sound, as if it had been a terrible blow up, and yet there was nothing of the kind. *Newsweek* printed an item saying that after a couple of weeks, or something, I had managed to alienate everyone in Hollywood. And that item came out before I had started because when I left *The New Yorker* I had a commitment to go to the hospital to have some minor surgery so before I got started they had printed that I had been this incredible fiasco, but that's sort of, you know, par. There's a great deal of hostility towards critics in general and toward a woman critic in particular, and an independent-minded one, and so you read an awful lot of stuff about yourself that isn't true.

OA: What exactly was your position?

Kael: It was just executive consultant and it was a very flexible position and I talked to anybody who stopped by and wanted to talk to me or any executive who wanted to discuss some of his decisions. An awful lot of the time in Hollywood was spent mulling over the same things because you talk to people and two days later they come back and talk over the same problems and I got very impatient. It's hard not to show it. It's hard to keep your mind open enough to consider the problems as those people face them. I was offered other positions afterward. But I really wanted out, I didn't want to go on in a different capacity because writing is, really, if you grew up as I did, the highest thing you could do and so the jobs where you make more money or wield executive decisions don't compare to the freedom of writing. It's the freedom that's fun.

OA: I'm interested in that whole term because when you think of your exalted position at the time and—

Kael: "Exalted" is putting it kind of strong.

OA: Well, as being the most important voice in movie criticism. There is a lot of significance in your trading movie reviewing for moviemaking.

Kael: Well, remember I did have a good position in that everyone in L.A. was incredibly nice to me, and they either respected me or feared me, or feared I was really there to write something nasty about them— which I would not have done. What [Warren] Beatty felt when he suggested the position was that what I did in my reviews in pointing out where a movie went wrong, I should be able to do before the movie was made, and so I should be very valuable in the industry. I think to some degree there was something to that but, really, the only thing that went wrong was I missed writing. I loved writing and I loved writing about movies and I had felt at the time—I was turning sixty—that maybe I was written out and that I was saying the same thing over and over again. But after I was there a few months and I read the reviews of other critics, I began to sort of hit the ceiling because people were panning movies that I saw merit in and they were panning performances that I thought were wonderful. I missed having my voice. No one was saying the things I wanted to say and so I arranged to go back to *The New Yorker*. I went back with sort of a renewed head of steam because I knew I really had more to say. I think I did some of my best work during those ten years after returning from Hollywood. I know that people who review me often say that my first book, *I Lost It at the Movies,* is my best work. I think they say that because it had a more original impact on them. I think my sensibility was fresher to them, but I think I knew more about movies in these last years. And I think I'm a better writer than I was then. I think some of the writing in the last couple of years . . . I'm not ashamed of. I don't feel I fell apart too much. There are places over the years where I think I got too wordy and too descriptive maybe, but it's partly in order to change. As a critic, as you get older you can't write the way you did. You have to find new approaches to movies, you can't tackle them the same way, and so you try to look at them differently and try to write with a different voice sometimes. You're trying not to be a repetitive drag and so I can understand if they like the early work, which was more hatchet-like, but I think there's more understanding of the movie process in the later work. Oddly enough when I retired earlier this year, I had the same reaction I had in '79 of, God, nobody's saying the things I want to say! It's driving me crazy, particularly when they pan things that I feel are good, but I know now I can't return. I'm not physically strong enough to go on with going into New York and waiting in lines and going to see the movies, so it's tough. But you have to recognize that you've reached a point. If I haven't said it now, I can't say it. But I still see movies and think, Why hasn't somebody pointed out this marvelous performance in the corner of this movie?

OA: Some people maintain that absolute power corrupts. In many ways—at least as a link between Hollywood and the audience—you are absolutely the most powerful voice in movieland. Of your Hollywood months you said: "People treated me as if I were a High Priestess!" It must have been hard—

Kael: You say very abrupt four-letter words when they do. You have to cut through that crap. I'm pretty good at being rude and cutting through it using rude language because I don't like being fawned on. I'm not built for people to fawn over, as they discover after a while.

OA: But you were in a position where people *did* fawn over you all the time—

Kael: Some did. But you can cut through that.

OA: Was it hard?

Kael: You can reveal that you're a person, not an eminence, and you know I never took to wearing capes or turbans.

OA: Was it a struggle ever? I would just think hearing praise over and over has got to be—

Kael: You hear a lot of ugliness too. You know there are people who are very hostile and that gets through to you too. Any number of male friends of mine have had to defend me against guys who wanted to beat me up and, in one case, a woman who wanted to.

OA: Did you have any preconceptions about working in Hollywood that materialized into reality?

Kael: Oh, I knew so much about it. I'd read so much and heard so much over the years. I felt a freedom in not having deadlines. I could stay up half the night talking to people, which was fun because I'm a very gregarious person, and when you're writing to deadline every week you

don't have much time to socialize. No, it wasn't bad. I enjoyed it, but I
enjoyed writing more. I felt as if I wasn't using my full brain.

OA: Do you enjoy going on movie sets and watching movies being
made?

Kael: I've only done that a very few times. It's excruciatingly boring
because they do the same thing over and over again, and mostly you're
standing around waiting for the lighting to be arranged for the next shot.
No, I really only did it for any lengthy period when I was doing the piece
"The Making of *The Group*" and it's very boring. I mean, I don't know
who has the patience to stand around movie sets. It's fun to drop in and
see what the locations are like and talk to the people briefly, but the
director's always busy as hell.

OA: A movie I saw a few times because I liked it was David Lynch's
Elephant Man. I understand you urged the right people to help get
it made.

Kael: I did. They had passed on it. They had turned it down. I had
never met David Lynch and I had no connection with the movie, but I
had read the script. I did not think it was a particularly good script, but I
thought the idea was such a good idea for David Lynch. I did know his
earlier work and I urged them to make the movie, to commit some money
to it. I was very excited when I saw the movie because I felt that Lynch
had overcome the weaknesses of the script. I was very sad that more
reviewers didn't respond to what went on in that movie because I thought
the kind of Victorian sensibility that he brought to it was fascinating. I
think people wanted to see it as simple sentimentality whereas I think it
had a kind of Dickensian grandeur.

OA: I find it hard to picture you attending the Academy Awards but—

Kael: I've never been there. So your instincts were right.

OA: They always award and neglect the wrong movies.

Kael: Almost always. Sometimes there's nothing to give it to. They
tend to go for certain kinds of pictures, and certain people, and others
are just systematically neglected. I've rarely agreed with the choices but
you get used to that. It's like books on the bestsellers' list—when are the
books you really like up there?

OA: How did your obsession with movies begin?

Kael: I don't think it's really an obsession. I know it seems that way,
because people have made it sound that way, but I was just as interested,
really, in books and theater and music and painting. I mean, I was almost
equally interested in all the arts. Somehow I think that I was able to write
on movies in a way that, perhaps, I couldn't write on other things because
all the arts came into play in them. I don't think it's really that I had that

much of a stronger involvement in them than a lot of other people do. But somehow, because I have been writing about them most of my life, it may seem like an obsession.

OA: You report that after college you "wrote plays fairly extensively for a number of years." Did you ever try to write a screenplay?

Kael: I was just never drawn to it as much. I really got into criticism fairly early, and once I'd gotten into criticism, I realized I could say what I wanted to say. I can make contact with people more directly that way. I'm too direct to be a screenwriter. I would be expressing myself rather than developing character.

OA: So even out of experiment's sake you never tried, since you began reviewing, a story or a screenplay?

Kael: I've played with it a couple of times, but I really love criticism and I think it's an honorable estate. For at least thirty years people said to me, Why don't you do something besides criticism?—as if criticism was something inferior. I think they're terribly wrong, and I think I can be more expressive as a critic than in other forms. I don't think people realize how much they enjoy reading criticism. I think people take it for granted because there are columns in the papers everyday.

OA: It is said that you never had to see a movie twice before writing about it. This is amazing because your reviews—by dint of their all-inclusiveness—always seem to be the result of more than one viewing. Did you *ever* have to see a movie twice to get a handle on it?

Kael: No, not to get a handle on it, but a couple of times I've gone to see a movie again because I wanted to be sure I was quoting a line accurately or was placing a bit of business in the right scene. I went to see *Godfather II* after I'd turned in my copy and it was in type, just to make sure there were no inaccuracies in it. I went to see *Casualties of War* after it was set up in type for the same reason, and *Nashville* I saw two nights in a row as a fluke. Most of the time, once is enough. I've got no great desire to see a movie again.

OA: Well, when you saw those three movies a second time did you pick up anything you had missed in your first viewing?

Kael: I wish I could be humble and say, Oh many things. Let's leave it at that.

OA: How should a person go about educating himself about movies?

Kael: Oh God, if he has to go about educating himself, forget it. I think that popular culture is something you pick up. It seeps into you. It's in the environment. I've heard of people getting jobs as movie critics and then watching ten classics to get educated in movies. The whole thought makes me want to throw darts at them. If you haven't picked up an education in movies from what's available in your area, from television and from VCRs, what's the point? You can never catch up. Sure, you can pick out some of the great ones to go see, but that's not the same thing as seeing what the great ones spring out of, which is all the crap. Part of getting to know movies is sorting out the great ones from the crap for yourself, seeing all those lousy Warner Brothers movies, out of which the really good ones came, and there's no way you can educate yourself in that.

OA: I've heard a few people say that they have stopped reading you because you have made them feel stupid at times for liking something they shouldn't. Have you ever—

Kael: Tough.

OA: I take it then that you never tried to tone down your criticism.

Kael: Sometimes simple humanity makes you do so. Oh sure, there are times when I'm not nearly as rough on a performance as I feel because it's just cruel. I mean, the person can't help being incompetent. There are a lot of actors or a lot of writers and directors who are just very bad and if you pan them once that seems to be enough. I try not to pan the same person over and over again. If I've panned somebody's work very harshly and then see another movie that's lousy in the same way, I don't review it because it's ugly to pan somebody over and over again. It's vicious. What can you do? Most of these people can't help it. It's much more to the point to try to spot who has talent in the movies than who doesn't.

OA: Has a critic of your work ever caused you to change?

Kael: It's hard to change. I've tried different things because of objections. Once a reviewer claimed I used the "I" form exclusively and so I didn't used the "I" form for a solid year, and the only person who noticed was a friend of mine who said, "Your work has become impersonal lately." But he didn't notice why and nobody else noticed either. I thought, He's right, it is becoming impersonal—it's losing something that was valuable there. So I went back to the "I" form. A lot of people have objected to my using the "you" form and they don't seem to realize it's a simple way of trying to be an American and not being a Britisher and saying, One thinks that. I hate the Anglicisms that have crept into critical writing. I loathe that "one" that you read all the time. You think, Who is that goddamn "one"? And so I try to write the way Americans talk and they use "you" very flexibly and so I use it even though I get rapped for it all the time. I'd say among the things I get rapped for the most that's probably number one and number two is my praise of Brian De Palma.

OA: We say "Y'all."

Kael: Sure, that's a way of getting away from "one" also. "Y'all" is sort of nice. It has a soft, easy quality. "One" formalizes everything.

OA: Is there a service in warning people away from vile movies?

Kael: Normally what I'm interested in writing about are the movies that I don't think get the praise that they deserve, but I do think it's important to use the destructive function of criticism. Sure, and I think that the thing is, if people aren't warned off certain movies they're not going to trust you on certain good ones. But I'd like to have gotten more people to go see a few oddball pictures that have opened. I'd love to have written about *Hearts of Darkness*. I really felt very strongly about that but I thought if I start writing about something I'll finish myself off in no time.

OA: There's a constant argument going on whether you should see the movie first or read the book first.

Kael: Well I don't think there's any question but that you should read the book first because the movie fixes its images in your mind so that you couldn't read the book afterwards without seeing it in the movie's terms. It would wreck a great book as in the case of *The Rainbow* by D. H. Lawrence. It would be heartbreaking to read it in terms of the actress [Sammi Davis] who played the leading role, because she was totally inadequate to it, and you would never see the dimensions of the character on the page. In any kind of honor to the book of a great writer you must read the book first because the movie is almost inevitably going to diminish the material.

OA: How would you describe *The New Yorker?*

Kael: I think it has been the best literary magazine in the country and I think most writers recognize that, but that doesn't mean it's anywhere near as good as it should be. It has been, though liberal, extremely conventional in many ways, and I think my column shocked regular *New Yorker* readers. The first few years I got very hostile responses from the readers and from a lot of the staff because the writing was colloquial and direct and deliberately so and deliberately crude in many ways. I felt the only way of being honest and writing about a popular form like movies was to try to write about them in the terms in which we actually experienced them instead of using the language of the classroom, which was more commonplace in film reviews then. In *The New Yorker* they expected a more genteel treatment and more respect for foreign films, and of course the first movie I reviewed for it was *Bonnie and Clyde* and that was sort of the opening shot of the new generation in movies. I had written the *Bonnie and Clyde* piece for *The New Republic,* where I was working at the time, and they had refused to print it. The arts editor of the magazine actually quit in disgust when the publisher refused to print the *Bonnie and Clyde* piece. He was deeply upset because he loved it and felt something new was happening in criticism and he just couldn't stand the publisher saying no to him. So I wasn't alone at least. And I had built up a certain following by then. I had been writing for various magazines for sometime, but that piece coming out of *The New Yorker* was a jolt to a lot of *New Yorker* staff people as well as readers. I don't think you would know the atmosphere of the times. The movie had been panned as an insult to the audience, as bloody and offensive, by just about every major critic in the country. And so the praise of it coming out in *The New Yorker* was quite a shock to people. And I do have a fairly strong voice, it's not a timid voice and that, coming from a woman in particular, added to the shock so that I remember getting a letter from an eminent *New Yorker* writer suggesting that I was trampling through the pages of the magazine with cowboy boots covered with dung and that I should move on out with my cowboy boots. William Shawn showed a lot of courage in sticking by me in those early years because I would get letters all the time saying, Why don't you get a job on a sports page and learn to write? People were more used to movies being treated in a magazine like *The New Yorker* as something a gentleman might condescend to now and then but wouldn't take very seriously. I felt that the truth of how we respond to movies, and the sexual aspects of movies, were far more important responses than critics wanted to acknowledge and so all that came out in the reviews too. But once people started getting used to me, the mail started changing. But I got angry responses whenever I panned anything that was liberal in intention or virtuous or European. European films have a respectability in this country that is way out of proportion to their merit.

OA: But *The New York Times* likes every European movie.

Kael: Over the years I've disagreed with so many of my colleagues that the public often gets confused, particularly when *The New Yorker* and *The New York Times* are so distant from each other. *The New York Times* shows more taste than most newspapers in the country and people in the East, in particular, want to regard it as some sort of exemplar of culture. And I think in general its critical press is really fourth rate and in movies it has not been a shining example of what it might be. The Sunday paper covers just about every foreign film as if it were an important cultural entity and people read all the praise of these incredibly terrible movies and go see the movies and can't disagree with *The New York Times* and so it's a shock to them to pick up *The New Yorker* and find the movie panned and so you have to deal with that over the years.

OA: You said *The New Yorker* is not as good as it could be. What do you think it needs to be better?

Kael: I think a certain Anglophilia crept into it very early on—when it was founded really. It started out with a sort of English tone and a kind of elite sophisticated Manhattan tone which was fake English. Even though it became political and much more democratic, and took very useful political stands during the Vietnam War years, it never got rid of that polite English tone. And it's too much a magazine that seems directed toward an educated reader. It never seems to invite people in. It's a magazine that could stand a little dose of multiculturalism in the fullest sense of that. It needs to be more open, less of the same circle of short story writers endlessly repeated. You get tired of the same words, all those long words Updike uses. It's great to have Updike but they should have a lot of people for whom words don't multiply so easily.

OA: I have trouble with *The New Yorker* ignoring the crime in the city.

Kael: That's part of the problem. It's not been very realistic about what went on in the city. It's as if it wanted to maintain a sort of elite tone even when the city had deteriorated and that tone was no longer in any way relevant to the city.

OA: In almost every one of your books you give thanks to William Shawn. How would you describe him as a person and an editor?

Kael: Well, he gave me a shot at something. He knew I was trying to do something different and he gave me a chance at it. I'm not sure that any other editor would have stuck by me the way he did, and he was a wonderful editor in the sense that you knew he wanted you to write your best. He was always interested in what I was saying, and if he liked a piece particularly, and didn't have a chance to tell me so at the office he would call me at night. He might call at midnight to argue about a comma, and I mean, it seems absurd, it *is* absurd, and yet you can't help loving and respecting someone who cares that much about the magazine and wants your writing to be as clear as possible. He made me clarify my thinking simply by his devotion to meaning. And he didn't care how long something ran. Sometimes I think he was wrong. There were a few times when I wanted to trim what I turned in and he said, No—he thought it was better at the full length. I'm not sure he was right, but the very fact that he felt that a writer had a natural phrasing and a natural length, and that a subject could be treated at a natural length, that you didn't have to cram everything into a half column, gave you a sense that what you were doing mattered. That's a very unusual editor, especially in New York in a glossy magazine on a weekly schedule.

OA: When *The New Yorker* was sold you were quoted as saying: "What

could endanger the tradition [of editorial integrity at *The New Yorker*]—
and would probably destroy the magazine—would be the appointment of
an editor from the outside to succeed William Shawn." Of course that is
precisely what happened. William Shawn was ousted and Robert Gottlieb, an outsider, was put in. How has the magazine fared?

Kael: I think what I said was fundamentally true. I think the magazine
has changed in some ways, some for the better, but a lot for the not so
good. I do think certain traditions have been broken down. There's an
awful lot of sloppiness in the writing in the front of the magazine in the
"Goings On" section, a lot of careless writing that sounds like advertising
copy. And I don't think the critical departments have fared very well. I
think in some ways the fiction may have improved. Gottlieb has more
open taste than Shawn did and is much less restrictive about the language
and theme and that has been good for the magazine. But I think, in
general, he has hired poorly in the critical departments. There are still
wonderful people. There's Arlene Croce, who is simply a magnificent
writer, and there are many fine writers who are posted in spots around
the world and do wonderful writing, but I think the weekly critical
columns are really part of the lifeblood of the magazine, and when those
become mediocre, the magazine is in trouble. You don't open the various
critical columns now with the excitement that you should. He has not
hired people, say, of the stature of Harold Rosenberg or some of the
others who held those posts. I find myself reading the critical departments
with disbelief often. Shawn read very widely, periodicals and books, and
tried to get the best person in the world for any kind of opening he had. I
don't think Gottlieb puts the same kind of effort and care into his
selection of people. The worst failure, I think, of Gottlieb's regime, is
that the book department is so bad. Everyone assumed that coming out
of publishing he would bring life to the book section and it's deathly. It's
so rare to read a review that you really want to go all the way through or
to read a new writer, read a new critical approach and feel, God, he's got
somebody hot on this. You just don't feel any heat in the book section
and that could be an important part of the magazine. There's an incredible
staff of people and having seen their devotion and their intelligence and
what they want to do, I'm often disappointed they don't get a chance to
get at livelier subjects in "The Talk of the Town." The title of it is an
embarrassment. What's in it is so rarely the talk of any town.

OA: Do you think Mr. Gottlieb has tried to maintain the tradition? The
look at least has not undergone too many changes.

Kael: I think the covers are better, not necessarily aesthetically, but
they have a little more vitality. They'd gotten to the point where you

couldn't tell one week's from the last week's. I do think Gottlieb has opened the atmosphere some, I just don't think he is as dedicated as Shawn was. I think he has other things in his life besides the magazine. He isn't thinking about it all the time and reading and seeing if there's a new voice somewhere that he should go after. That was the great thing about Shawn, that he would go after new voices. Let me put it this way: I think Gottlieb wants to put out the best magazine he can. I'm not always sure he's as daring in what he prints as he might be and that holds particularly in the book section. There are old fogey voices in the book section much too often.

OA: You are a TV news junkie. Isn't it kind of depressing to see the way politicians, or candidates, get away with so much?

Kael: Yeah, but it's fascinating to see what they get away with and how much. I don't understand people who say, There's no point in reading newspapers because they all lie. Teenagers say that or: There's no point in watching the news—they don't tell you the whole truth. That seems to assume that you can't piece anything together or learn anything, and of course you can.

OA: Are you working on anything now?

Kael: I'm making notes on something. There's been a lot of stuff to clean up. I was behind on correspondence. I hate not answering things promptly, but things have piled up on me, and a lot of mail has come in, so I'm behind on that. I feel that I should clean up the mail before I sit down to write—which is silly. I'll never clean it up. There are a couple of subjects that I want to write about but I don't want to talk them to death before I write about them. The other thing is, I don't have the energy I used to have. I used to be able to count on just being able to go all night and day. You know, sometimes I wouldn't see the movie I wanted to write about until the night before my deadline at the magazine, but I knew I could stay up all night and write the piece and I'd be in the clear. I just can't count on energy like that anymore.

OA: Have you cut back on going to movies since your retirement?

Kael: Yeah, there are a lot of stinkers, at least I assume they're stinkers on the basis of what they're about and who's made them, that I figure I'll wait for and watch on TV, or on HBO. But generally when they turn up, they're such stinkers that I don't have the interest in watching them on HBO anyway.

OA: Sounds like a sort of retirement gift.

Kael: Yeah, it is a gift. If you have any brains at all, you can't watch the mediocre movies all your life. I mean, there has to be something else going on in your head. There are a lot of things I want to do. It's more fun to be with people than to watch some stinky movie.

OA: Is a person lucky to be a movie critic?

Kael: It really is a wonderfully exciting field to write about when the movies are good. When they're not so good, it's to despair. The really bad movies you can write about with some passion and anger. It's the mediocre ones that wear you down. They're disgusting to write about because you can feel yourself slipping into the same mediocrity and stupidity. And you feel you're boring the readers and yourself. When you start falling asleep while you're writing a review, you know how dull the movie is. The danger for criticism is that people will want to become critics in order to become television celebrities, rather than enjoying the pleasure of writing and the excitement of trying to define and describe what you've seen.

OA: Do you miss writing reviews?

Kael: Yes, but I know I've got to adjust to it. That's part of adapting to getting older. You've got to recognize that the time for certain things has passed and, I'm not an idiot, I know I would not write at my best if I went on. You know, you start repeating yourself—you write the same phrase, you write the same descriptions. I've already had the problem of working on a paragraph that I thought was pretty good and looking up what I said about that director's work the last time I wrote about him and finding out it was almost exactly the same paragraph. Well, you know, it's time to quit.

Kael Talks

Hal Espen / 1994

From *The New Yorker* 21 March 1994: 134–43. Reprinted by permission; (c) 1994 Hal Espen. Originally in *The New Yorker*. All Rights Reserved.

Espen: Why do you refer to objectivity as "saphead objectivity"?

Kael: I hate to spell it out, but here goes: Our responses to a movie grow out of our experience, knowledge, temperament—maybe even our biochemistry. I always thought that the reason Stanley Kauffmann and I so rarely agreed on things was clear if you looked at his measured walk versus my incautious quick steps. I'm just naturally attuned to jump-cutting.

I tried to put my background and predilections right out on top, so that the reader could know what my responses came from. And I tried to suggest perspectives on moviegoers' emotions, because we're all susceptible, in varying degrees, to dramatic pressure.

Ideally, criticism is a matter of your intelligence and all your intuitions coming into play. Yes, a critic should be disinterested, not have a stake in the outcome of a movie at the box office, but you can't make an objective judgment in any of the arts, and this should be perfectly clear about movies, because they touch people's responses on so many levels.

Espen: What makes you read a movie critic regularly?

Kael: Flashes of insight—epecially about what the movie means and how it affects us. But I'll gladly take them about a performance, the sets—whatever. I'll even settle for a good phrase. There are eminent critics—steady, intelligent—who have never had a perception that could spark a fresh thought in anybody. They're so higher-degree educated they're drained. You read them and think, Yah, yah, yah. I'll read anyone who makes me laugh and is on target.

Espen: Which did you like more, to pan or to praise?

Kael: Panning can be fun—you roll up your sleeves and head into the Augean stable. But it's also showoffy and cheap—it isn't sustaining. If you really like something, writing becomes humble and stirring. You give yourself to the work you're describing. You want to do it justice, and you want to share the pleasure it has given you. Writing about it intensifies your own pleasure.

Espen: Did you ever think you'd been cruel?

Kael: Yes, and I knew it at the time I was writing. It wasn't being cruel to be kind, either. There's so much intellectual sloppiness out there that sometimes you have to be ruthless to keep a sane basis for writing about pop culture. And sometimes a cruel remark—even if it's an overstatement—is the best way to get a point across.

Espen: Do you think there are many independent-minded critics at work now?

Kael: Some—there are always some. But the vast majority are swept up in the campaigns for movies and in the atmosphere at the time. For example, Woody Allen's *Manhattan Murder Mystery* is, I think, the most enjoyable movie he's made in years, but it was passed over, maybe because it's so light in tone, or maybe because it wasn't fashionable at that moment to like a Woody Allen movie. The picture is a dud as a mystery, but it's a lovely marital comedy. Maybe co-writing once again with Marshall Brickman helped restore Allen to the timing he used to have. And when he and Diane Keaton get a rhythm going it's as if they'd never stopped being comedy teammates.

Espen: Some people say that you tell young critics what to think.

Kael: Yes, I've read that I run a conspiratorial network of young critics. The evidence seems to be that young writers often parrot me. But who wants to be imitated? A number of critics take phrases and attitudes from me, and those takings stick out—they're not integral to the writer's temperament or approach. I hate it when I read a piece in a magazine and hear echoes of things that I wrote years ago, on totally different subjects. If I told critics what to think, do you suppose they'd be acclaiming *Unforgiven* and *The Piano* and *Naked?*

Espen: How do you deal with the possibility that your reaction against something like *The Piano* may grow out of your having seen so much?

Kael: You try your best to clue in the reader. Sometimes the less there is going on under the surface of a daydream movie like *The Piano,* the more moviegoers project into it. They make it theirs. So there mightn't be much purpose in my comparing the image of the piano on the beach to the imagery in Polanski's short film *Two Men and a Wardrobe,* but I'd definitely try to contrast *The Piano* with *Utu,* the 1983 New Zealand film by Geoff Murphy, in which a band of Maori guerrillas vandalize the farmhouse of a British couple and pound on the piano before smashing it out the window. The piano represented the wife's last connection with the culture she'd come out of, and it represented the culture the Maoris wanted to desecrate. Its destruction has a lot more resonance than anything in *The Piano.* But then in *Utu* the woman played Beethoven. Holly Hunter plays New Age trills.

Espen: What about the director, Jane Campion, who's viewed as a great new talent?

Kael: She does have a gift for imagery. But she's totally arbitrary, in an art-school way. Things don't hang together in her movies. The symbolism never really registers fully, because you can't tell what she's symbolizing, though you know damn well it's symbolic. *The Piano* could be a silly erotic fantasy and still be fun if it didn't have so much unexamined feminine smugness. That's what sets it apart from, say, a romantic gothic that would lull an audience with sweet dreams. This movie congratulates its heroine for any damn thing she does.

Espen: You used to answer a huge volume of mail. Do you still answer letters?

Kael: Well, the volume is way down, but I can't answer them all anyway. I want to, but, with Parkinson's, I can't get my hand to oblige.

Espen: What do people write about?

Kael: Mostly, they want to know what I think of a particular movie— Streisand's *The Prince of Tides,* for example, or *The Crying Game.*

Espen: And what *do* you think of them?

Kael: If Streisand were more tough-minded, *The Prince of Tides* could be enjoyable camp. But her sincerity—the naked emotionalism she pours into it—makes it somewhat embarrassing. I think that the emotionalism is what affects people and what they find a little bewildering. As for *The Crying Game,* watching it I kept thinking, If the hero's lover had been a clinging-vine woman who built altars to her men, she would have been considered a sick chick, and the hero advised to get away fast. With a transvestite in the role, many people found the relationship weirdly romantic and kicky.

Espen: People just really went for that kind of secret, although it was an open secret by the time the movie came out.

Kael: Well, it was open the first time some of us looked at the guy. His wrists and his voice. But I think it wasn't just the publicity gimmick. The picture had a romantic pull for many people. It had something they'd been missing in movies—the magnetism they'd have shrugged off in a boy-girl picture.

Neil Jordan has got to extend his territory. In *Mona Lisa* he had a man falling in love with a lesbian; in *The Miracle* he had a man falling in love with his mother; in *The Crying Game* he has a man falling in love with a transvestite. Still, Jordan has a wonderful gift for atmosphere. A number of silent-film directors gave audiences a sense of magical possibility—of romantic enchantment. Neil Jordan is one of the few new directors who have that lyricism.

Espen: People felt very protective of *Rain Man,* and were convinced that it did something serious. You got a lot of complaints, didn't you?

Kael: I got very angry mail from people who felt that I didn't appreciate the real-life seriousness of autism, because I didn't appreciate the movie. The press, in general, publicizes what the director says he's doing, and afterward the reviewers tend to review his intentions rather than what's on the screen. If some of us then point out what's actually up there people get upset, because we're not respecting that artist's wonderful hard work for humanity. Not many reviewers have a real gift for effrontery. I think that may be my best talent.

Espen: It's a talent that could be viewed as a detriment to one's professional success.

Kael: Oh, sure. But if you can't make fun of bad movies on serious subjects what's the point?

Espen: Your review of *Shoah* was one of your most controversial, and you had to fight William Shawn to get him to run it. Do you have any regrets about that particular battle?

Kael: No. I was being honest about what I knew and what I felt.

Espen: I suppose that I can understand editors facing the fallout of running something like that, and preferring to leave it alone.

Kael: Sure. But, on the other hand, editors who show courage in some directions maybe could be pushed to show it in other directions. I mean, a Holocaust movie should not be sacrosanct simply because of the subject. I think most of the reviewers were willing to call the director of *Shoah* a great filmmaker because he'd taken on a great subject. They used to treat Stanley Kramer as a great filmmaker, too, especially when he made the nuclear-disaster movie *On the Beach.*

Espen: Did you know when what you said was going to cause a ruckus?

Kael: In this case, yes, but not always. People take offense at things you never would have guessed at. A friend of mine told me that he took a date to see a movie that had delighted him, and afterward she walked so far from him on the sidewalk she might have crossed the street. I sometimes felt as if *New Yorker* readers kept crossing the street. People almost deliberately want to misunderstand what a critic is saying. If a movie touches a nerve, they accuse you of the wildest sorts of things.

Espen: The whole social dimension of moviegoing is something that just doesn't exist in television. I can remember so many kinds of strange emotional aftermaths of moviegoing, whether I was on a date or with a bunch of friends.

Kael: If you disagree about too many movies, it's very hard to sustain a friendship.

Espen: There aren't many other art forms, or public forms of entertainment, where that's really the case.

Kael: No. If you go to a dance concert, or an opera, you're relatively safe. But if you go to a movie you never know what's going to be dug up. I know people who can't talk about movies they've seen to friends on the telephone when their spouse is in the room, because they disagree and it has become a sore spot.

But, of course, there's the other side, too—the friendships based on shared movie tastes.

Espen: I'm curious about some of your early moviegoing experiences—about what films affected you strongly, in the way that films can when you're very young.

Kael: I saw so much. It was movies in general that drew me. When García Márquez says that he wouldn't have written novels if he'd been able to make movies, it's clear what he's saying, because there are so many elements that go into movies that he could have used. It's a supreme art form, and for a while there Coppola and Altman and Godard and Bertolucci and a dozen others ran with it. That's why when I think it's used badly I'm so derisive. I want so much from it because the possibilities are there. On dates, my enthusiasm would often be condescended to by the fellow. He would think it was his mission to straighten me out. And, you know, if you hold forth about why something's great with a guy who just wants you to calm down it's a flattening experience. You learn to shut up, or you find another guy. Or you don't.

Espen: I wanted to ask you about one feature of your writing that bothered some people—the use of "we" and "you."

Kael: It was never an imperial "we"—it was "we" in the audience, or "we" as a group. I always used it right alongside "I," to make the distinction between my reactions and what the collective audience might be reacting to. I used "you" in an indefinite way, to represent "you people" or "one" or "I," and relied on the context to make the meaning clear. I used it in the way we use it in conversation, where you say, "You know that such-and-such." About once a year, I used "one." I avoid "cinema" the way I avoid "one," because where I grew up only pretentious phonies said they were going to the "cinema" or referred to themselves as "one."

Espen: I'm fascinated by the idea of what kind of person it takes to be—to become—a movie director.

Kael: Let's be brutal: It takes a person who can raise the money to make a movie.

Espen: And also what kind of career a director can have. I mean, there are such odd inconsistencies and ups and downs in a director's career.

Kael: I think you're being a bit dreamy. Educated people often now speculate about directors' lives the way less educated people used to fantasize about the stars. And they read *Premiere* the way stenographers used to read *Photoplay*.

Espen: I take your point, and I'll throw one back. What about the issue of relationships with filmmakers, whether it's just a critical relationship or actually a kind of deeper affinity that crosses over into friendship?

Kael: Do you mean, "Is it O.K. to hang out with the people you write about?" Let's say it's dicey. I think the deeper affinity is deeper than friendship. There are directors I personally don't feel any warm response to whose work I care for intensely. That's one of the surprises in the arts. You think that you would like somebody personally if you like his work, and that may not be the case at all. Anyway, I've very rarely had personal relations with directors, even the ones I've written about a great deal.

I knew Jean Renoir very well. I knew him perhaps better than I've known any other director. One night in the fifties, I was at home in Berkeley working on displays for the theatres I managed, and there was a knock at the door and Jean Renoir stood there; we fell into each other's arms, and I guess you could say we never fell out. Somebody had sent him some things I'd written about him; he had gone looking for me at the theatres, and was directed to my house. We remained in close touch until his death, yet his later movies—from the period in which I knew him—I didn't care for very much. He knew that, and it was a source of pain to both of us.

I knew Peckinpah fairly well. It's a funny combination, Renoir and Peckinpah. But most of the directors whom I've been said to be on close terms with I know hardly at all. I've only seen Brian De Palma to say "How do you do?" to two or three times.

Espen: I've heard people criticize you for having what they view as a kind of unseemly loyalty to a filmmaker or engaging in special pleading for him, and yet sometimes the same people seem infuriated by what they see as a kind of perverse fickleness.

Kael: I know. I suspect that behind all this is the notion that a woman can't be a true critic—that she has pets, and also that she's vindictive. It's simply natural in the arts to have preferences. You wouldn't be a critic if you didn't have emotional involvements with the work of certain artists of the past and the present.

Espen: Am I right in thinking that you're disappointed in Scorsese?

Kael: He has become a much more proficient craftsman, but the first films he did that I responded to intensely—*Mean Streets* and *Taxi Driver*—had a sense of discovery. He was looking into himself and the world. I was disappointed in *GoodFellas,* and I thought *Cape Fear* was just a terrible mistake. *The Age of Innocence* is really Merchant Ivory terrain. Even though Scorsese shows what he can do with it in some ways, he doesn't shape the material. I thought the movie disintegrated.

Espen: When you think of Scorsese working with Daniel Day-Lewis—

Kael: You want more. Day-Lewis is the kind of actor that De Niro was as a young man. You don't want just to see him anguished.

Espen: What about De Niro?

Kael: It's a long time since he's shown the fervor of his work in *Godfather II* or the intensity of *Taxi Driver* and his restless bopper in *New York, New York.* I enjoyed him in his brief performance as Al Capone in *The Untouchables.* I liked him in *Brazil.* But in the big performances something sluggish and stolid has crept into his acting. When he attempted comedy with Sean Penn in *We're No Angels,* it was Penn who made me laugh. I find De Niro heavy-spirited.

Espen: What do you think of Michelle Pfeiffer?

Kael: It may be because she has such a great camera face that she hasn't got her full due as an actress. She seems the most American of the women stars, but she has surprising range. You see her opposite Sean Connery in *The Russia House* and you accept her as Russian without fuss or doubts. I accepted her as Catwoman. She was lovably nasty.

Espen: You clearly have favorite directors also.

Kael: Yes, of course, and I have blank spots, too—such as Fassbinder. Ozu, too. But if you mean do I play favorites, I don't think so. It's apparent to anybody who reads me that I think Altman has some real achievements to his credit, even though I've been disappointed in many of his films. I used to say that he made a good one and then a bad one, and so on. He made both in *Short Cuts.* It has some of his worst work and some of his best.

Espen: Can you give me an example of each?

Kael: Sure. The little boy trudging home after he's been hit by a car is almost unbearably fine. The camera fastened on Jack Lemmon's back as he walks down the hospital corridor pushes its point—it's awful. Lemmon tries so hard he has a special mood-altering quality. He seems to be pleading with you, and you think, What is it he's pleading with us for, in movie after movie? What does he want from us? Of course, in *Short Cuts* you also have Tom Watts and Lily Tomlin, and Bruce Davison, and Madeleine Stowe, and others who are in character.

Espen: What other directors do you feel a bond with?

Kael: There's a deviltry in Paul Mazursky's films that makes me laugh. I often read stories that make me think, Paul Mazursky should make a movie of this—like Lore Segal's "Her First American." Oh, and when I read Saul Bellow's "A Silver Dish" in *The New Yorker* I thought Mazursky could make a classic short film for TV out of it.

Let me put it this way: We all know that people in the audience have their own special tastes in directors and performers. Well, so do critics. Maybe they think differently from the guy who just wants to see sullen, pouty, slutty women; maybe they don't. The difference between the layman and the critic is not that the critic is "objective" but that he probably has more background in the art and, if the gods smile on him, he can write. And perhaps the critic's work has sharpened his tastes. For example, there's an intelligence in Judy Davis's acting in *Husbands and Wives* that I find exciting—it's a more controlled and sophisticated form of what Bette Davis had for some of us in the thirties and forties. You felt there was a drive there to express herself via acting; some people found it rather repellent. But, on the other hand, I respond to what I think the large audience responds to in Julia Roberts. There is something about her in *Pretty Woman* that's enormously touching. That broad smile gets to just about everybody. But Julia Roberts not smiling is like Tom Cruise meditating.

Espen: You know, that whole group of women stars of the thirties and forties didn't make any impression on me as a kid.

Kael: Maybe they would have if you'd been born earlier and been a girl. Bette Davis's nervous sass got to me. It was as if she were saying, "I'm more alert than women are supposed to be and I'm not afraid to be a cartoon."

Espen: Did Katharine Hepburn do that, too?

Kael: She made an impression of a very different kind. She was like no one I'd ever imagined. She made a style out of affectation and then, at her best, transcended it. I'm thinking of movies such as *Little Women* and *Alice Adams* and her great performance in *Long Day's Journey Into Night*.

Espen: How is it different with actors now?

Kael: It's a period of sensational acting, even though actors don't often get a chance at shaped characters. When they do, as in the small roles that Holly Hunter and Gary Busey had in *The Firm,* they pop up like jack-in-the-boxes. Kelly Lynch pops up even in turgid melodramas, and Suzy Amis really takes the camera. Tim Roth seems to be able to give shape to each role he plays. And Susan Sarandon becomes more richly sensual.

TV is a good medium for actors—I'm thinking of Albert Finney in *The Green Man,* on A&E. Two-parters and three-parters give them a chance to develop a character. But performances on TV don't vibrate in memory the way big-screen ones do, because there's usually even less of an imaginative structure supporting them. And there isn't the interval of thinking them over while going home. But some stay with me—James Woods as Roy Cohn on HBO, Brian Dennehy in a whole batch of roles. Kelly McGillis surprised me in Jeff Bleckner's *In the Best of Families.* And Andre Braugher on *Homicide* is about as good as acting gets.

Anybody who cares about acting might take a look at Mercedes Ruehl's performance in Martha Coolidge's version of *Lost in Yonkers.* Or Robert Duvall in *Days of Thunder.* Or look at Jeff Bridges as the ex-con in *American Heart.* Every little physical detail is right. The picture maybe has too much integrity and not enough dramatic imagination; you get a whiff of virtue. But Bridges is the real thing.

Espen: What about the kinds of roles that actresses are getting today?

Kael: Taller, stronger-looking actresses play revamped cliché heroines but with titles such as Doctor or Captain. They can throw a punch like a man—they're toy boys. As moviegoers, we get to watch these wonderful amazons: Sigourney Weaver, Daryl Hannah, Geena Davis, Uma Thurman, Laura Dern, and all the others. But only a few—Angelica Huston, Christine Lahti, Joely and Natasha Richardson—have, on occasion, landed real women's roles. Still, you know, the situation isn't much better for men.

Espen: Is sexual politics getting into movies.

Kael: A lot of it is. Most conspicuously in the rabble-rouser *Thelma & Louise,* a revenge movie for women that distorts the issues it poses much as the Charles Bronson *Death Wish* movies used to. Along the way, the heroines destroyed a working-class man, the man with the rig, because he had the wrong style. He had low-down sexist attitudes, and the women were outraged by them. If he'd been upper-class, he wouldn't have talked like that. It's a class-unconscious movie. And then the doomsday finish! The women punish men by killing themselves—they're heading for an all-girl heaven.

Espen: Did you see *The Fugitive?*

Kael: Yes. Tommy Lee Jones ran off with the picture. He would have run off with *JFK,* too, if it hadn't been such a load.

Espen: Are you still as committed to Brian De Palma?

Kael: Yes, of course I am. His *Carlito's Way* has a tired script, and Pacino, good as he is here, has played his role before. But Sean Penn gives one of his sneakily witty performances, and De Palma himself knows how to set up certain kinds of scenes better than practically anybody else ever has. He does sequences that are similar to ones he's done before, but he does them with more ingenuity, more finesse. It may be a while before he does anything again that's as phenomenal as *Casualties of War,* but he's one of the few directors who keep developing in technique.

It's one of the frustrations of writing movie criticism that so many of the people who will take the trouble to read reviews have leather-bound tastes. They'll wait in line for the Merchant Ivory *Remains of the Day,* but they won't go near a gangster picture even if, in visual terms and in sheer movie-making skills, it's far more complex. I understand why. Literate people like the literate sound, the commas in place. It all stands for decorousness, for safety. I think they mistake their priggishness for high standards. To be fair, *Remains* is very well acted—I particularly liked Peter Vaughan, who played Hopkins' father—and Ivory has become accomplished at what he does. Even his unvarying pace achieves a dull splendor. But the picture is almost a parody of repression: the culmination of nothing.

See, I put my leanings right out there for you.

Espen: A few years ago, you wrote, "The only fresh element in American movies of the eighties may be what Steve Martin, Bill Murray, Bette Midler, Richard Pryor, Robin Williams, and other comedians have brought to them."

Kael: Yes, I think that's right. When you saw Richard Pryor alone onstage in a concert film, you felt the flipped-out truth of what he was saying. The performers—especially the standup comics crossing over—brought a roughhousing charge to eighties movies. They were as marginal as we felt ourselves to be. (See, there's a "we" that represents the hip audience.) Whatever they were, they weren't square. That's changing. When you see Steve Martin starring in a dull "family" movie like *Father of the Bride* or *Parenthood* or *Housesitter,* or Bette Midler in *Beaches* or *For the Boys,* you may feel a thud in the chest; and that was a depressingly bad production of *Gypsy* that Midler was in on TV. At one point, I couldn't stand listening to the musical cues anymore, and got up and put a rap CD on.

Espen: Which one?

Kael: Salt-N-Pepa.

Espen: Why are you so rough on harmless family comedies?

Kael: I know that sometimes I treat mediocrity as if it were criminal. I don't think I can explain that except with the totality of what I've written. I love low comedy and I love high comedy, and I like mixtures of the two, as in *Soapdish.* But when I see entertainers play down to the public—turn wholesome—I want to cry foul.

Espen: What do you think about the esteem in which Clint Eastwood is now held?

Kael: As a director? It's a delicious joke—further proof that there's no such thing as objective judgment in the arts. I did think Eastwood's performance in *In the Line of Fire* was one of the best he's ever given, perhaps the best. But when he was fun in his early movies it wasn't because of his acting skill, and now that he has a little skill he's lost the spaghetti sexiness that made him fun. He's all sinews. He has become a favorite of intellectuals just when he's losing his mass audience. It has to be a consolation prize.

Espen: I don't think anyone before you had talked about movies the way you did. I'm thinking of things like the line in your Goings On note for *Mr. Smith Goes to Washington*—"No one else can balance the ups and downs of wistful sentiment and corny humor the way Capra can—but if anyone else should learn to, kill him."

Kael: I literally, physically, can't respond to that stuff the way some people do. Loving movies is a very peculiar love-hate relationship. I mean, you love what they can be, but you also love the crap they are. I have my limits, though.

Espen: You also loved jazz, and I've always associated the unsentimental, fast, cool appreciation of virtuosity in your writing with jazz.

Kael: It wasn't conscious, but I think that by temperament I wanted to approximate something of the speed and feeling of jazz.

Espen: Did you ever think about becoming a jazz critic?

Kael: I might have gone in that direction, but I didn't. I love gospel, too, and I'm sort of tickled that I admitted to you that I like rap.

Espen: *(Laughs)* Why tickled?

Kael: Because people find it out of season in someone who will be seventy-five in a few months. They think that I couldn't possibly enjoy the music, that I'm just trying to be a swinger. People are still outraged when I say I like rock. I also like Handel and Purcell and Gluck. But, God, what I don't like is Broadway show tunes. I love movie musicals, but there's something about the stale Broadway approach! The musicals I love tend to be things like *Singin' in the Rain, Cabaret,* and the M-G-M *Pennies from Heaven.* I loved *Little Shop of Horrors* and *Phantom of the Paradise* and *Saturday Night Fever,* and other movies that used a little bit of a shiv in them. I'm not crazy about the soft Americana musicals.

Espen: The musical seems to me a genre of movies that is, perhaps, at a dead end.

Kael: But it shouldn't be. We've had the singers, we've had the music. Elvis Presley was trashed early on; most of the rock and soul people weren't used at all. There was about five minutes of Aretha Franklin in *The Blues Brothers;* when Tina Turner did her number in *Tommy* and the camera travelled up her legs, it was like an explosion, but movie producers didn't seem to notice.

Espen: I was amazed when I heard that *New Yorker* messengers taking proofs to Mr. Shawn on a Saturday would go up to his apartment and be invited in and he would be watching *Soul Train.*

Kael: Isn't that great? He loved all of show business. When I turned in my review of Richard Pryor's concert movie, he was overjoyed, because he had worshipped Pryor and had followed his career from the beginning. I mean, he had many sides that didn't come out, really, in the way he ran the magazine. He played terrific jazz piano. But he also had a series of taboos that were part of his creed of good writing.

Espen: Did you have confederates at *The New Yorker,* people who encouraged you, and said, "I'm glad you're here," or was it kind of an uphill struggle?

Kael: When I started to appear in the magazine, some of the writers—the ones whose prose seemed to be rolled like an English lawn—wrote me hideous letters. You know—"Get out of here, with your cowboy boots."

Espen: Oh my God.

Kael: Some of them were from people I had admired—and that was really a shock.

Espen: What color were your cowboy boots?

Kael: I didn't have cowboy boots. I've never had cowboy boots. It was their idea of my writing—trampling manure on the pages of *The New Yorker.*

Espen: Well, there is a certain kind of literary sensibility that seems to be profoundly aggrieved by your style.

Kael: They were—some of them—the kind of people who said they didn't have a TV except in the kitchen, for the maid. That was sort of the approach to movies. E. B. White represented the essence of *New Yorker* style, and I couldn't evoke the movies in that spare, lucid E. B. White language.

Espen: Why did you take that break in 1979 and go out to Hollywood?

Kael: I thought that maybe I was written out—that I needed a change.

Espen: But you didn't like it in L.A.?

Kael: I missed writing. Pictures were opening and nobody was saying the things I wanted to say. I was like a firehouse horse hearing the bell.

Espen: There were stories in the press suggesting that you were a failure out there.

Kael: When I left *The New Yorker,* I had a commitment to give some seminars and lectures at a couple of universities in the South. So I hadn't yet reported for work at the studio when one of the newsweeklies ran an item saying that in my first weeks in Hollywood I'd managed to alienate everyone. That was picked up and elaborated on all over the world: it was what people like to read. The movie people in L.A. treated me incredibly well. I think they were terrified that I was really an Eastern spy, that I was going to write an exposé of some sort.

Espen: By 1991, were you afraid you weren't strong enough to find fresh ways of talking about things?

Kael: It had become too hard for me to go in to New York to see the movies, and my balance was so bad that a few times I fell smack on my face on the sidewalk. But it wasn't just me. Movies by then weren't setting off the kind of sparks in me that they had in the seventies; I didn't think they spoke to what was going on in the country in the way *The Godfather* did, or *Nashville.* Wonderful movies turn up, but movie criticism now is often a report on a vacuum.

Espen: I always walk out of a theatre nowadays with a deep sense of regret that I'm not going to read what you thought. Which films of the past couple of years do you regret not writing about?

Kael: *Hearts of Darkness,* the documentary that included footage Eleanor Coppola took during the shooting of *Apocalypse Now.* It dealt with Coppola's manic-depressive swings. It was like the naked, honest-to-God version of Fellini's *8½.* You heard Coppola saying that he didn't know what he was doing, that he was failing, and then heard him convince himself that he'd brought it all off.

I was sorry not to have been able to write about *The Fisher King,* because I had often found flaws in Terry Gilliam's work—in the way he overscaled his pictures—and this time he scaled it right, and Robin Williams, Jeff Bridges, Mercedes Ruehl, and Amanda Plummer did great teamwork. That hairy leprechaun Robin Williams talks so fast that what he says hits you like a double take—he and Amanda Plummer are like boy-and-girl Marx Brothers. I'd like to have written about Carl Franklin's small film *One False Move.* And there have been little, unimportant pictures that were very satisfying, like *Rambling Rose* and *Diggstown.* Soderbergh's *King of the Hill* is a wee thing but nicely detailed.

Lately? Well, two movies I loved. Fred Schepisi and John Guare's *Six Degrees of Separation*—a drawing-room comedy that rises to such heights it becomes a genre of its own. It's amazing that it ever got made.

(The ending is a disappointment: you don't want Nora, but you don't want Mary Tyler Moore, either.) And Jim Sheridan's *In the Name of the Father,* an Irish movie without any malarkey. It's sane—that's a high compliment—and forceful. And what a situation: a son who doesn't get along with his father is imprisoned with him, and the father monitors everything he does. The movie has substance.

Espen: What about *Schindler's List?*

Kael: I'm not sure there's much more to be said about it. Do I think it's a masterpiece? No. The basic material is great; the movie itself is a very fine melodrama, made with the skills of a superb moviemaker and with deep love. It doesn't have the moral complexities of *In the Name of the Father,* but within its limitations it's just about the best of its kind. *Schindler's List* is Spielberg's attempt to be a grownup artist; I hope he won't lose his most inspired side—his access to the child's emotions we all have in us, what came out so strongly in *Jaws* and *E.T.*

Espen: Are you still gluttonous about movies?

Kael: Perhaps a little less so than I used to be, but I'm gluttonous about all the arts. When I went dancing, I never wanted to stop. If I start a novel in the evening, I still stay up half the night to finish it, even though I know I'll feel hungover the next day.

Espen: What have you been reading?

Kael: Except for my greater tolerance for pulp on the screen, my taste in books is very similar to my taste in movies. I've been reading a lot of Edna O'Brien and Lee Smith—I just finished her *Fair and Tender Ladies.* In its own way, it's almost as good as her novel about country music, *The Devil's Dream.* I've just read Anatole Broyard's *Kafka Was the Rage.* It's a memoir of life in Greenwich Village in the forties, the memoir of a sensualist and amoralist. Sentence by sentence, it's as beautifully precise as any contemporary American work I know. I laughed out loud at Philip Roth's *Operation Shylock.* It's the most daring and, of course, obsessive of his novels. I haven't been startled into laughter like that since *Naked Lunch* came out.

Espen: What about nonfiction books about social issues or politics?

Kael: I tend to read those things more quickly. I slow down for something like Frederick Crews' *The Critics Bear It Away.* Crews' gamesmanship is insidious, it's so entertaining. What a good time he has taking scholars apart! But I tend to whip through most nonfiction books; they're often written to be informative, and I read them to be informed. I really love reading writers who care about how the words go together.

Espen: Do you read any fiction about movies?

Kael: I liked Michael Tolkin's book *The Player.* It has an anger that's quite different from the movie's lightness of tone. Tolkin got at the conflict between the executives and the writers in a mean, funny way.

Espen: About *The Player*—what happened when the novel was made into a movie?

Kael: The book is about how writers are mistreated, and Robert Altman is notoriously not interested in writers or fidelity to writers. He turned it into an amused satire of Hollywood. The fact that the writer—the wrong writer—got it in the neck seemed a minor matter. The movie itself is minor—enjoyably so.

Espen: Are there any young writers you've particularly admired in the last few years?

Kael: I liked "My Appearance" and "Lyndon," two of the stories by David Foster Wallace in his collection *Girl with Curious Hair.* "My Appearance," the one about the actress scheduled to be a guest on David Letterman, is very distinctive.

Espen: What was it about?

Kael: The woman's husband was worried about what would happen to her, whether Letterman would cut her to ribbons, and it's a legitimate fear. On talk shows, you never know what you're up against.

Espen: Have you had bad experiences?

Kael: Generally, it's been a disaster for me. I've been put in false positions, asked vacuous questions, most likely by an edgy, hostile host, and accused of liking only highbrow European films or violent American pictures.

Espen: I guess I don't need to ask if you'll be doing TV interviews for the new book.

Onward. People have criticized you for being an amoral sensualist.

Kael: Just what I love Broyard for.

Espen: And people say that you have an obsession with violence and sex, and that you have a dirty mind.

Kael: The better to write about movies. As for violence, I have a wonderful quotation from Tolstoy.

Espen: Was that the one that you had pinned up in your office at *The New Yorker?*

Kael: Yes. Now I have it at home. The paper has yellowed. He said this in 1908, on the eve of his eightieth birthday: "I am seriously thinking of writing a play for the screen. I have a subject for it. It is a terrible and bloody theme. I am not afraid of bloody themes. Take Homer or the Bible, for instance. How many bloodthirsty passages there are in them—murders, wars. And yet these are the sacred books, and they ennoble and uplift the people. It is not the subject itself that is so terrible. It is the propagation of bloodshed, and the justification for it, that is really terrible!''

As I see it, there are the moviemakers who use violence for a turn-on; they put you on the side of the bullies. Examples: The rape scene in *A Clockwork Orange*. The emotionless killing in the *Dirty Harry* films, such as *Magnum Force*. The gory opening of *Wild at Heart*. Then there are the moviemakers who sensitize you to what violence does to its victims. Classic examples: *Grand Illusion, Casualties of War*. I think it's the job of a reviewer to make the moral difference clear and to try to make it clear that some movies—such as *The Wild Bunch*—blur the distinction. There are also movies that use violence for casual, bang-bang effects; most action films do. They're childish—pre-moral—and a lot of people enjoy that freedom from judgment. What I'm getting at is that violence has a whole range of meanings; simply to condemn it is mindless.

Espen: People in the government also jump on the incessant quality of it. You know, the fact that violence is a convention and that you just absorb so much of it.

Kael: I don't know what to say about that. I don't have the answers.

Espen: People asked me about asking you to handicap the Oscars.

Kael: Phooey.

Espen: It holds no interest for you?

Kael: It goes against the grain of what I think criticism should be. I mean, trying to dope out what the big winners will be.

Espen: What about how an Oscar might affect or help an actor's or actress's career?

Kael: This is why I've stayed off television.

Espen: You once wrote, "It says something about the nature of movies that people don't say they like them, they say they love them." It's safe to say, isn't it, that you still love them?

Kael: Yes.

Espen: Then, if you feel you can't write, why shouldn't you do monthly interviews?

Kael: Because it's not the same. This is just off the top of the head—it's not like giving yourself to a subject.

Espen: Do you feel that you're in a painful predicament now?

Kael: Getting old isn't fun, despite Betty Friedan's thesis. She must have a fantastic constitution.

Espen: To assert that it's a wonderful new stage of life?

Kael: Balls.

Four Stars for the Counterculture

Evelyn Renold / 1994

A slightly shorter version of this interview appeared in *New York Newsday* 12 December 1994: A21. © 1994 by Evelyn Renold. Reprinted by permission.

Question: Are there film critics you enjoy reading now?

Pauline Kael: There are some pretty good ones, though not a lot of strong voices. What I miss are people who could make you want to see something, who could bring up some obscure film that you'd barely heard of and send you to it, who could make you argue with them. The critics are a little too genteel now, almost academic some of them.

Q: Why are there so few strong voices?

PK: It takes a certain amount of courage and audacity to stand by yourself and simply say what you think. There's a conventional response system that builds up. And it's safer to string along with what others are going to say. I mean, people don't really want to say how bad *Interview with the Vampire* is. It's hardly possible to sit through the picture.

Q: What about the people who review movies on television. Are they undermining film criticism?

PK: No, I think it's the movies themselves. Movies are terrible at the moment. There are only a few good ones each season, and some of those don't get a very big public response. Over the last few years, I can think of only a handful of movies that were worth intensive criticism. *In the Name of the Father. Six Degrees of Separation.* More recently, *Pulp Fiction* is very enjoyable; I don't know how much there is to say about it, but it's very funny, and I think it could be talked about in terms of certain kinds of humor. And the Chekhov film, *Vanya on 42nd Street,* is really worth talking about. There are action films that are unobjectionable like *Speed,* which was a very entertaining little film, but it isn't worth more than a critic's paragraph. You can't become euphoric about a film that just fulfills certain expectations.

One aspect of criticism now is that the critics have become part of the apparatus of advertising. When you look at the ads for movies, you see a long list of people from various TV and radio stations, and most of the names you've never heard of. And when there's a chorus of praise for something like *Love Affair,* you just have to assume that those people are incompetent or really don't care. I don't mind trash that's lively. I quite enjoy it; I think it has its place. But with something that's as enervated as *Love Affair,* you really have to be part of the system to praise it.

Q: In 1980, you wrote a famous essay called "Why Are Movies So Bad?" Are the problems pretty much the same today?

PK: I think so, but everything that I described—the conglomerates taking over the movie companies and the heads of the studios being anxious for their jobs—has become even more so. And it's reached a point where it's just about lethally impossible for somebody to do good work in the system. They're fought every step of the way.

Q: Will there be another big upheaval in Hollywood as there was in the late '60s?

PK: I hope so. I don't know what will happen. I don't expect anything very unusual out of the triumvirate of Spielberg, Katzenberg and Geffen. Spielberg is a great moviemaker but he's not a great innovative movie-maker. He's not a real thinker. And most of what he's promoted on films and on television has been very mediocre. He himself transcends the mediocre by his skill. He is really a marvelous entertainer. But I wouldn't expect him to have ideas that would be exciting as a producer.

Q: What about the smaller, independent films?

PK: The distribution of smaller films is better now, but the films themselves are not. The big hit was *The Piano,* which was a triumph of salesmanship. It's soft and squishy and flattering to women in ways that women are very susceptible to, and I hope they're pulling out of. It goes into the virtue of being a victim. The woman is so victimized that it seems all right for her to be an utter bitch to everybody. Everything she does seems justified by the movie, starting when she tells off the captain of the ship for offering her some assistance. There's no way for men to behave in some of these movies.

I also think *The Crying Game* was a fluke hit. A love story between a man and a woman would not have been taken nearly as seriously as a love story between a man and a transvestite. It's very unusual to have a man and woman love story on the screen now that has any authenticity.

Q: So movies don't have the primacy they once had.

PK: No, I don't think they do. When they're interesting now, they tend to be oddball, strange hits. And sometimes that can be fun. But in the '70s they dealt with things that were much more primary to our experi-ence at the time. We've had nothing like *The Godfather,* or *Nashville,* or *Shampoo,* or *McCabe & Mrs. Miller,* or any number of movies that said something about the times we lived in. We've had nothing like *Mean Streets* or *Taxi Driver* for a long time now. Instead we have the directors of those movies doing remakes of old films. I mean it was depressing that it was [Martin] Scorsese remaking *Cape Fear*.

Q: I know you weren't a fan of Scorsese's *Age of Innocence*.

PK: It was an honest effort, but wrong-headed. I think nothing could be as foreign to his sensibility as Edith Wharton. I mean, he didn't seem to share her revulsion at those moneyed, vulgar people. He made the dinner look good.

Q: What happened to filmmakers like Scorsese?

PK: They lost their sureness about what they should be saying. Very often they lost confidence in their own gifts. I think once the counterculture was over and the Republicans came in [in 1980], people lost heart. I mean the people who make movies. It was as if a blanket had fallen over everybody. All the enthusiasm, all the feeling that something new was going to happen that the counterculture had represented, it all ended. And now, once again, it's hard to believe that the counterculture is being used as if it were a negative thing, as if it hadn't loosened up American society and made so many things possible.

Q: Is anything taking the place of movies?

PK: No. Movies are such a great art form that people are going to go for the little that it gives them. I mean, it's still better than nothing. Also, movies are trumpeted so much you feel you're out of it if you don't see them. Right now, I sometimes wonder if I've seen a movie or only heard so much about it that I think I've seen it. And sometimes I see more than I want to see when there's a director or an actor selling a movie on a talk show. He may tell you the movie is a dog even while he's selling it.

Q: For instance?

PK: The Kenneth Branaugh salesmanship for *Frankenstein*. The more glib he became, the worse the movie seemed to me.

Q: So movies are on a downward spiral?

PK: In some cultures, in Asian society and in some European countries, movies are still serving a positive purpose. Even though the movies may not be very good by our standards, they're still progressive forces in many backward countries. And they express things that the government doesn't want expressed.

Q: What's good about American movies?

PK: I think acting has never been better in movies and on television. People take it for granted, but if you compare it to the acting of 20 or 30 years ago, you see how much better it is.

Q: Which actors or actresses do you admire?

PK: There's a whole slew of forthright, independent young women on the screen, who seem to be willing to do daring roles and take risks that actresses didn't take in the past. Picture after picture, I see women who are quite remarkable. Kelly Lynch, who played Matt Dillon's girl in *Drugstore Cowboy,* Julianne Moore and Brooke Smith who are in *Vanya on 42nd Street.* I adored Judy Davis in *Husbands and Wives.* And all those tall goddesses—Sigourney Weaver, Uma Thurman. We have some marvelous actresses. It's hard to be better than Diane Keaton and Jessica Lange when they hit their stride, when they get a good role.

Q: And the men?

PK: They're not as good as the women at the moment. Sometimes they seem very promising but they don't go beyond that. I think John Cusak is awfully good, particularly the work he did in *The Grifters,* but he isn't a very strong presence on the screen.

Bruce Willis is a much better actor than he's generally given credit for. He's often good in movies that aren't very good. We tend to take certain people for granted; if they seem silly and unpretentious and do action well, we don't see the acting that goes into it. Michael Keaton I think is misguided. He's very talented, but he's playing leading men who aren't funny enough. Still, for his work in *Beetlejuice,* I will be his fan forever.

Harrison Ford showed a lot of talent in the Indiana Jones pictures—that kind of spontaneity and easy-going quality is good—but when he plays a serious role, he's deadly. These spy thrillers in which he plays a diplomat or an army officer, you can hardly wait to escape. We have a lot of actors who can't play men they think are serious. When Jack Nicholson has tried it, he's been deadly too. They need a kind of casual exuberance or they can't come across.

Q: How about the Harrison Ford of *Working Girl?*

PK: He was okay, but just okay. Tom Hanks is better at that kind of thing. But Tom Hanks sounds as if he wants to be James Stewart. And that could be pretty lethal. When they start being virtuous and kind and gentle and lovely it's time to run out of the theater.

Q: Which brings us to *Forrest Gump.* How do you account for its success?

PK: It struck me like *Field of Dreams* and other movies that people suckered themselves into reacting to. Somehow there's a softness in people's thinking. They're saying to themselves, You don't have to be smart, you only have to be good. But you can barely get around the corner on goodness in this society now. These movies do speak to something in the culture, which is a desire to regress, to believe in certain kinds of values that never did operate. It's very strange, because *Forrest Gump* was made by a director [Robert Zemeckis] who's done some of the most cynical, funny movies I've ever seen, such as *Used Cars.*

Q: You've said in the past that some of the best movies that get made in this country don't get seen.

PK: It's a pity. *Cattle Annie and Little Britches,* with Burt Lancaster, was one of our best modern westerns and very few people saw it. It's sort of a tragedy. In one scene, Lancaster bathed nude and you could see that he had a belly and that his body had gone to hell, and you couldn't help but think what a gallant, courageous actor he was. It's a terrific movie. *Vincent and Theo* is another unsung movie. They talked about Robert Altman making a comeback when he did *The Player,* but he'd made *Vincent and Theo* just before and it's a far more interesting and unusual movie.

Q: Are the other arts in as much trouble as the movies?

PK: The theater is in much worse shape than the movies, I would say. Our society has been in a stagnant slump culturally, except for pop music to some degree.

Q: What happened to movie musicals?

PK: Musicals really died out as a genre, just as popular music in this country was reaching some pretty high points. Somehow or other, movies and music never really got together. They're not using the talent that's in music on screen. Maybe they're afraid there isn't a big enough international audience for it, I don't know. It's amazing that Michael Jackson never played the lead in a Hollywood movie—I mean, when you think of what happened in the 1930s, how music brought movies to life.

Pennies from Heaven, with Steve Martin, was the best American musical of recent years. I say recent, and it's almost 15 years ago. I'd say *The Bodyguard* had something, but the structure was very stale and it was very ineptly done. *For the Boys* was just a tragic mistake. Bette Midler doesn't seem to be aware of how embarrassing it was watching her being cheered on for her wonderful nobility. I mean, there's a talent just blown away.

Q: You've written a lot about movie violence. Is anyone doing anything interesting or provocative now?

PK: I thought Brian De Palma used violence beautifully in *Casualties of War.* He used it the way the Greeks did in *The Trojan Women,* and it made you hate violence more than you'd ever hated it before. Then of course there's the playful use of violence in *Pulp Fiction.* It's so grotesque and so sudden, it's funny. In Oliver Stone's *Natural Born Killers,* violence is used in the worst, exploitive way. It's used to hit you and make you get all buzzed and silly.

Q: Now that you're no longer reviewing, do you feel the same compulsion to see as many films as you can?

PK: Well, I spare myself some of them that I suspect are going to be dogs. But I still have the same interest in seeing things. And if I miss them in theaters, I watch for them on HBO, or I see them on tape.

Q: Is the moviegoing experience any different for you now?

PK: Not really, except that I don't make notes now. When I see something I love, I still have the same desire to communicate it. I saw *Vanya on 42nd Street* on tape because there's no other way to see it up here in the country, and I still felt the same old excitement.

Q: In the introduction to your recent anthology, you talk about your working relationship with William Shawn, when he was editor of *The New Yorker*. How do you think you might have gotten on with Tina Brown?

PK: I don't think she would object to what I have to say, except perhaps in things that affected her own preferences. It might be difficult if I panned the work of, say, someone she just arranged to have write for *The New Yorker*. But there are always those problems with different editors. Even with Shawn. Once when I turned in a review making fun of someone, he said, "You don't understand, he's like a son to me." I delivered an obscenity, and Shawn published the piece. But I think had I not been fairly popular with the readers at that point, he might not have.

Q: What do you think of *The New Yorker* under Tina Brown?

PK: I've never known the magazine to be livelier than it is now or to be talked about more. On the other hand, it isn't loved or respected as much. I'm not sure young writers would hold it up as the ideal, the place where they most wanted to be printed. Even when I was a student at Berkeley in the late '30s, when we were rather derisive about the slickness and the fancy advertising and the rather genteel condescending prose style, we still respected *The New Yorker*. We knew those were terrific writers who wrote for it. I don't have that sense now. I see new writers in the magazine who are not terrific, and the fine writing is sacrificed to topicality. But the topicality makes it more newsworthy and makes people respond, too. I don't know, you balance one against the other. Sometimes people labored too long over the fine writing.

Q: Do you think we have anything to look forward to in the movies?

PK: There are always surprises in the arts. I mean, there's some kid in middle America who's writing a screenplay or something that's gonna knock our heads off. I hope. And I think there will turn out to be some wonderful surprises from women. Maybe we'll have our own Leni Riefenstahl. I mean, it's an indication of how crazy the arts are in a way that the most marvelously gifted woman moviemaker of all time should have been a Nazi. Things aren't fair, are they? But you have to acknowledge talent where it is.

A Message from Our Leader

Ray Sawhill / 1994

From *The Modern Review* December–January 1994–95: 6–7. ©
1994 by Ray Sawhill. Reprinted by permission.

Ray Sawhill: If you were starting off now, would you write about films?

Pauline Kael: In this period of movies, in terms of what's being done now, I doubt it . . . I'm not sure.

RS: People don't talk about movies the way they used to.

PK: How can you talk about special effects for more than a minute? You say, how was that done? And someone explains how it was done, and you think, why did I ask?

RS: Is it because movies so thoroughly take over your consciousness that, even when they stink, people are still fascinated by them?

PK: I think so. Even a dumb movie has a lot going on in it.

RS: I know in San Francisco you worked on experimental films.

PK: It interested me a lot at the time, but my talents, such as they were, probably tied in more with entertainment movies than with experimental movies.

RS: How do you explain this?

PK: Because of my interests, which were primarily in films reaching large numbers of people. There is something rather closeted about experimental films. They seem like part of the foundation world, or the art gallery bureaucracies. And I love the idea of the democratic medium of the motion picture. Whitman's poetry reached out to people in a way that early movies did too.

RS: Have movies lost that?

PK: Well, now they're made for subliterate cultures. American action films travel so well all over the world. Whereas the films that try to do something unusual are trapped.

RS: Doesn't that make the action film even more democratic?

PK: It's democratic in the worst way. It degrades the mass audience. If there's nothing else in movies but action it's just one special effect thrill after another. And people learn to settle for that.

RS: What do you make of critics' eternal search for a great new B movie?

PK: A mystique has built up that B movies were really the all-American

183

goods, and if you can bring that quality to bigger movies you've got
something. But the trouble with B movies is the B conception of character. You don't have characters with many sides. The characters are really
a function of the plot.

RS: Do A movies today offer anything more than B movies used to?

PK: They still have more interesting performances, particularly in the
smaller roles. A bum actor in the leading role will be surrounded by
whizz-bang players to keep the picture going.

RS: What direction might your life have taken if William Shawn hadn't
been a fan?

PK: I don't really know, because I was at the point of giving up. I had
just quit *The New Republic* because the publisher had dumped some
reviews of mine, and chopped up another while I was out of town. And I
was in bed with the flu, and I thought, well, it's really hopeless. Shawn
phoned when I was at my sickest and offered me to start the following
Monday. He had printed the pieces that *The New Republic* had rejected—
"Movies on Television" and "*Bonnie and Clyde.*" Shawn liked movies,
he cared about them. Most editors are just not that interested.

RS: There's a roomful of editors waiting for you to speak to them.
What do you say?

PK: I'd say, stop assigning so many stories and listen to what the
writers want to write about. The worst thing that's happening in magazines and newspapers is that people get trained to write on assignment,
and they cook up fake stories about whatever the editors have heard a
little buzz about. If it was a story they really cared about, they could do
some independent research, and they might have some background in it,
and it might be something they believed in.

RS: Where does the "buzz" come from?

PK: The publicists, often. They take their cue from the executives in
the movie companies. It starts with what the executives think is going to
be the hot picture. And it goes all the way up to what's featured on
magazine covers and TV talkfests.

RS: Why do editors trust what they're told?

PK: Because they don't trust themselves. They go out with important
people at dinner parties or at openings. They trust what they hear or
overhear more than they trust their own critics.

RS: Was the magazine world at the time you were getting going similar
to the magazine world today?

PK: No, but it was terrible in its own way. Things were chopped up
and hacked, but I wasn't told in advance what to write about. After I

wrote about something, then the editors would get their fists in it. One way or another they get you.

RS: It's an editor's world.

PK: In many ways *The New Yorker* wasn't a dream, either. There were movies I couldn't review because the thought of them upset Shawn so much. For example, I didn't publish a review of *Deep Throat*. He simply wouldn't allow it.

RS: If you had been Paul Kael, how might things have been different?

PK: (laughs) I don't know who can say, because I very specifically took a woman's point of view. And I used bitchery as a tool. So I can't say I wasn't putting myself ready up there for it.

RS: Why did you so deliberately take a woman's point of view?

PK: Because so many movies were being judged in what I thought were absurdly masculine terms. Cowboy movies and war movies, and everything else, too.

RS: Would a woman critic starting off now be badgered as you were?

PK: I think she might have it easier than a man. Where before editors wouldn't consider women critics, now they're looking for them, because they think there is a kind of political advantage in having them.

RS: What is it that success does to entertainers?

PK: They begin to view themselves as having a responsibility to the public. And that generally means a responsibility to view themselves as ideal characters. They'll no longer do the things they did earlier on.

RS: Some people go to pieces.

PK: Often they start on drugs or high living or new marriages or new sex lives. They just can't handle it. But often it's a matter of wanting important pictures with important themes. I think there are directors who have more talent than brains—Spielberg, Demme, maybe Scorsese. Streisand. Some of them are technically and emotionally incredibly gifted, but they don't know what they should be doing with their gifts. They pick terrible material. It's almost incredible that a man of Spielberg's gifts should have made *Always*. And when you hear him making speeches about how everybody should see *Schindler's List*—as if it were a duty— you lose heart.

RS: Is Coppola an example of someone who couldn't handle success?

PK: I think it was overpowering for him. It was really at the peak of the counterculture and of the drug culture, and I think he got swept up in it. Certainly the people he worked with got swept up in it. By the time he was going to Cuba and being fêted by Castro, and was announcing he was going to buy Belize, he'd really become a saviour. And I think he still has something of that grandiloquence.

RS: Did you ever feel bad panning someone?

PK: You can't help knowing that you're hurting a person. I've sometimes had accounts of how so-and-so went to bed for three days after reading my review. It's a comedy, but it's also awful. You realise that months out of their lives had gone into this role, and suddenly they feel they're subjected to public ridicule. But it's part of working in the arts that you have to accept aesthetic criticism, and Lord knows I've been panned, so I know how it feels.

RS: People often don't realise that as a critic you're a public performer. They think all you're doing is—

PK: —attacking other people. They don't realise you're on the line too. And as a critic you get attacked with a particular hostility that people reserve for critics, because they think of them as parasites.

RS: Are they parasites?

PK: The subject a movie critic writes about is movies. It seems to me as legitimate an object of contemplation as any other. (laughs) I think it's a great subject, especially how movies interact with our lives. It's difficult to be a good critic. There are very few great ones, a handful—Hazlitt and Shaw, Virginia Woolf with the Common Readers, D.H. Lawrence in *Studies in Classical American Literature*. Tynan early on in *Curtains* wrote stunningly on actors.

RS: How important is it for a movie critic to be right?

PK: There's no standard to judge right or wrong by in any of the arts. You have to go on whether other people see something different in the work because of what you've written. In movies, judgment is often not so important in a critic as responsiveness to what a movie feels like, and where it's heading and what its vision is.

RS: There's a roomful of Pauline Kael imitators waiting for you to speak to them. What do you say?

PK: "Cut it out!" (laughs) I don't see how you can develop your own responsiveness if you keep using somebody else's vocabulary or attitudes. It's the attitudes that they take over, which are sort of tough-girl attitudes, and seem aberrant in male critics.

RS: Are there works or artists you find yourself unable to respond to?

PK: Yeah. Fassbinder I never got on with. I just didn't see what the fuss was about. A lot of later Bresson didn't interest me. There are big names I don't care for very much. For me, Zhang Yimou joins Ozu and Tarkovsky. I find Zhang Yimou's pictures mostly very tiresome. They seem like a reprise of what was done in the Twenties and early Thirties, and slower and more pictorial.

RS: What do you think of the British movie critics?

PK: Graham Greene could summarize a movie in two or three sentences that were just about unforgettable. He could do it with a phrase. And he had a strong point of view about what kinds of movies he believed in. There are some remarkably smart critics now, but you feel they could be writing about almost anything. It wouldn't have to be movies.

RS: Is that a failing?

PK: It's a failing in terms of a strong movie sense. They don't have a strong feeling of what they want movies to be, besides better entertainment.

RS: The *Modern Review* gang seem to be the first Brits who don't condescend to American pop culture.

PK: They're still on a high from it. They haven't yet had too much of that high. We're overdosed on American pop culture. We could stand a little something else.

RS: Some of us Americans get tired of having our nervous systems raped.

PK: Sure.

RS: Why does pop culture take over everywhere it's introduced.

PK: Because it's so basic, and charged with energy. Why does rock music or country music take over? Because everybody can take part in it, everybody can feel it. You don't need an education for it. It gets to you instantly. And American pop movies have the same instant accessibility to people. The emotions and drives are so simple.

RS: It's like sugar. In every culture where sugar was introduced—

PK: It swept the country. Sure.

RS: The Sixties' exhilaration about pop culture left a lot of people thinking there was liberation of some sort to be found in pop.

PK: It was fun bombarding people with pop culture and getting them to agree that they really enjoyed it. Because academic people had been talking about it as if it wasn't worth discussion. And the fact is it has basic qualities that often have gone out of serious fiction and movies. But it's not all we want. Pop culture in its most extreme form is what you get in the action film.

RS: Well, now that pop culture has been admitted into polite society—

PK: There is no polite society.

RS: So has the fight for pop culture been won?

PK: It's been won in a terribly distorted way. I don't think anybody who wanted a recognition of it wanted it to be recognised as the sole art of America.

RS: So where in the Sixties you were arguing for people to recognise the virtues of pop, you would now be responding to people who have become addicts of pop?

PK: That's right. Those who resent anything that requires more attention than the simplest forms of pop do.

RS: How do you explain this resentment?

PK: If people grow up on pop music, how do they respond to more complex music? Are they willing to make the effort, or do they scorn it because it doesn't have the immediate pleasures for them?

RS: What might be ideal?

PK: What you get in Renoir or Satyajit Ray, or Preston Sturges at his best. You get it in *McCabe & Mrs Miller,* in dozens of films: *The Maltese Falcon, The Wild Bunch.* Not just action. A vision.

RS: A vision that at the same time doesn't deny the popular aspect?

PK: That's right.

Index